THE REVEALING OF GOD

Book One in the *Revelation in Our Time* Trilogy

Hugh Shelbourne

Innovo Publishing

Published by
Innovo Publishing, LLC
www.innovopublishing.com
1-888-546-2111

Providing Full-Service Publishing Services for
Christian Authors, Artists & Organizations: Hardbacks, Paperbacks,
eBooks, Audiobooks, Music & Videos

THE REVEALING OF GOD
Book One in the *Revelation in Our Time* Trilogy
Copyright © 2011 by Hugh Shelbourne
All rights reserved.

Library of Congress Control Number: 2011929472
ISBN 13: 978-1-936076-76-5
ISBN 10: 1-936076-76-4

Cover Design & Interior Layout: Innovo Publishing, LLC

Printed in the United States of America
U.S. Printing History

First Edition: June 2011

TABLE OF CONTENTS

THE VISIONS REVEAL THE SPIRITUAL DRAMA OF THE AGES

ACT ONE: THE STRATEGY OF JESUS:
THE TIMES OF THE GENTILES

SETTING THE SCENES
John is given his task.

Act I, Scene 1

THE RISEN LORD SPEAKS TO HIS CHURCHES

JESUS DEFINES THE CHURCH'S MINISTRY
The Churches are to be Lampstands

JESUS DEFINES THE LEADERS' MINISTRY
Church leaders are to be stars in Jesus' right hand

JESUS REVEALS THE CHURCH'S APOSTASY;
HE DEFINES THE TRUE BELIEVER
All Christians are to be conquerors

Act I, Scenes 2, 3 & 4

THE WAY INTO GOD'S THRONE ROOM IS OPEN

THE LAMB OF GOD TAKES THE SCROLL
He is the only one fit to take and open the scroll
in God's right hand.

THE HEAVENLY HOSTS WORSHIP THE LAMB

THE LAMB OPENS THE SCROLL   as 4 seals are opened
THE CALL TO "COME"
THE FOUR HORSEMEN ARE SENT OUT
TO PATROL THE EARTH

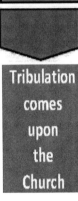

Tribulation comes upon the Church

JESUS REMOVES ALL RESTRAINT ON INIQUITY

Act I, Scene 5: SEAL 5 IS OPENED
THE TESTING OF BELIEVERS BEGINS
THE ANTICHRIST IS REVEALED
THE RAPTURE

DANIEL'S PROPHECY: WEEK 70 / 7 YEARS

Act I, Scene 6
6TH SEAL IS OPENED; GREAT TRIBULATION COMES
    UPON THE WORLD

Act I, Scene 7
SEALING OF 144,000 IN ISRAEL
    Preparation for Great Tribulation

Act I, Scene 8
MULTITUDES ARE SAVED OUT OF GREAT TRIBULATION

Act I, Scene 9
7th SEAL IS OPENED—WRATH OF GOD ON THE EARTH;
    TRUMPETS 1-6

Act I, Scene 10
PROPHECY OF THE WRATH TO COME ON NATIONS

Act I, Scene 11
TWO PROPHETS IN JERUSALEM

Act I, Scene 12
THE 7th TRUMPET

JESUS IS DEALING WITH ISRAEL

ACT TWO: GOD'S FAMILY

Act II, Scene 1
THE PREGNANT WOMAN BRINGS FORTH HER CHILD
    FOR GOD; SATAN SEEKS TO DEVOUR THE CHILD
    AT BIRTH AND FAILS; THE RAPTURE OF THE
    CONQUERORS; THE BATTLE IN HEAVEN; SATAN
    AND HIS ANGELS THROWN DOWN

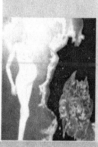

ACT THREE: SATAN'S STRATEGY

Act III, Scenes 1, 2, & 3
THE ANTICHRIST & THE FALSE PROPHET REIGN

ACT FOUR: GOD ACTS

Act IV, Scenes 1-6
GOD'S WRATH ENDS WITH DESTRUCTION

JESUS REIGNS

Act V, Scenes 1, 2, & 3
JESUS REIGNS FOR ONE THOUSAND YEARS
SATAN IS RELEASED: REBELLION

GOD IS ALL

Act VI
THE GREAT WHITE THRONE JUDGEMENT
JESUS DELIVERS THE KINGDOM TO GOD

Act VII
NEW HEAVEN AND NEW EARTH

GLORY

INTRODUCTION

THE WORD OF GOD IS ONGOING, CREATIVE REVELATION: GENESIS BEGINS IT; REVELATION COMPLETES IT

The Bible is a comprehensive narrative through time, revealing the reality and truth of God our Creator, and the *Revelation* is its dramatic conclusion. Any course of study that seeks to unlock the secrets of the last and most mysterious book in the Bible must begin in Genesis. All books are designed to be read from the beginning to the end so that their story may be properly and fully communicated to the reader, and the Bible is no different. The mistake is to uncouple the wonderful *Revelation* from all that has gone before it, when in fact the solving of its mysteries is entirely dependent upon the previous books, and especially upon Genesis, the "beginning." The apostle John, who wrote *Revelation*, when earlier writing his gospel, was profoundly conscious that he was not able to record everything that he had heard and seen Jesus speak and do, but he was confident that what he had written was enough.

> *"But there are also many other things that Jesus did; were every one of them to be written, I suppose that the world itself could not contain the books that would be written"* (John 21:25).

By the same token, we can assume that what is written in the Bible is sufficient for God's purposes and what is omitted is not essential to the story he is telling. The Bible is unique in its claims to be the certain Word of God. It is indeed God's book, *designed to reveal him to his people.* Everything we will ever need to know about him is there, and everything there is necessary to our lives as Christian believers. Thus, as we take Bible study seriously and in its totality, we are engaging with the God who created us, and everything else, for himself.

> *"For ever, O Lord, thy word is firmly fixed in the heavens. Thy faithfulness endures to all generations; thou hast appointed the earth, and it stands fast. By thy appointment they stand this day; for all things are thy servants"* (Psalm 119:89–91).

David, the great king-poet of the Bible, who wrote many of the psalms, knew well that God's Word is always truth and that as he read it in faith, it had power to change him and his circumstances. But if the Bible is not *God's Word and words* to us, then it is simply literature that we understand intellectually, and its power to change us is not apparent.

The task of reading and absorbing the whole Bible is a formidable one and is not accomplished easily, but God has promised to help and reward those *who seek to know him* through it. His divine guidance is available to us immediately as we begin to do the hard work of discovering the truth about him. Of course we must be able to read, but, given that, a decision to study the Scriptures with the purpose of knowing him is an appropriate response to our responsibility to search for him in life.

Paul spoke strongly and publicly to his Athenian audience in words that would shock us today:

> *"The God who made the world and everything in it, being Lord of heaven and earth, does not live in shrines made by man, nor is he served by human hands, as though he needed anything, since he himself gives to all men life and breath and everything. And he made from one every nation of men to live on all the face of the earth, having determined allotted periods and the boundaries of their habitation, that they should seek God, in the hope that they might feel after him and find him. Yet he is not far from each one of us"* (Acts 17:24–27).

It might seem obvious that an acceptance of God's existence is a prerequisite to receiving *revelation* from him through his Word. But such an acceptance cannot be relied upon in an age of positivism. The Bible shows us that the *"fear of the Lord is the beginning of wisdom and the knowledge of the Holy One is insight"* (Proverbs 9:10). However, "God is spirit" (John 4:24); that is, he is not material and by definition he is unknowable to a material/physical world. Unbelief in God, therefore, militates against true wisdom because it stifles *revelation* of the spiritual dimension of human existence. Thus, anyone opening the Bible to read and study it makes a choice. He either subjects what he reads there to a nonspiritual, intellectual worldview of life, or he chooses to seek revelation from the Author himself through prayer. While it is true that many men did the actual work of writing the books of the Bible, God inspired every writer, and he can just as easily inspire every reader. Thus, reading the Bible with prayer is to engage directly with the Spirit of the living God.

> *"Whoever would draw near to God must believe that he exists and that he rewards those who seek him"* (Hebrews 11:6).

A point-blank denial of the existence of God in the face of the evidence afforded by his creation, of which we are an integral part, is actually dangerous. Indeed, far from exhibiting wisdom, it is the intellectual fool who says, *"There is no God"* (Psalm 14:1), for his attitude cuts him off from his Creator completely. This is not a pejorative use of the word "fool" but a divine description of the unwisdom of acquiring and holding a worldview without God as its source. Paul is unequivocal on this point:

> *"For the wrath of God is revealed from heaven against all ungodliness and wickedness of men who by their wickedness suppress the truth. For what can be known about God is plain to them, because God has shown it to them. Ever since the creation of the world his invisible nature, namely his eternal power and deity, has been clearly perceived in the things that have been made. So they are without excuse"* (Romans 1:18–20).

Despite protestations based on scientific evidence or speculative theories, God insists that this creation—the beauty and wonder of the skies and stars, the weather systems providing an exquisite environment to meet our needs, the lush and varied vegetation, the marvellous creatures all conformed to an ordered pattern of existence for our benefit—provides incontrovertible evidence of his existence. These wonders, properly considered, constitute a convincing body of evidence that will lead us inexorably to faith in him as the Creator if we will allow it. Such a step of faith is available to us all by an act of our will. To ascribe our creation to chance or accident is insulting to God and unforgivable, because it is a willful denial of him. It constitutes a direct denial of him personally—his integrity, his truth, his validity, his authority and the power of his Word—and without an admission of error and a deep repentance, such an attitude will permanently cut us off from any future relationship with him.

> *"By faith we understand that the world was created by the word of God, so that what is seen was made out of things which do not appear"* (Hebrews 11:3).

In Scripture we find that God is his Word. Thus, without his Word we have no insight into the purpose of our present existence and no hope for a future one. The apostle John well understood this. His gospel records his personal testimony of what he had seen and heard as he lived and ministered with Jesus, including seeing him publicly humiliated, flogged, and cruelly crucified. And yet, despite this, he opens his gospel with a stunning *revelation*.

> *"In the beginning was the Word, and the Word was with God and the Word was God. He was in the beginning with God; all things were made through him, and without him was not anything made that was made"* (John 1:1–3).

This man, a beaten, bloodied human being hung on a cross to die, was the Creator of the universe! Jesus' existence as God predated creation. *Jesus always was, and always will be, the Word of God.* Interacting with the Father and the Holy Spirit, he personally brought the creation into being and then entered into it as man to rescue it by dying for his fellow men.

> *"He reflects the glory of God and bears the very stamp of his nature, upholding the universe by his word of power"* (Hebrews 1:3).

Despite who he was, Jesus allowed himself to be despised by his own people and rejected by the world at large. *Why?* The revealing of God through his Genesis creation account is but the beginning of the whole *revelation* that we need in order to know him maturely. Our Genesis knowledge of God is complemented by the revealing of him in Jesus Christ and through his ministry to the world, the Bible being our witness to both. The last book of the Bible takes all that has preceded it and reveals its stunning conclusion.

But receiving *revelation* of God is not simply a matter of reading and believing something intellectually, as if it were simply information to be taken on board. When it is God's Word that we absorb, we are recreated by it. Our new understandings and insights change us.

The people of Israel fell into devastating error when their leaders began to limit their covenant with God to that of keeping a written set of laws—as if they were just a catalogue of right and wrong behaviour defining the way they should live. God intended it to be so much more than that to them, and to us. Yes, the Old Testament is a legal code. It reveals that God will never accept sin. But it also reveals that God wants a relationship with his people and that he is prepared to provide a basis for restoring them to favour, subject to their continuing in obedience to his Word.

Genesis is there to show us how a man, created perfect by God, became a sinner, thus passing sin on to us all. The legal code of the Old Testament is God's law, not only defining sin for Israel, but also providing the basis on which all mankind will be judged, as he reveals in *Revelation*.

The new covenant superseded the old as a further expression of God's grace and mercy. It did not diminish the seriousness of sin but made possible personal holiness through faith obedience for the first time since Adam's fall. God's grace, revealed in the sacrificial death of Jesus, is a mystery that we celebrate in the breaking and eating of bread as his body and in the drinking of the wine as his blood. This vividly symbolises Christ's becoming part of us. Under the new covenant, we become literally a tabernacle ("a meeting place with God") where worship takes place.

To keep his Word as God intended is discipleship. It is to receive Jesus personally into our hearts and to breathe the Holy Spirit constantly so that we are changed to become like him. For this to happen, the whole Word must not only be read and understood but also chewed and digested, so changing our minds and then changing us. If the book of *Revelation* is excluded from our diet, inevitably we shall grow up to be spiritually deficient. Paul wrote:

> *"I became a minister according to the divine office which was given to me for you, to make the Word of God fully known, the mystery hidden for ages and generations but now made manifest to the saints. To them God chose to make known how great among the Gentiles are the riches of the glory of this mystery, which is Christ in you the hope of glory. Him we proclaim, warning every man and teaching every man in all wisdom, that we may present every man mature in Christ"* (Colossians 1:25–28).

Maturity in Christ is achieved only by our spiritual growth over a period of time. It is the purpose of discipleship. It has a clearly defined path and, as Paul makes clear, the journey is mandatory for every believer. But we all have some practical problems to face.

It is a shock to discover in God's Word that Satan (a fallen angel) is the father (or progenitor) of lies in the world (see John 8:43–47). Thus, by our everyday conversation we reveal who our spiritual father really is. Three times in the last two chapters of *Revelation* the liar is included in the lists of those who will find no place in heaven. We are going to discover that personal integrity and honesty matter a great deal to God. Should we lie or use deception in any guise, we deny the integrity of our newborn spirit, and each deception turns the screw on a full and proper enjoyment of our salvation. It is the process of sanctification alone, obedience to God's Word, *the truth*, which reverses this progression and sets us free from the past to be what God wants us to be.

> *"Blasphemy against the Spirit will not be forgiven . . . Whoever speaks a word against the Holy Spirit will not be forgiven, either in this age or the age to come . . . For out of the abundance of the heart the mouth speaks. I tell you, on the day of judgement men will render account for every careless word they utter; for by your words you will be justified, and by your words you will be condemned"* (Matthew 12:31–37).

God is true to his Word. Just as with us, his spoken words are the expression of himself, and since he is holy, his Word (the sum of his words) is absolute truth in every aspect. Were it not so, he would cease to be God. We have seen that Jesus too is God, the perfect expression of God the Father. The Holy Spirit also is God. He came into the world from the Father as the unseen witness to the truth of the Word of God (see 1 John 5:7), thereby convicting the world of sin and righteousness and judgment (John 16:8).

> *"When the Spirit of truth comes, he will guide you into all the truth; for he will not speak on his own authority, but whatever he hears he will speak, and he will declare to you the things that are to come. He will glorify me, for he will take what is mine and declare it to you. All that the Father has is mine; therefore I said that he will take what is mine and declare it to you"* (John 16:13–15).

So God's Word is absolute truth revealed by the Holy Spirit. We need God's truth as personal *revelation* in order to become what God wants us to be in this life. But it is a tough truth. It brings light and reveals darkness. It changes us only as we agree with it and live it out. "The truth" includes the *Revelation*. We cannot have Holy Spirit *revelation* of the *Revelation* unless we are already seeking to live in obedience to his *revelation* of both the old covenant and the new covenant.

All *revelation* begins in Genesis.

> *"In the beginning God created the heavens* (the spiritual arenas) *and the earth* (the physical-material arena). *The earth was without form and void* (empty), *and darkness was on the face of the deep* (it was covered in water); *and the Spirit of God was moving over the face of the waters"* (Genesis 1:1–2).

In this preliminary statement, God sets the scene for the next thirty-three verses. Our planet, the earth, is shown us as a sterile globe floating in space by itself, empty and lifeless. There are no other planets around, and nothing is happening. We are not given details of how it had become like this, nor are we shown how long it had been lifeless, but we know that at a point in time, God began to take action.

The Holy Spirit began to move above the waters. In five days, by the spiritual power (or divine energy) of his spoken words and *out of nothing material*, God brought life to the earth, creating a dynamic physical, fully functioning world, and so clothing the previously barren planet Earth with life much as we know it today.

It is not to be thought that God was acting on the spur of the moment in doing this. It is evident that everything had been carefully planned in advance, down to the minutest physical detail, smaller even than our most powerful microscopes can penetrate. God had a master plan covering not only all the material details of the universe but also the spiritual details from a timeless past to the timeless future.

> *"He chose us in him before the foundation of the world"* (Ephesians 1:4).

> *"He was destined before the foundation of the world but was made manifest at the end times for your sake"* (1 Peter 1:20).

> *". . . everyone whose name has not been written before the foundation of the world in the book of life of the Lamb that was slain"* (Revelation 13:8).

Everything in creation is designed by God for a purpose to be achieved at a future date. With this in mind, we understand that the sun, moon, and stars (in that order) were created on the fourth day for the sole purpose of establishing signs and seasons and days and years on a now living earth—the divine prophetic calendar and clock, showing us that God had already ordained and detailed the world's future. Nothing takes God by surprise. Although we choose to call the unexpected disasters that strike the world from time to time, "acts of God," putting the blame on him (even if we don't believe in him!) for the havoc they cause, every "act of God" is pre-known to him. Each one is to remind us of his sovereignty and encourages us to look to him for our assurance rather than to the resources of the world. Each part of his creation he described as being "good," as he completed it. That is to say, it was perfect for its purpose and without flaws. In just five days, God made the earth ready for its human occupants; he was turning his plans into a material reality.

The wonder of the galactic system, in its unfathomable immensity, with all the precision and complexity of its moving parts, are beyond human comprehension (even today!). The planet upon which we dwell is held in a cat's cradle of interlocking forces of nature so ordained by God that we are able to sustain perfectly an otherwise precarious place in the universe. *It is all comprehensively perfect.* We are to understand that not only was it all created by the energy and power of God's spoken words, but also *it is sustained on a daily basis* by those same words, as it will be until his purposes have been completed. Only then, when they have been fully achieved, will the earth, our seemingly substantial and permanent home, be declared redundant and be replaced with a new heavens and a new earth of even greater wonder.

Then, when all was ready and good, on the sixth day God made *the central object of his creation—Man!* Man, we know, was created in the image of God and, in fact, in the likeness of Jesus. And for this reason, the manner of his making was startlingly different from all the other creatures. Jesus took up dust from the precreated earth and fashioned man physically from it. Of course this was not just an act of model making; it was a miraculous, creative act to transform dust into the complexity and harmony of the human body. Today with our advanced technology we are able to probe and scan the foundation blocks of physical life, and as we do so we gradually uncover and expose the breathtaking skill and inventiveness of the master Creator. And yet we are severely limited in this because we see only that preliminary, physical part that was made from dust.

After this, even more wonderful to recount and quite beyond our scientific comprehension, God breathed his own divine life-breath into physical man—the breath of eternal life—and *man then became a living soul.* The dusty body is wonderful, but how much more the eternal soul that indwells it? God could easily have created man by speaking appropriate words; but in choosing to do it this way, he shows us that the precreated heavens and earth and the six-day creation were both essential parts of an in-line process leading to the creation of man.

It is important that God did not speak man into existence like he did the animals and the rest of creation. We are to see from the order in which the creation took place that the earth was first conceived in God's heart as the "womb" for man. In the first stage of creation (Genesis 1:1), the planet Earth (made of dust) was already "pregnant" with dust-man. Then, during the six-day creation, man was literally taken out of the earth and for the earth. Unlike the animals, however, he was given spiritual life from within God in order to live on the earth. The idea of the Earth Mother is found here. God the Father created the earth by his Word and then formed man (Adam and Eve together: husband and wife as one person) from the physical substance of the earth. Then his Spirit, breathed into dusty, physical man, generating him into full, spiritual life with an awareness spanning both material earth and spiritual heaven. He was a "son of God." In the next phase, Adam and Eve were separated physically and given gender, becoming God's children (*but still spiritually at one with each other and with their Father*). God gave "them" together dominion over his new earth and the task of populating it on his behalf. We shall see later in this book that this mysterious "spiritual unity" of a plurality of people is central to our understanding of God's purpose and to the book of *Revelation* itself.

Adam's tragic rebellion changed everything. But, while it may first seem to us that God's purposes were thwarted by the Fall in Eden, the Bible gradually reveals that this is not so. The *Revelation of Jesus Christ*, to give the last book of the Bible its full and appropriate title, is critically linked to the book of Genesis, although that link is not immediately obvious. Genesis begins with the account of the creation of our universe and the fall of man. *Revelation* ends with the account of new heavens and earth and the redemption of man. Between these two events lies the whole history of mankind, during which God will achieve the objectives for which he initiated the world in the first place. The book of *Revelation* is the completion of the revelation of God that begins in Genesis.

Only by faith can we embrace and receive God's *revelation* of our world's origin, its tragic history, its devastating and dramatic end as portrayed in John's *Revelation*, and God's great purpose in it all. Without an intention to embrace Jesus (the whole of God's Word) each day in every situation, it is unlikely that we can stand through all the events that will come upon us. Without responding to his continuing presence in us, we must go backward in our faith, and that may have eternal consequences.

In this book, I seek to set out the *revelation* that I have received over a lifetime of study and ministry, claiming it to be consistent to the words of God in the Bible and coherent with the Word who is Jesus. Although we have human teachers and ministers in our churches, each of us has the responsibility to do the work, seeking, researching, and receiving truth for ourselves, and as we do this, the Holy Spirit will teach us all things.

THE SWORD OF THE SPIRIT IS NECESSARY FOR PERSONAL SALVATION

1. The Word is heard as God's *revelation*.
2. The heart is convicted of sin (iniquity) by the Holy Spirit (see Mark 7:20–21).
3. The will initiates repentance in response to the Holy Spirit's conviction.
4. The mind agrees with God's Word as truth, putting away old lies and confessing past disobedience and sin.
5. Confession and repentance brings forgiveness and renewal to body, soul, and spirit through the indwelling Holy Spirit.

THE NEW COVENANT

Salvation is a generic term that describes what God has done and what he is doing in the life of a born-again believer. By his grace we are justified and reconciled to him. As we seek to obey God in everything, we are sanctified. On the day of Jesus' return we will be glorified.

Sanctification is a process of willing change in character and lifestyle as a result of obedience to the Holy Spirit and God's Word, by which a disciple is preparing himself for the second coming of Jesus.

The whole Word of God (from Genesis to Revelation) is necessary to us for our sanctification:

1. The Word of God is to be studied, learnt, and digested regularly.
2. The heart (will of the spirit) goes on being convicted of the need for our sins to be forgiven and our iniquity to be changed into righteousness as we grow to spiritual maturity.
3. Through careful and thoughtful repentance each day, the old nature (in body, soul, and spirit) is put to death and replaced by the new nature.
4. Renewal is the deliberate putting off of the old nature and putting on of the new, through which process we are a new person (without condemnation) and we live a renewed life as a child of God.
5. By faith the disciple stands firm in the testing of the enemy.
6. As we are living in this process, we are ready for the Lord's return at any time.
7. The Word, made up of the two books of covenant, will be the basis of the judgment of all those in the last days whose names are not found written in the Book of Life.

SETTING THE SCENE

Strictly speaking the whole Bible is prophetic because it reveals God's will for his creation. The Bible (the Word of God) is the sum of God's words, encompassing the past, present, and future of our world. Although about 30 percent of its writings are predictive, foretelling or warning of future events, the primary meaning of the word "prophecy" is the revealing of God's will. The Word, which we know as the Bible, embodied within the person of Jesus, existed before the beginning of time. God made his Word formally available to mankind in four stages as was appropriate with the passing of time. First came Moses' account of the first generations in the Pentateuch. The history of the nation of Israel as God's chosen people is encompassed in the following books of the Old Testament. Then we have the gospels, Acts, and the epistles detailing the New Covenant. Finally, in *Revelation* we discover the details of the end of our world as we know it.

A strong narrative thread through each part of the Word is that both time and timing belong to God. It is clear that the writers are all aware of a destiny of individuals and nations that is controlled by God. Both have a beginning and an ending. God gives us a brief span of life to use as we will, but we will each answer to him for it.

The Bible also suggests that the fate of each one of us is known to God from the beginning, and in this sense our fate is predetermined. However, although we neither know the end of our life nor the timing of it, we are to know his purposes for us within it. The *when* of our end is shrouded in mystery, but as long as time lasts the opportunity to know God still exists. Once we understand that the time given us by God is finite, we know that each day of our lives has significance for our relationship with him whatever our circumstances may be.

Thus, accepting that everything in this world takes place within the timing and foreordained purpose of God is not a form of fatalism. Rather, it is essential to our faith in God's intrinsic goodness, and provides assurance that everything that happens to us, including suffering and even death, is for our ultimate good if we will receive it. The unfulfilled promises we now have by faith in his Word, we shall see and possess in reality when we have achieved his spiritual objectives for us, and our time here is over.

> *"Blessed be the God and Father of our Lord Jesus Christ, who has blessed us in Christ with every spiritual blessing in the heavenly places, even as he chose us in him before the foundation of the world, that we should be holy and blameless before him . . . For he has made known to us in all wisdom and insight the mystery of his will,* **according to his purpose which he set forth in Christ as a plan for the fullness of time**, *to unite all things in him, things in heaven and things on earth"* (Ephesians 1:3–4, 9–10).

In the *fullness of time*, at each stage of the *revelation* of himself to man, when God has achieved his objectives in that stage, he moves on. Not only Paul in his New Testament letters, but all Scriptures make it clear that God's will in the world is bound up with his relationship with the men and women who currently occupy it.

The detailed study of Scripture reveals a sad account of man's failure in this respect. It seems that no matter what arrangement God makes, man somehow contrives to mess up. Adam was only the first of many. He famously failed in his responsibility to protect Eve from her foolishness. By eating the forbidden fruit they both sinned, and so losing their perfection and their harmonious marriage, they were driven out of Eden; and as God had warned, death came upon the human race.

According to the Genesis account, mankind's behaviour over the next 1500 years gradually degenerated to such an extent that human beings became incorrigibly offensive to God (see Genesis 6:5–6). A time came when only one man among all the multitudes was found as a "man of faith." Drastic action was called for, and so God cleansed the earth by means of the flood, and made a new beginning with Noah and his family. Before too long, this arrangement too was spurned. Nimrod masterminded a religious coup, only the first of many, attempting to replace God altogether by raising a temple to imaginary gods so that he could control the people. The subsequent confusion of languages and the scattering of the peoples by God's command led to the worldwide, rebellious and competitive society that exists today.

Abram (Abraham) was born in the mid-twentieth century BC, and with him begins the Old Testament account of how God began to restore mankind to a relationship with himself. Abraham was used to reveal the great principle of "faith-obedience" as the means by which man would be considered to be righteous before God. Those coming after, who would follow his example, would become "children of God." But even Abraham needed grace. He "failed" in the testing of his faith, and the consequences of that failure, manifested in the twelve tribes that came from Ishmael—plague our world today.

> *"The promise to Abraham and his descendants, that they should inherit the world, did not come through law but through* **the righteousness of faith"** (Romans 4:13).

Later, God offered an amazing deal to the people of Israel through Moses, the old covenant—a promise of extraordinary blessing for obedience, backed by an assurance of punishment for disobedience. We know from the record that although God exhibited extraordinary patience with them for 1500 years, the people and their leaders were rarely compliant with his Word. The warnings of the prophets and their predictions of a calamitous future are there for us to read. So when their long-expected Messiah came, Jesus did not fulfil their misplaced expectations and they rejected and slaughtered him in unbelief.

We know now that this disaster was the necessary preliminary for the next phase of God's plan. Temporarily abandoning Israel to their promised punishment, God turned to the Gentiles. At that time, two thousand years ago, God extended his offer of grace to all mankind by means of a new covenant. In the new circumstances, a "called-out church" would become his family—a united people drawn from every tribe and tongue and nation who would make him known throughout the world by their holiness and self-denying lifestyle.

> *"I therefore, a prisoner for the Lord, beg you to lead a life worthy of the calling to which you have been called, with all lowliness and meekness, with patience, forbearing one another in love, eager to maintain the unity of the Spirit in the bond of peace.* **There is one body and one Spirit, just as you were called to the one hope that belongs to your call, one Lord, one faith, one baptism, one God and Father of us all, who is above all and through all and in all"** (Ephesians 4:1–6).

Under the new covenant, the priesthood passed from the nation of Israel to those individuals who would be his church. This relationship, unlike that with Israel under the old covenant, would be a great mystery in the world. The true church, undefined by human structures and organisations, was the affianced *"bride of Christ."* The spiritual unity of husband and wife so disastrously lost in Eden was now restored under the new covenant. The marriages of its members were to be a visual model of Jesus' relationship with his "bride." To these members of the new united body, anointed and appointed by the Holy Spirit to be "a royal priesthood," was given the responsibility to worship God in his temple in spirit and truth. Jesus said that in the future his brothers and sisters must worship God as Father.

> *"But the hour is coming, and now is, when the true worshippers will worship the Father in spirit and truth, for* **such the Father seeks to worship him**. *God is spirit, and those who worship him must worship in spirit and truth"* (John 4:23–24).

Without worship in spirit and truth it is impossible to have a relationship with God our Father. The New Testament church, consisting of Jews and Gentiles, was wonderfully and powerfully established at Pentecost, when the Holy Spirit was poured out so dramatically on the new believers. However, despite its promising beginning, a mere seventy years later things had gone seriously wrong in the new churches.

How disappointed John must have felt as he looked back at his life. He well knew the chaotic events that had taken place in Israel since Jesus died. He had been there on the Day of Pentecost, when the Holy Spirit came in such power. He had seen the gospel preached boldly throughout Israel with amazing signs and wonders giving testimony to its source. *But, once again, the Jewish nation and its leaders had rejected the gospel of Jesus Christ.* John had witnessed the political chaos that arose in the nation, leading to an outright rebellion that had inevitably prompted an invasion by the Roman armies. The tragic fall of Jerusalem and its temple in AD 70 had finally destroyed the pretensions of Israel to be God's people on the earth. He had seen the breakdown of law and order and the dispersal of the Jews, and he remembered Jesus' words that had so precisely predicted all of this (see Luke 21:20–24).

John also knew that Paul and his fellow apostles had travelled far and wide into many nations, preaching the gospel to the Gentiles and establishing churches as Jesus had instructed them to do. After a promising and exciting beginning, there had come a *falling away of so many churches.* Jewish hostility, political animosity, and the effects of false teaching and false apostles from within, combined together to cause doubt and the falling away of many. They had been led to expect that Jesus would soon return and put things right. John himself, anticipating that the Antichrist would appear (perhaps in the form of one of the Caesars in Rome) as the immediate prelude to Jesus' return, had written:

> *"Children, it is the last hour; and as you have heard that* **antichrist is coming**, *so now many antichrists have come; therefore we know that it is the last hour"* (1 John 2:18).

But Jesus had not come. It was inevitable that disillusion would set in and Bible teachers would become less confident in their predictions. By the time of his exile, John too must have been puzzled. For sixty years he had faithfully ministered against great opposition as had his fellow apostles; one by one they had died, until it seemed he alone was left of all those who had been with Jesus. Now, an old man, he saw a persecuted and apostate church that appeared to be collapsing under the combined pressures of public hostility, government disapproval, and the venality of the world. Banished and alone on the island of Patmos, he could only worship God and continue to pray in faith for Jesus to return.

Throughout those first years, the imminent return of Jesus was fundamental doctrine in the churches. In the midst of much political upheaval and social disintegration, his soon return was their constant hope. Indeed, Jesus had enshrined such an attitude in his teaching. *"You must be ready,"* he had said, *"for the Son of Man is coming at an hour you do not expect"* (Matthew 24:44).

The whole church, it seemed, was longing for the Lord's return, an attitude sadly despised today but commended by the writer of Hebrews, who pointed out that the Lord was coming a second time to take to himself *"those who are eagerly waiting for him"* (Hebrews 9:28).

Paul had even found it necessary to refute certain wild stories and wrong expectations that were circulating to the effect that Christ had already come back. Paul wrote his second letter to the church at Thessalonica to refute forged letters purporting to be from him, which said that the Lord had already returned. Paul gave the Thessalonians precise details of what they must look for before Christ's return so that they would not be deceived. This prophetic *revelation* was a warning to the churches of the time, but it holds for us today also. Paul warned that "apostasy" would overtake the churches in the last days, and he had no doubt about the tragic consequences of this. Later he wrote to Timothy, making clear what such "apostasy" would look like.

> *"Now the Spirit expressly says that in later times some will* **depart from the faith** *by giving heed to deceitful spirits and doctrines of demons, through the pretensions of liars whose consciences are seared, who forbid marriage and enjoin abstinence from foods which God created to be received with thanksgiving by those who believe and know the truth"* (1 Timothy 4:1–3).

> *"But understand this, that in the last days there will come times of stress. For men will be lovers of self, lovers of money, proud, arrogant, abusive, disobedient to their parents, ungrateful, unholy, inhuman, implacable, slanderers, profligates, fierce, haters of good, treacherous, reckless, swollen with conceit, lovers of pleasure rather than lovers of God,* **holding the form of religion but denying the power of it.** *Avoid such people"* (2 Timothy 3:1–5).

Prior to receiving the *Revelation*, John certainly had expected Jesus to return in his lifetime. His wonderful gospel is full of information and personal anecdotes about his life with Jesus, and there was much more that he could have said. But he included only that which was essential. When he recorded some of Jesus' last words spoken to Peter, he did so because he knew they were important.

> *"If it is my will that* **he remain until I come,** *what is that to you?"* (John 21:23).

These enigmatic words were afterward interpreted by many as a signal that Jesus would come again before John died, but John himself was clear that there was more to it than that. It is not until we read the opening two verses of *Revelation* that we have the explanation of what Jesus had said some sixty to seventy years earlier.

God chose John, the apostle of Jesus, to be the prophet who would make his end-times will known to his churches. John was a direct link with the man Jesus, his special friend. He had walked, ministered, and lived with him. John, a man full of the Spirit, of unimpeachable integrity, was known to all believers as the beloved and trusted friend of Jesus. He had been tried, tested, and proven in his faithfulness, and so was qualified as one fit and reliable to bring the final great *Revelation of Jesus Christ* to the churches.

So it was, on one wonderful day, that everything changed for him. Out of the blue—with no prior warning—*the living Jesus came to him!* In complete accord with his promise, but not in any way that could have been imagined, Jesus came. In all the glory of his risen majesty, he came to John with a clear purpose. To this faithful, beloved servant and brother, a true conqueror in the spiritual realm, one tried and proven in the fires of adversity, Jesus was going to give a detailed and comprehensive *revelation* such as no man had ever been given, greater even than the prophetic visions of Ezekiel, Daniel, and those other great prophets of old. In God's perfect plan, the time had come for him to take action to help his church. It was time to give a further, and this time final, *revelation* of his will to his people.

He would do this by first subjecting the existing churches in Asia to a searching and critical analysis for the benefit of those who would come after, and second by setting out in detail what must happen in the future. The opening verse of the *Revelation of Jesus Christ* declares his purpose; God wants his people to know what will happen in the future.

Jesus perfectly well knew the failed state of his churches. So for those of them who "have ears to hear," he would provide the spiritual sustenance they need to see them through the difficult times they must face. On their behalf, faithful John was to see and know the full purposes of almighty God in creation. God was now ready to use this apostle, a man honed and worn by years of arduous ministry, to bring his full and final *revelation* to the church, present and future. He was going to show him *"what must soon take place,"* for, he said, *"the time is near."* In order to accomplish this, he was going to take John on a free-ranging tour through time past and time future. Men had exiled him to a remote island, but God was going to take him into the very throne room in heaven. Men had sought to cut him off from communion with his friends, but he was going to walk and talk with angels, and God would fellowship with him. And why was this happening to him? *So that we who would come after him, no matter the state of our church or the world, by our faith in the words John would carefully write, might see what he saw and so, having understanding, be ready for the Lord's coming at any time.*

John was to be the human conduit through whom people in succeeding ages would be able to meaningfully disengage from their immediate circumstances and the discourses that dominate the world to understand the greater truths of God. The *Revelation* given to him would provide a spiritual context and a satisfying understanding to history past, provide insight into the spiritual relevance of present-day life, and define the destiny of mankind in eternity.

A firsthand account of Jesus' life, death, and resurrection had been available to the early church through the apostles and other witnesses. But with their passing, the generations that followed would be dependent upon the written record of God's Word. In the ever-changing, but always hostile environment of the secular world, they needed something more than a historical record that related to past events and mostly to Israel. The Lord was fully aware of the society and its challenges within which he had called his disciples to learn and exercise their faith. The *Revelation* would provide an authoritative statement sent directly from God to his churches to enable them to do this with confidence.

Humanly speaking, John had an impossible task. How could he possibly convey to others the scenes and sensations that he was to experience within the limitations of human language? But of course he was not doing this task by himself in his own strength. It was vital that John get it right. As with Moses at the beginning, and down through the ages since, the Holy Spirit was willing to use a man to record God's Word to men. Never before had it been said of a portion of God's Word.

> *"Blessed is he who reads aloud the words of this prophecy, and blessed are those who hear, and who keep what is written therein"* (Revelation 1:3).

And never before had such a warning been issued against any who should tamper with what God had caused to be written for his church.

> *"I warn everyone who hears the words of the prophecy of this book: if anyone adds to them, God will add to him the plagues described in this book, and if anyone takes away from the words of the book of this prophecy, God will take away his share in the tree of life and in the holy city which are described in this book"* (Revelation 22:18–19).

With such strong words from God to give it authority, how can it be that this last book of the Bible has come to be so discredited for the church that few have regard for it, and most fear to attempt to understand it? It is true that the *Revelation* has been a source of much controversy ever since it was given. It is true too that cranks, cults, and sects have used it and abused it. But such things only emphasise the need for an answer to our question: Why is this great book of unique prophecy, sent direct from God to his churches, so neglected by the people who need it most? In whose interest is it that such wonders should be discredited?

It is a reasonable hypothesis that if the *Revelation* is a key book for God's people, then it must be one of the main targets for the great enemy of God to attack, and it seems he has achieved considerable success! As we have seen, Satan has been working in the churches from the beginning. His aim is always to separate God's children from God's Word by questioning its integrity.

> *"Now the serpent was more subtle than any other wild creature that the Lord God had made. He said to the woman,* **"Did God say,** *'You shall not eat of any tree of the garden?'"* (Genesis 3:1).

For generations, because the integrity and relevance of the *Revelation* is denied by church authorities, the churches have been separated from the great *Revelation of Jesus Christ*. That first astonishing question posed to Eve still holds its power today, **"Did God say . . .?"** The only proper answer to it is, **"Yes, he did!"** The idea that Satan could be at work within churches will seem incredible to most modern Christians, but in all Bible prophecy, including the *Revelation*, God shows us the reality of the terrifying iniquity that has bound his people all through the ages. Unbelief in his Word as truth, encouraged by Satan, will deliver countless souls to a judgement they can avoid (see Ezekiel 33).

In the very last days, terrible and frightening things will indeed occur on this earth. Fearing to read about it, and in denial of their spiritual impotence, the churches refuse to access the light they need to deal with the darkness they are in. God wants us to be looking forward to the return of Jesus and to know what will happen before he comes back so that we will be ready. It will not be an easy time for anyone and the *Revelation*, having spelled it out in uncompromising terms, like all good prophecy, reveals to the Lord's people how they should prepare in order to pass through these times successfully.

In a limited sense, the "day of the Lord" is at hand for us all, for the *"dead in Christ will rise first,"* Paul says (1 Thessalonians 4:16b). So the New Testament writers were not wrong in injecting a sense of urgency into their ministry. The use of the word "soon" has for us a meaning that normally denotes just a short period of time before something happens. Evidently, however, in the New Testament it denotes an attitude of expectancy toward something coming, the precise timing of which is not predictable. So there is urgency in this, for none of us know when we will die. On the day we do, our opportunity to prepare ourselves for glory is over. In the end, the second coming of Christ will be too soon for many people.

Having understanding of the *Revelation* is important to every believer in every age, but it is possible only within a context of the reader's hungry anticipation of Christ's return. So in the first few verses of the *Revelation* reference is made to Christ's return and its manner. As he went, so he will certainly come, and every eye on earth without exception will see him—and for those who are not looking forward to his coming, there is only anguish in store.

Consider the greeting John brings:

> *"Grace to you and peace from him who is and who was and is to come, and from the seven spirits who are before his throne, and from Jesus Christ the faithful witness, the first born of the dead, and the ruler of kings on earth. To him who loves us and has freed us from our sins by his blood and made us a kingdom, priests to his God and Father, to him be dominion for ever and ever. Amen.*

> *"Behold he is coming with the clouds and every eye shall see him, everyone who pierced him; and all the tribes of the earth will wail on account of him. Even so. Amen.*

> *"'I am the Alpha and Omega,' says the Lord God who is and was and is to come, the Almighty"* (Revelation 1:4–8).

It is hard to imagine a more solemn and authoritative statement than this one. It summarises everything we know about Jesus up until the *Revelation*. He was resurrected to life and reigns even now from heaven. He was faithful in his ministry, even to death. His lifeblood shed on the cross is the basis of our forgiveness. He has made us to be a royal priesthood to his Father. He is already Lord of all, having recovered the *dominion* ceded by Adam to Satan. He is coming in the clouds, and his coming will not be welcomed by the world. The *Revelation* is given both to bolster biblical doctrines and to assure the believer in his expectation of future glory so that he can be joyful at all times.

> *"The revelation of Jesus Christ, which God gave him to show to his servants what must soon take place . . . for the time is near"* (Revelation 1:1, 3).

> *"He who testifies to these things says, 'Surely I am coming soon'"* (Revelation 22:20).

Who is it testifying to these things? It is no one less than the Creator himself, the one who is Alpha and Omega, encompassing all, the Lord Almighty. The time is near. He is coming soon.

SUMMARY

❖ God's purpose in giving the Revelation:

    i) to reveal matters that have never been revealed before

    ii) to tie together and coordinate all the end-time prophecies of Scripture

    iii) to comfort and assure his people through inevitable times of difficulty and disaster

❖ All disciples, men and women, are anointed and appointed to be priests to God here and now in preparation for their role in heaven.

❖ God's church is the bride of Christ. The spiritual oneness of the church is invisible but manifested to the world in Christian marriage.

❖ The *whole* of the Revelation is essential knowledge for God's people and must be taken seriously by each one.

❖ God is the beginning and the end of everything—he alone knows the whole truth, and he has a divine strategy for achieving his objectives.

❖ Jesus is coming back soon, and to have a balanced spiritual perspective on life, we *must* be looking forward to his coming on that day.

❖ In order to have understanding and insight, the student of *Revelation* must be in the Spirit as John was.

❖ In the introduction, we have been given a quick preview of the three great subjects Jesus is going to deal with in the *Revelation*:

    i) the priesthood created by Jesus, its role and destiny (1:6).

    ii) the local churches as the expression of Christ's purpose in the earth

    iii) the second coming of Christ and its consequences for all creation (1:7)

JOHN'S VISION OF JESUS
REVELATION 1, 2, AND 3

Act I, Scene 1—JOHN'S VISION OF JESUS   **Time: AD 90**

Place: Island of Patmos   **People: The Seven Churches**

We know nothing of John's circumstances on the island of Patmos, nor are we given any information concerning the terms and conditions of his exile. We know from our maps that the island is off the west coast of Turkey, and we can presume that in those days it would have been relatively remote, barren, and unpopulated. We can presume too that it was the objective of the authorities to remove John to a place where he would no longer be a nuisance to them. Clearly, earlier efforts to silence him had been ineffective, so this old man was banished to Patmos with the expectation that he would soon be forgotten. It would have been difficult for John and his people to believe at the time that these authorities were acting in accordance with the plan of God for John's life, and yet it was to be through their ill-intentioned actions that this great servant of God would imprint his name and influence on the church down through all the ages yet to come.

The churches John left behind would have been very upset at the loss of their apostle in such a manner. How could God have let such a thing happen? What was behind this cruel banishment? But we know now that God had a superior purpose in these events, as he always does. By his long experience and his faithful ministry of God's Word to the people, John had proved himself to be uniquely qualified for the task God had for him.

Many generations before, there had been another friend of God, Moses, and through many trials and testings he too had proved himself to be a faithful servant of God. He was a man upon whom God could rely, and to him was given the *revelation* of the beginning of the world and its early history. He recorded what we know as the first five books of the Bible: an amazing work of scholarship by an old man. Now, to John, another old man of God, a once intimate friend of Jesus, was given the great *Revelation*: what we know as the last book of the Bible and the completion of God's written revelation of his purposes for the world that he created.

It seems that all personal details of John's detention on Patmos are irrelevant to the *Revelation*, for we are given no idea of how long he had been there, what his daily routines were, or how much liberty he had. We know only that John was exactly where God wanted him to be.

John tells us he was *"in the Spirit on the Lord's day"* (Revelation 1:10). He does not think it necessary to explain what he meant by this phrase; he can only have presumed that it would be a condition well recognised by those reading his words. John himself was a member of the spiritual priesthood ordained by Jesus. He knew full well the nature of worship that was acceptable to his Father. Had he not written about it in his gospel and his epistles to the churches? Here we find him in that dimension of the spirit that is known only through the Holy Spirit's deep ministry in us. That this is not a trance state is clear, for upon hearing a voice behind him, John responds quite naturally by turning around to see the one who is speaking to him.

It is important to comprehend that being in the Spirit (or in spirit) is an extra-internal dimension of our current being, of which it is an integral part. It is not a separated, mystical state in which we become unconscious of our ordinary condition of body and mind. It is not achieved by the suspension of our faculties. Much harm can result from seeking for mystical experiences. Outside of our relationship with Jesus, the spiritual world is real enough but occult in origin and inevitably harmful. Quite simply, as was his habit, John was in intimate communion with his Father on the Lord's Day when suddenly and without warning, he heard a great voice sound out behind him. All his responses to this extraordinary experience are human, both physically and emotionally.

"Write what you see in a book and send it to the seven churches" (Revelation 1:11).

It is likely that these seven churches were John's own churches, to whom he had faithfully ministered for many years: the beloved family he had left behind when he was exiled. How he must have been thinking of them and praying for them all. Was God about to answer his prayers and give him a message that would encourage and strengthen them in his absence?

It is never easy to write about a dramatic occurrence without the use of hyperbole, but in his account of all that he saw John manages to do this. He writes only what he sees, exactly as he has been told to do. There must be no exaggeration in what he writes, no introduction of his own feelings and emotions; nothing must be added to make the account more dramatic or exciting, even if that were possible. The plain truth of what he sees is what the church needs; under the leading of the Holy Spirit God's people are to interpret the meaning of these wonderful visions for themselves. So we find almost nothing of John himself in the account, except on just one occasion when he is overcome and cannot help weeping, and perhaps at the very end when he allows himself a comment or two. In fact, he is at pains to make the account as stark as possible, presenting the bare truth, while at the same time being precisely accurate in the details he gives.

It is necessary for each one of us reading his account to allow that same Holy Spirit who directed John in his writing to direct and enlighten us in our studies. Each one who enters into the labyrinth of the *Revelation* is to become a part of what is unfolding. We cannot stand outside as if we were some impartial observer who is intellectually appraising what is going on. We have to enter as one already committed and convinced of the uniqueness and authority of God's Word, as one who is hungry for the righteousness it brings as we respond to it. Only then can its deepest meanings satisfy our souls.

John's first response to the events he describes in chapter 5 is to burst into tears, and we too shall be moved emotionally as we study the book. God is certainly not unemotional, and in the *Revelation* we will discover the deepest feelings of his heart. This is no cold, calculated exercise of an uncaring and superior being. The contrary is true. We disciples are to have the privilege of *knowing*, and so by definition loving, our God and Father in an intimacy enjoyed by very few in the course of history. As we allow the Spirit of God who searches the deep things of God to enlighten this revelation to us, we must be willing to experience his deep pain as well as his joy.

When John heard the voice like a trumpet behind him, it was a shock. He turned around to face the speaker and saw Jesus in his glory!

There had been nothing so dramatic since Moses met with God on the mountain. On this occasion John tells us in some detail about the appearance of this Person; he wants us to see what he saw. The whole *Revelation* is alive with colour, sound, and movement, and John finds himself at the limits of his vocabulary in trying to convey to us what he sees. We read in the Old Testament the account of Daniel's great visions of God and how the powerful, almost overwhelming effect of these made him physically ill. Now, John's own response to being in the presence of the glorified Jesus is to collapse as if dead, his senses being totally unable to cope with what he is seeing. What possibility could there be of fellowship between such a glorious being and a mortal man?

John had been the one who was so close to Jesus during his earthly ministry. He had embraced him and sat with him. He had seen him transfigured on the mountain. But now he was cast down before him. So different is the heavenly from the earthly creation that there can be no fellowship across the boundary apart from God making a special provision to enable it to take place.

Jesus lovingly touches John. This is a moment of restoration to life and relationship. John now receives from Jesus' touch the power to sustain the experience. *"Fear not,"* he said, for he knew what was in John's heart. Will any human be able to swagger before the living God? If righteous, faithful John feared, how much more will the unrighteous have to fear when they too stand before him?

> *"I am the first and the last, and the living one; I died, and behold I am alive for evermore and I have the keys of Death and Hades"* (Revelation 1:17–18).

Jesus announces himself with the unequivocal statement that consigns all other faiths and religious pretensions to the realm of futility. This can only be wonderfully true as a statement or an outrageous lie. It is the message that the church must continually bring to the world.

The glorious "Son of Man" identifies himself. There is no room for a mistake. Jesus makes a totally satisfying statement of truth that brooks no argument or spiritualisation. *"I am"*: God in the person of Jesus, the one who left his throne in heaven to come to earth to die, is here with John in person. He is eternally alive, and it is time to manifest himself to his people.

John is meeting with the Living One who will never again be changed. The keys of death and Hades are symbolic of what he has accomplished by his submission to death and the grave. If we wish to specially honour someone, we give that person the freedom of the city. We issue the person a set of keys as a symbol of the right to come and go as he or she pleases. Once the person has that honour, the honoured one can bring in or out anyone he or she chooses. Previously, Jesus had the keys of the kingdom of heaven (Matthew 6:19), and Satan had the keys of death and Hades (or the grave). Now Satan's power over death and everything else is broken.

Of course, Satan is still the liar he always was; he pretends that nothing is changed, but he has the keys to nothing. Death and Hades have not yet been dealt with finally, for they are still with us, but both are totally subject to Jesus. Any residue of power that Satan has is by divine permission in order that God's purposes may be fully accomplished.

John describes what he sees in some detail, and it is an instructive picture for us. He sees Jesus dressed in priestly robes, standing among seven beautiful, golden lampstands. John must have been lost for words. His narrative conveys a picture that his senses received rather than a photographic image. He has a sense of white light streaming out of the head of Jesus and, seeking for a suitable metaphor, he speaks of his head and his hair as being like the purest of washed and brushed wool. Today we might speak of there being a halo of brilliant light around his head.

Then he describes the eyes. Such eyes! As they looked at him, it was as if a flame of fire was washing over him—not with a sense of burning or of pain but with a sense of purging of everything unclean. Perhaps this is akin to the experience Paul refers to in 1 Corinthians 3:13–15, where he makes it clear that the unperfected souls of some of his saints will be tested by fire.

As if to draw attention to the glorified nature of the whole of Jesus' body, and to counter the thought that he was some ethereal, ghostly figure, John particularly mentions the feet of Jesus. These gleam like burnished bronze. Because we shall be like him, we too shall be a beautiful bronze colour in heaven. We are to understand that the heavenly body is totally human in form, with hands, feet, hair, face, and body just like our own, but marvellously glorified.

While John is struggling to absorb these visual impressions, he hears the sound of the Lord's voice. It is a majestic, rolling sound, full of cadences and minor harmonies like the sound of deep waters coming together. This is far different from the still, small voice by which God, in his great mercy, speaks with us in our hearts today by his Spirit as we have ears attuned to hear him.

John sees that Jesus is holding seven stars in his right hand. Without referring to his left hand at all, John proceeds to describe the sharp, two-edged sword issuing from Jesus' mouth. Again, it is as if John describes what he is seeing not only by its appearance but by its immediate effect on him. This technique is used much in the *Revelation*, and as we read the words, we too need to allow the visions to affect us. As he heard the great voices and saw Jesus' mouth forming the words, so he experienced deep within the effect of a scalpel being wielded by a master surgeon cutting out that which is unclean and harmful. The sense is entirely faithful to the passage in Hebrews (4:12–13) that describes the effect of God's Word when wielded by the Holy Spirit in us.

Just as John knew that the deep things of his heart were being exposed to view by that scalpel of Jesus' Word, so we all, one day, will know that same sensation. If John had had any darkness to hide, it would have been exposed at this time. We can only guess at the horror of any such a thing being exposed in us. But we can also reflect on the mercy of God that he had so prepared John that, having been refined in the fires of life, he was found fit to stand with his Lord.

Who can look upon the sun when it is shining at full strength? It is so brilliant that it is actually dangerous to try to do such a thing, and yet this is the face of Jesus. No wonder John had no visual recognition of him. But what a wonderful hope it affords us, for John himself knew, and assured us all of it (1 John 3:2), that when Jesus comes for us, in that same day we will be like him. Jesus too made reference to this beautiful state (Matthew 13:43), almost casually it seems, and yet it is a part of the hope that all Christians need to carry with them.

> *"Then the righteous will shine like the sun in the kingdom of their Father. He who has ears let him hear"* (Matthew 13:43).

This must have been a wonderful moment for John. After all his years of faithful ministry, he was face to face with his living Lord once more. It is impossible to believe that the life he found flowing in him after Jesus laid his hand upon him is anything other than the most wonderful infusion of grace, carrying with it the full knowledge of love, joy, and peace beyond anything he had ever known before. Now he is ready to undertake his onerous task.

> *"Now write what you see, what is and what is to take place hereafter"* (Revelation 1:19).

John is now given the great time clock of the *Revelation*. Only two periods of time will be dealt with. The first relates to the current situation of the church in John's day—*"what is"*! And the second relates to an unspecified future period—*"what is to take place"*! Each period has relevance and deep significance for the other. As with all true prophecy, what is predicted for the future has immediate implications for the present. Jesus will use his analysis of those seven churches in Asia to prepare all the churches of the coming ages for the day of his coming.

Every picture and scene that John sees is a puzzle that the reader must resolve for himself. The clues to the proper interpretation of each are to be found within the details that he gives us. When these are properly observed and then related to other Scriptures in an appropriate way, the meanings gradually become clear. You should not think that the *Revelation of Jesus Christ* merely repeats, or perhaps enhances, what has already been revealed. No, each picture must be considered as essential new material without an understanding of which our comprehension of truth is severely limited.

What does the scene of Jesus standing as a priest among the seven gold lampstands mean? That the lampstands are symbolic of the seven local churches under John's oversight in Asia is made clear to us. The stars in Jesus' hand are his chosen messengers, each with a special task to fulfil in relation to one of the churches. But, as with all biblical imagery, the picture is used to convey much more than a photographic image, and we need to use all our emotional and intellectual capacity, under the enlightenment of the Holy Spirit, to get out of it what God intends.

This picture shows us Jesus in his role of high priest, attending to the lampstands so that they will give an effective light. For some two thousand years, Jesus has personally and patiently tended his churches so that they will truly be a light in the darkness. But do we need this picture today? What relevance, if any, does this obscure picture of seven lampstands have for us two thousand years after it was given?

Clearly, the picture of the seven lampstands is allegorical. The purpose of allegory in part is to hide the meaning from the uninitiated, rather like Jesus' use of parables. Here, Jesus is revealing what he means by *church* and what he always meant his churches to be. Surely, we might say, after two thousand years we understand the purpose of the church. But do we? By means of this vision, Jesus intentionally challenges our inherited, traditional views of what church is about. In doing so, he exposes the tragedy of what passes for church in much of the world today. But Jesus uses imagery that will make no sense to those who do not value the Old Testament as essential to our comprehension of the gospel.

> *"To you it has been given to know the secrets of the kingdom of God; but for others they are in parables, so that seeing thy may not see, and hearing they may not understand. Now the parable is this: the seed is the word of God. . . . As for the good soil, they are those who, hearing the word, hold it fast in an honest and good heart, and bring forth fruit with patience"* (Luke 8:10–15).

The imagery of the lampstand will be understood only by those for whom it is intended, and to understand it we must go far back in time. A study of the original tabernacle design reveals the important role of the lampstand. It stood in the small, covered tent known as the Holy Place, which served as a kind of entrance lobby to the Holy of Holies. These two sections of the tabernacle were covered over so that without some artificial lighting, it would have been impossible for the required rituals to be carried out.

When the high priest entered the Holy of Holies on his annual visit on the Day of Atonement, he had to pass through the Holy Place; and he was able to make his way to the veil only by means of the light from the lampstand. The daily rituals of the sacrificial offerings made on the altar that stood immediately in front of the veil and the preparation of the bread of the Presence on the adjacent table were all activities that could be carried out only by means of the illumination provided by the seven lamps on the lampstand.

We read in Exodus 25:31–40 that the lampstand was to be constructed to an exact specification, the pattern for which had actually been shown to Moses when he met with God on the mountain. In Exodus 26:35 we read of the exact positioning of the lampstand, and then in Exodus 27:20–21 we read of the *"pure beaten"* oil, which is to be burned in the lamps and of the continual attendance of the priests to keep the lamps burning. The great significance of this seven-branched lampstand to Israel is clear because its proper functioning is to be *"a statute forever"*; that is, it is to be observed by the people of Israel throughout their generations. This piece of furniture in the Holy Place is given a unique role for Israel—the light must never be allowed to go out! Should it do so, it would signify that *the functioning of the tabernacle as God's dwelling place among his people had ceased and God's presence had been withdrawn*. The temple of God thus would become *"ichabod"*—a dreadful situation!

The lampstand also spoke prophetically of the churches that God would bring into being one day, each of which would be a light, so that under the terms of the new covenant, countless men and women would be enabled to come into his presence to worship just as the high priest had done, but now not once a year but constantly.

In the *Revelation*, the vision of Jesus surrounded by seven lampstands gives the original symbolism new meaning with a practical application to our times. Now, the attending priest is the risen Lord Jesus himself, and he is robed accordingly. He uses this means to show us what his role will be during the age of the church.

In prophetic language, the use of a number conveys special and consistent information about its subject. Thus the seven lampstands *of Revelation* stand for all the churches of Christ down through the ages. The number seven has this significance because all through Scripture it stands for the completeness of God's handiwork, as in the seven-day week of creation and earlier in this chapter (1:4), where we have the description of the Holy Spirit, unique to the *Revelation*, as *"the seven spirits who are before his throne."* On this same basis, we can see the seven lampstands as representative of all those churches that make up God's one church throughout time. Thus this teaching is extremely important for every church and fellowship in every age. Jesus is building *his* church, just as he said he would. He is the head of his body, and here he shows us how he exercises that responsibility in order to make each lampstand effective. The question must then follow: *if a church is not an effective lampstand, can it be his church?*

The directness and immediacy of Jesus' oversight is remarkable. We see no sign of hierarchy or denominational structures involved. The seven stars are shown to be in his right hand, and these emissaries, most probably the leaders of the seven churches, are there to carry dispatches from him directly to their individual churches. The identification of the stars visible to us in the heavens with the invisible angels is consistently used in Scripture, perhaps to remind us of their great numbers and their continuing presence as God's ministers on the earth. In this case, the church leaders are sharing the ministry of the angels.

[It is worth noting that in these prophecies we find no popes, archbishops, bishops, or governing bodies serving as intermediaries between Jesus and his churches. All church leaders are to be servants of his churches—God's messengers—who, just like John and the angels, are to find their ministries at the throne of God.]

The messages these angels are to bring to the seven churches are not theological propositions; they are highly specific and practical, relating to the behaviour and condition of each church at that time. Each message apparently is to be ministered to the whole church by its pastors, and Jesus expects each individual within the church to hear the message with spiritual ears and to know its significance.

Concerning angel-ministers we read:

> *"Are they not all ministering spirits sent forth to serve, for the sake of those who are to obtain salvation?"* (Hebrews 1:14).

The implication of this must be that the Lord intends to directly and consistently communicate his view of each church and its doings to the church through a specific messenger, *one who gets his messages directly from Jesus.*

The Greek word *aggelos* is sometimes used in the Bible of humans who are messengers of God (e.g., John the Baptist). From this it can be argued that church leaders themselves are intended to be divine messengers, in which case they are the stars in Jesus' right hand: a picture of completely devoted men and women who live in his presence and who hear his voice for their churches. Can this apply to today's church leaders? Is Jesus still sending his angel messengers? Are the leaders hearing the messages? Are they living examples of the messages they bring? Is this Jesus' description of the proper ministry of apostles, bishops, and other church leaders—to be his special messengers? Such ministry can be fulfilled only by those who, having ears to hear and hearts to obey, are themselves disciples and *conquerors* and therefore examples of what they teach, as was John.

These angels are men and women who are spiritually mature. Like John, they know what it is to be "in Spirit." They live from God's throne room.

> *"Therefore, brethren, since we have confidence to enter the sanctuary by the blood of Jesus, by the new and living way which he opened for us through the curtain, that is, through his flesh, and since we have a great priest over the house of God, let us draw near with a true heart in full assurance of faith, with our hearts sprinkled clean from an evil conscience and our bodies washed with pure water"* (Hebrews 10:19–22).

Certainly, as our churches generally recognise, we are to have a united, shared theology and doctrine accurately derived from Scripture and revealed to us corporately by the Holy Spirit. But accurate theology and doctrine need to be applied within the context of each local situation. The truth that leads to personal conviction at a given moment is not formal theology or unchanging traditional practices; rather, immediate revelation of truth is what brings conviction. An angel messenger responsible for a church (whether spirit or man) must derive his or her messages and teaching directly from God. These certainly will accord with orthodox doctrine, but they will also reveal the practical application within the context of that church as we see with the seven churches Jesus addresses in the *Revelation*.

The *Revelation* shows us that each leader, church, and individual is continually being measured against the standard of God's Word; and as part of the lampstand allegory, each of us lives under specific direction from him. On this basis it quickly becomes clear that at least five out of seven church leaders he was addressing were failing their Lord and their people.

If the application of this vision was simply for a limited time in the early days of the church, then it would not be very helpful to us. But in the same way that the maintenance of the tabernacle lamplight was to be a statute forever to Israel, so we can take it that this wondrous picture of the church-lampstand is to be a statute forever, until Jesus himself will change it once more by removing his church to glory.

If each church is to be a representation of the main body of the lampstand, then we can see that Jesus views each church as being beautifully fashioned and intricately wrought from pure gold. It pictures a people of harmony and holiness with all their impurities (iniquities) purged away. The light itself proceeds from the seven individual lamps that stand on the top of each branch of the lampstand. Each almond-shaped cup represents an individual within the church. Each has its own wick and its own supply of oil. In the temple, the duty priest had to see that each wick was properly trimmed so that it did not give an uneven light and that each cup was filled with the best oil so that the wick should not smoke or the lights fail.

The allegory mirrors the parable of the vine and the vinedresser (John 15:1–11), where the branches are totally at one with the vine but still must be pruned in order to be fully effective. It is against the standard of this beautiful, light-giving lampstand that each church is constantly being weighed by Jesus.

Just as the lampstand was specifically placed to provide illumination for the daily routines of the attendant priests in the Holy Place, and also to light the way into the Holy of Holies for the sanctified high priest to make atonement once a year, so the specific purpose of the church is to provide spiritual light for the daily worship of God by his priests (see Revelation 1:6), enabling us to come into his presence in the holiness given by Jesus.

THE STARS
REPRESENT
ANGELS

THE LAMPSTANDS
REPRESENT
JESUS' CHURCHES

Surely this is the definition of the work of the church that is an effective lampstand: *to teach and minister to the saved so that they know they are called not only to enter God's presence but also to live with him there. As we learn to enter and abide with him, he will use us to lead others into his presence.*

That this is a spiritual mystery is incontrovertible, but if we miss this truth because it presents us with difficulties of comprehension, then our ministry can never do justice to the wonderful salvation that Jesus brought us. By this vision of the "lampstand-church" Jesus sets the scene for the remainder of the *Revelation*. Everything that follows turns round this central theme of his intentions for his church in this world. As he began the work of introducing the new covenant to Israel and the world, Jesus said:

> *"The time is coming, and now is when the true worshipers will worship the Father in spirit and in truth, for such the Father seeks to worship him. God is spirit, and those who worship must worship in spirit and in truth"* (John 4:23–24).

As Jesus said this to the Samaritan woman at the well, he was already anticipating the cross and preparing the way for the "lampstand-churches" that would come into being as a result of his death and resurrection. By his own definition, "temple worship" as was then experienced in Jerusalem was to be changed to a new "temple worship" that could take place only within the hearts of those who are themselves physical temples of the living God.

To encourage the seven *Revelation* churches to conform to his challenge to be effective lampstands, Jesus offers incentives. In these promises the great purpose of God in creation is revealed. These guarantees show us what God has made possible for his children to achieve; but if the believer is to inherit the promises, *he or she must become a conqueror*, just as John had written about in his first epistle.

For any who might think heaven is a dull place, these promises open the understanding to an incredible reality. There are at least fifteen privileges that God wants to bestow upon those brothers and sisters of Jesus who persevere in their commitment and obedience until the day of the Lord's coming or until death overtakes them, whichever is first. These great privileges, to be received by the conquerors in that day, are part of their inheritance as joint heirs with Jesus.

These wonderful promises reveal the heart's desire of Jesus. Although our minds struggle to understand them, they are indications of what our oneness with Jesus now will mean in eternity. When the Father delivers these gifts to his children in heaven, his original purpose in creation will have been largely achieved. They are there for us to look forward to. They are intended to carry us through the dark times, through the persecutions, pains, and sufferings that must come. We can become so focused on blessings in this life that we fail to appreciate that suffering is necessary to our achieving the promises of God in the next life (see Ephesians 1:15–23).

It is questionable whether or not we can be those who "conquer" without looking forward to the promises of God awaiting us in heaven.

THE FIFTEEN PROMISES OF GOD FOR THE CONQUEROR

TO EPHESUS *To him who conquers:*
1. *I will grant to eat of the tree of life which is in the paradise of God* (Revelation 2:7).

TO SMYRNA *He who conquers:*
2. *shall not be hurt by the second death* (Revelation 2:11).

TO PERGAMUM *To him who conquers:*
3. *I will give some of the hidden manna,*
4. *and I will give him a white stone, with a new name written on the stone which no one knows except him who receives it* (Revelation 2:17).

TO THYATIRA *He who conquers and who keeps my works until the end:*
5. *I will give him power over the nations, and he shall rule them with a rod of iron, as when earthen pots are broken in pieces, even as I myself have received power from my Father;*
6. *and I will give him the morning star* (Revelation 2:26–28).

TO SARDIS *He who conquers:*
7. *shall be clad thus in white garments,*
8. *and I will not blot his name out of the book of life;*
9. *I will confess his name before my Father and before his angels* (Revelation 3:5–6).

TO PHILADELPHIA *He who conquers:*
10. *I will make him a pillar in the temple of my God;*
11. *never shall he go out of it,*
12. *and I will write on him the name of my God,*
13. *and the name of the city of my God, the new Jerusalem which comes down from my God out of heaven,*
14. *and my own new name* (Revelation 3:12).

TO LAODICEA *He who conquers:*
15. *I will grant him to sit with me on my throne, as I myself conquered and sat down with my Father on his throne* (Revelation 3:21).

When we have this insight, the questions that must always follow are these: Am I ready now for Jesus' return? Am I living in conscious awareness that I am a temple of the living God in which worship takes place? Do those who come to seek God through our church find that illumination, which leads them personally through the process of discipleship right into Father's presence in the Holy of Holies?

The seven churches Jesus assessed in the *Revelation* were all more or less failing by comparison with the yardstick by which Jesus judged them. Only those suffering from persecution came off very well in his assessment. It seems that though they were doing many "good" church things, none of the seven churches understood that their task was to *make conquerors of their disciples.*

Bad teaching, immorality, legalistic "old covenant" practices, loss of first love, lukewarmness, powerlessness, pride, and even idolatry—all marks of apostasy—were tarnishing the lampstand. The lamps themselves were smoking and sputtering in unwilling obedience to the Holy Spirit and the Word of God, and so giving a deceptive and flickering light.

There are many detailed teachings that can be drawn from the ministry of Jesus to those seven churches. There will be no attempt here to carry out a detailed exegesis but rather an attempt to draw out those points that have particular relevance for the study of the rest of the book.

Jesus' criticisms are always trenchant. His comments lack our modern "spiritual," sanitised language. In four of the seven churches, Satan is named directly as being involved with the problems being encountered. Do we really understand the serious nature of the spiritual battle we are called to fight?

Jesus' primary concern was not and is not for the state of society. His concern is that his churches (and their angels) should so minister truth to his children that they are led by his Spirit into his presence and know his presence in them. If the churches are not visible lights (i.e., effective lampstands) in this dark world, then we are presenting something substantially less than the whole gospel, which is no gospel at all. Prosperity without holiness is the devil's deception. As is so clearly laid out for Israel in the Old Testament, holiness must precede prosperity.

The picture of the pure gold lampstand is given to inform us of the error of our alternative objectives. It shows us what Jesus is determined to achieve in us individually and through us corporately. If he cannot do this, then he must remove the lampstand so that pretence of truth and spiritual authority will no longer deceive people. What a tragedy! It is frightening to see how many lifeless churches there are, churches that possess neither life nor power for life, yet still go through the motions. Indeed, how many lampstands has Jesus had to remove already?

It is apparent in these last days, as with those seven churches of *Revelation*, that in many churches the lack of the Holy Spirit's presence in the ministry will be compensated for by good works, religious exercises (including prayer, music, and singing), and even occult healing practices. All these can touch the emotions and deliver a feel-good factor to the flesh, but they do not bring the personal changes inside that alone evidence holiness and enable us to worship in spirit and truth. This situation is entirely consistent with prophetic New Testament teaching of what can be expected in the churches of the last days. The New Testament writers are quite explicit: there can be no acceptance of anybody or any work that does not begin with the cross and does not go on in discipleship under the direction of the Holy Spirit. The *Revelation* reveals that the conqueror is one who is living daily in God's presence with God's presence in him. It was when the seven churches fell away from these absolute standards that they offended their Lord.

On two occasions, John writes of people who "*say that they are Jews and are not, but are a synagogue of Satan*" (Revelation 2:9; cf. 3:9). Judaism and Islam are both examples of the terrible deception of inherited legalistic religion. Their adherents respect their "God" but fear death and the afterlife because they have no forgiveness of sins and no assurance of God's favour. Like all other religions, they are ruled by controlling demons who seek their worship. There can be no compromise with them, for this is similar to the idolatry of the nations that led Israel astray. Such unfortunate peoples are subject to the harassment and control of the unclean spirits who torment them (see 1 John 5:17–21).

The New Testament is filled with warnings for the church of the last days, and *Revelation* spells it out once more. Jesus shows the seven churches that they have failed to guard against false apostles, false prophets, and false teaching. As a consequence, there is immorality, apathy, lukewarmness, pride, slumber, and self-satisfaction. The extensive lists of faults are not exhaustive, but Jesus calls his people, and especially their leaders, to be unequivocal in confronting them. They are not to be tolerated. As they are uncovered, they are to be a cause for repentance by the whole church, leading to reformation.

All churches need to submit themselves to this searching of the Spirit, through Jesus' prophetic words in *Revelation*. Now, as then, Jesus makes it clear that his purpose is not to bring condemnation but rather freedom from error, which will lead to blessing. The analysis of each of the seven church situations is accompanied by a call either to repentance or to perseverance in suffering.

One cannot couch the *revealing* of the lampstand-church in moderate and reasonable language, for the truth is that many churches are desperately in need of root and branch revolution if they are to be the lampstands that Jesus intends. Leaders *must* be "angels" who find their messages at God's throne, and the saints *must* be "conquerors" if they are to inherit God's promises. The Word of God is the *only* light to our path, individually and corporately, and the Holy Spirit in us is the *only* means of our being led into all truth.

In the *Revelation*, Jesus coins the special word "conqueror" to replace other words popularly used to describe Christians, many of which have become debased in their meaning; he does not speak of believers, Christians, church members, or even disciples. Seven times he makes the statement, "To him who conquers I will give . . ." He is speaking of those who are living in the whole work and purpose of salvation. This is simply orthodox, biblical Christianity.

It is conquerors who make up the hidden body of Christ: those saved ones from among his churches who are living in the painful process of being sanctified. These conquerors are the ones who are being changed into the likeness of Christ. They are pressing on to spiritual maturity, knowing God and knowing his presence in them.

Seven times Jesus said, *"He that has ears to hear, let him hear what the Spirit is saying to the churches."* It is clear that God holds us all individually responsible for hearing what the Holy Spirit has to say. Any one Christian can go on with God, even if his whole church is out of order, although the struggle will be very painful and difficult.

To conquer, or to win the victory, means that one is in a conflict with an enemy. There is a discernible opposition, and there is a battleground where the fighting takes place. With his clarion call for each of us to conquer, Jesus propels us into an otherworldly scene. We are warriors in a war that is being fought totally unobserved by mankind in general and by much of the church in particular. It is a bitter battle, and it is for life or death.

Until we are born anew, our natural mind is the arbiter of our decision-making processes, drawing on our past, our education, our memories, and our feelings, all learned in the world. Once we are "saved," our mind is to be trained to a new perspective by the *Revelation of Jesus Christ*. That new perspective is provided as the *Revelation* amplifies and completes the whole Word of God. The Holy Spirit will introduce us to hidden realities, beginning even before the events of Eden, and then lead us daily, through a battle with our flesh, the world around us, and Satan and his forces to a spiritual victory that will take us eventually to the glory, which awaits us in eternity.

SUMMARY

❖ The *Revelation* is intended first for the seven churches in Asia that are under John's pastoral oversight. They now serve as an example for all churches through time.

❖ The work and ministry of the churches is that of being lampstands.

❖ The work and ministry of Jesus is that of the priest responsible for cleaning each individual lamp and filling it with pure oil.

❖ Jesus is now Lord of all, and he alone holds the keys of death and the grave.

❖ Jesus' continuing judgement of his churches is based upon the absolute standard of the lampstand that stood in the Holy Place in the tent of presence (the tabernacle) as a perpetual light—does it give a pure, steady light?

❖ The lampstand was there to give light so that the priests could carry out their functions in the Holy Place, and the high priest could enter the Holy of Holies once each year.

❖ The lampstand-churches' function is to make conquerors who come into God's presence to worship.

❖ All God's people must fight and win the spiritual battle and so be conquerors.

❖ The conquerors may be defined as sons of God: those who know his presence in them and who know their presence in him.

❖ The fifteen promises of Revelation are for those who are conquerors.

THE THRONE ROOM OF GOD
REVELATION 4

Act I, Scene 2—THE THRONE ROOM OF GOD

Time: Eternal

Place: Heaven

People: All Mankind

"After this I looked, and lo, in heaven an open door!" (Revelation 4:1).

Each time John introduces a new vision, he signals it by using a brief phrase such as, "Then I saw" or "Then I looked." At this point in the *Revelation*, without preliminary, a stunning sight opens before him (and us). A door in heaven is opened, and John hears the voice of thunder again, saying, "Come up hither!" This was no vision; a human being was to walk in heaven for the first time. He was to enter the throne room of God and then report what he had seen to the churches.

Had John simply received the seven, very detailed prophetic messages for the churches, that would have been remarkable enough; but now the voice promises, "I will show you what must take place after this" (Revelation 4:1). In previous times, God had personally met with Adam and Moses on the earth. Some others, like Daniel, Isaiah, and Ezekiel, had seen wonderful visions of heaven. But John uniquely was called to visit with God in his throne room. His experience was on behalf of all those who would be "conquerors." He was to know and report to the churches what it is like to actually stand in the throne room. God purposed to encourage his lampstand-churches by giving them insight into their certain destiny. The promise of our being seated with Christ in the heavenly places right now is given substance beyond anything revealed in the Bible up until this time.

There is nothing casual about this occasion. It is of huge significance for the churches and for each one of us individually. This was not an experience calculated to impress or dazzle John; he did not need that, nor is that God's way. In God's mercy, this wondrous experience was given to John so that all other Christians might share with him the marvel and glory of the occasion and understand that it has ongoing, daily significance for us. Primarily, it causes us to know with certainty what our hope is for our future. It also confirms the Old Testament prophets as being faithful in recounting the visions given to them for Israel. This detailed and comprehensive experience is given to John for each one of us personally, and it is a vital help for us in our battle to conquer. *It is the revelation of Jesus' "throne room strategy" for his churches.*

The call, *"Come up hither,"* was a unique occasion for John for a special purpose. All members of Christ's lampstand-churches are called into God's presence (see Hebrews 10:19–22). The difference between us and John is that our call is to be in God's presence in spirit because of his experience. John's task was to write down "all that he saw." What a task! Think how all his senses must have been reeling under the impact of being in the glorious, living, moving environment of heaven and in the presence of God almighty. John has written it down for us, making it our task to appropriate and apply his experience to ourselves as the Holy Spirit leads us into the reality of it.

The immediate and central figure in the throne room is God himself, the centre of the glory and the object of worship. John was unable to distinguish much detail because his senses were overwhelmed and the impact of God's sensational appearance had him grasping for adequate metaphors. He could see the outline of a man, but as he looked, what came into his mind were the vivid colours he associated with rare and precious stones; he knew of jasper and carnelian, both of which possess a similar opaqueness and brilliant colour.

Around the throne was a most glorious rainbow, with a predominantly emerald hue to it. But still it was as if the source of the colours was God himself, a multicoloured light, living and moving in an ever-changing beauty. This aura of colours was intermittently punctured by great pulses of lightning emanating from the throne and accompanied by peals of rolling thunder, giving the impression of great voices speaking. Perhaps the living creatures were conversing with God.

John could see other thrones also. Altogether, he could make out twenty-four of them, and their occupants were much more discernible. Somehow he knew that these men clothed in white garments and wearing crowns were elders drawn from the ranks of the saints from the past.

The flaming torches in front of the great throne spoke to John of the seven spirits of God. Was he reminded of that great day of Pentecost, when the tongues of heavenly fire had fallen visibly on all those who were gathered together, thus equipping them for battle with the prince of this world? It must have seemed a distant memory.

How could he describe the translucent floor on which they were all standing? It was like a sea, clear and sparkling and deep, made from pure crystal and yet solid enough to bear his weight.

His senses registered further details. There were some other very wonderful and awesome creatures attending the throne. These beings he called "living creatures," upright although not human in form. Each was distinctive from his neighbour in his features. He had an impression of many eyes, active eyes, all-seeing eyes. The features of one called to mind a lion, a second reminded him of an ox, the third was not unlike a man, and the fourth like an eagle. They each had six wings with which they covered themselves—and they sang!

We can hardly imagine the beauty of such heavenly singing. The throne room was filled with it. As John listened, it swelled up to a crescendo—a beautiful, rolling cadence full of crosscurrents and hidden harmonies. This was music such as he had never known, but it found an echo in his own heart. The song seemed to be a universal hymn of praise,

> *"Holy, holy, holy is the Lord God Almighty,* **who was, and is, and is to come***!"* (Revelation 4:8).

> *". . . for* **thou didst create all things**, *and by thy will they existed and were created"* (Revelation 4:11).

In their song of praise, the heavenly hosts delight to link Jesus with the past, present, and future of all creation. What an authoritative confirmation this is of the Genesis story.

Before we continue with the detailed sequence of events that John saw, let us pause and consider the profound significance of this vision for ourselves and why God gave it to us.

We can assume that like all of the *Revelation*, this vision is an important part of the equipping of the saints so that they can be conquerors. But how does it fit in? In his second letter to the Corinthians, Paul wrote of the experience of all Christians who are filled with the Holy Spirit. As they behold *"the glory of the Lord"* (3:18), they are in a constant process of change. He is writing of our being constantly in God's presence as a function of our spiritual lives, and thus always being conscious of his glory. This is not by means of fleshly senses or even feelings, but something we receive by faith with increasing maturity. We can "see" the Lord's glory only as we are with him in the throne room in the Spirit.

We know that Jesus is in heaven, but more than that Jesus is in each of his disciples. *"Do you not know that you are God's temple and God's Spirit dwells in you?"* writes Paul (1 Corinthians 3:16). Jesus also promised:

> *"If a man loves me, he will keep my word, and my Father will love him, and* **we will come and make our home with him***"* (John 14:23).

By faith, we are to receive Jesus in all his glory into our hearts as a permanent resident. This is a mystery that we are required to work out for ourselves. Without his presence we cannot conquer. In salvation we each become a new covenant tabernacle. We are each made a priest with the duty to minister to God within the tabernacle, *"the tent of meeting,"* which is our heart. These are profound spiritual realities for us to take hold of every day. We will have suffering and temptations to pass through in this life, just as Jesus did. And while Jesus will not live life for us, he will stand with us as we live our life for him—no matter what. In other words he expects us take our full responsibility in the spiritual battle in this life. We make the choices and decisions, and we make mistakes and get things wrong from time to time; but as long as our desire is to obey him, we may be sure that he is with us and will bring us through.

> *"For it was fitting that he, for whom and by whom all things exist, in bringing many sons to glory, should make the pioneer of their salvation* **perfect through suffering***. For he who sanctifies and those who are sanctified have all one origin. That is why he is not ashamed to call them brethren"* (Hebrews 2:10–11).

We know that our Father wants us to receive this experience of John's, to take it into our hearts, and to allow the Holy Spirit to minister its significance to each one of us personally.

> *"But God, who is rich in mercy, out of the great love with which he loved us, even when we were dead through our trespasses, made us alive together with Christ (by grace you have been saved), and raised us up with him, and* **made us sit with him in the heavenly places in Christ Jesus***, that in the coming ages he might show the immeasurable riches of his grace in kindness toward us in Christ Jesus"* (Ephesians 2:4–7).

This vision of God in his throne room is eternal and unchanging. We must receive it, keep it, and cling to it as part of that hope, which is ours in Jesus. The glory we see here in heaven is far more real than any temporary glory the world may offer us. The throne room is the place of our being in the Spirit. This glimpse of home is like a living photograph for us to relish while we are physically away at the battlefront. We are present with him in the Spirit even as he is present with us, until the time when he takes us home and we shall be one with him forever. Our Father awaits our arrival, and he assures us that everything is made ready.

What a wonderful day that will be when we share his throne. Like all else in Scripture, we are to receive the promises by hearing with faith. Is our faith able to receive this insight into our destiny? Is this not what Christ promised to the ones who conquer? Consider again the promise God makes to the conquerors of Laodicea:

*"**He who conquers, I will grant to sit with me on my throne**, even as I myself conquered and sat down with my Father on his throne. He who has an ear, let him hear what the Spirit says to the churches"* (Revelation 3:21–22).

I believe that this wondrous experience opened John's understanding to the intimacy and immediacy of his relationship with his Father. What was impossible for Moses on the mountain is made possible for us through Jesus under the new covenant. We are with him, and he is with us, always! Just as the Father and Jesus were one in everything, so are we. We are so afflicted by feelings of unworthiness (reinforced by constant exhortations of our need to improve) that we do not believe or understand the magnificent victory of our salvation. Jesus' prayer for us *is* answered!

*"I do not pray for these only, but also for those who believe in me through their word, that they may all be one; even as **thou Father art in me, and I in thee, that they also may be in us**, so that the world may believe that thou hast sent me.*

*"The glory which thou hast given me I have given them, that they may be one even as we are one, **I in them and thou in me**, that they may become perfectly one, so that the world may know that thou hast sent me and hast loved them even as thou hast loved me.*

*"Father, I desire that they also, whom thou hast given me, **may be with me where I am, to behold my glory** which thou hast given me in thy love for me before the foundation of the world.*

"O righteous Father, the world has not known thee, but I have known thee; and these know that thou hast sent me.

*"I made known to them thy name, and I will make it known, that **the love with which thou hast loved me may be in them, and I in them**"* (John 17:20–26).

This prayer of Jesus is truly amazing in what he asks for. It provides us with a summary of the purpose of salvation, and it defines for us the proper meaning of the word "reconciliation": it is "oneness" with God. To be a conqueror is to live in the whole truth of what Jesus achieved for us on the cross. To be a conqueror is to come out of the bondage of the world (its morals, standards, aims, methods, and entertainments) in the Spirit and to come into the heavenly place (the tabernacle) also in the Spirit. It is a new life lived in two dimensions at the same time. While we are in a world dominated by the flesh and the devil, Jesus is in us. And when we are in heaven, we are beyond the world, for we are in Jesus.

God answered Jesus' prayer even as he prayed it, and this throne room revelation is a reminder for us of the unchanging purpose of God in every generation since he prayed it.

TAKING THE SCROLL
REVELATION 5

Act I, Scene 3—TAKING THE SCROLL

Time: Immediately before Pentecost

Place: The Throne Room of God

People: All Mankind

In *Revelation* 5, John recounts a brief scene that is crucial to our understanding of the integrity, coherence, and harmony of all scriptural prophecy. In his time, Daniel had received remarkable prophetic dreams and visions that span the years of history from Nebuchadnezzar's reign to Jesus' second coming. One would expect there to be an important symbiosis between Daniel's writings and John's, and there is.

Daniel depicted a time to come when a "son of man" would be given everlasting dominion over all of God's creation. Now John sees the detailed enactment of this moment.

> *"I saw in the night visions, and behold, with the clouds of heaven there came one like* ***a son of man****, and he came to the Ancient of Days and was presented before him. And* ***to him was given dominion*** *and glory and kingdom, that all peoples, nations and languages should serve him; his dominion is an everlasting dominion, which shall not pass away, and his kingdom one that shall not be destroyed"* (Daniel 7:13–14).

Revelation 5 begins with another dramatic scene in the heavenly throne room. John writes, "And I saw," so denoting a change in what he was seeing. Now he sees that the one seated on the throne is holding a seven-sealed scroll in his hand.

It seems that John recognises that this scroll is of great significance to the destiny of mankind. He understands that there is a supreme urgency for it to be opened; and yet, unless a man can be found who is fit to open it, it must remain forever sealed up. He weeps passionately; he knows that should it not be opened, then his world would be without hope of redemption.

It is significant that this is the only time in the whole of his *revelation* experience that John gives way to emotion. What, then, is this wonderful scroll that can be opened only by someone very special? What are the qualifications to open it? Who indeed is worthy to do so? Who could have earned the right?

Thankfully, one of the twenty-four elders responds to John's distress.

"Weep not; lo, the **Lion** *of the tribe of Judah, the* **Root** *of David, has conquered, so that he can open the scroll and its seven seals"* (Revelation 5:5).

The elder was reminding John of Jacob's great prophecy concerning Judah *("Judah is a lion's whelp")*, made on his deathbed many centuries before (Genesis 49:9–10). The elder links it to Isaiah's great prophecy of a coming saviour *("There shall come forth a shoot from the stump of Jesse, and a branch shall grow out of his roots")*, a conqueror who will one day transform the world with peace and righteousness (Isaiah 11:1). All those prophecies find their fulfilment in Jesus, the one who by his obedience in death is fit to take the scroll from God's hand and open it.

Then John witnesses a remarkable scene. Between the throne and the four living creatures, and among the elders, he sees not a fearsome lion as might be expected but a little lamb standing: the Lamb of God, the one destined to be slain from the foundation of the world to take away the sins of the world—Jesus! In this vivid picture of Jesus, the Lord of all glory demonstrates for us what it is to become a conqueror. He was lamblike in his obedience to his Father, and that made him vulnerable even unto death itself at the hands of wicked and foolish men. He did not use his lion-power and authority to save himself. He that was truly a lion became a lamb so that we too, becoming lambs in his likeness, might follow him to glory.

What universal joy there was in heaven at this special moment! No one in heaven itself was legally entitled to open that important document. If Jesus had not paid the price, then it would have remained closed forever, and the consequences for creation would be inconceivable. Despite the record of history, the vain belief continues that man is capable of ordering his own life without God. Although we hate to acknowledge it, the truth is that mankind acting outside of obedience to God always degenerates and is quite incapable of helping himself or improving himself.

It was this moment that Jesus spoke of to his disciples when he gave them the Great Commission:

> "**All authority** *in heaven and earth is given to me. Go therefore . . .*" (Matthew 28:18).

After his death, he went down into the grave. Then at his resurrection he went to his Father in heaven and received the scroll. Then he appeared to his disciples once more. Then it was time for Pentecost. It was time for the next phase in God's plan to begin.

In the earliest days, by the time of Noah, Scripture tells us:

> *"The Lord saw that the wickedness of man was great in the earth, and that **every imagination of the thoughts of his heart was only evil continually**. And the Lord was sorry that he had made man on the earth, and it grieved him to his heart"* (Genesis 6:5–6).

Much has happened since then, but of our generation Jesus said:

> "**As it was in the days of Noah, so will it be in the days of the Son of Man.** *They ate, they drank, they married, they were given in marriage, until the day when Noah entered the ark, and the flood came and destroyed them all"* (Luke 17:26–27).

Jesus prophesied that the moral decadence afflicting mankind at the end of the age will be exactly as it was in Noah's time (not much noticeable evolutionary improvement there!).

What then is this important scroll? Wherein does its significance lie? As with other mysteries in the *Revelation*, many theories have been advanced in answer to this question, but the clues to the correct answer are to be found in Scripture itself. In Jeremiah 32, we find a detailed description of Jeremiah's purchase of a field from Hanamel, his cousin, in which the title deed of ownership of the property plays an important part. This account sets out for us the way that property transactions were handled in Israel according to the provisions of the law and cultural practices of those times.

We can learn too from Naomi's decision to sell land. When Naomi wanted to dispose of a parcel of land that she owned, by protocol she had to offer it to her next of kin first (see Ruth 4:3). If he could not or would not pay the price fixed by the elders, then the one who came next after him in the bloodline could buy it. In this case Boaz, a relative of Naomi's late husband, became entitled to make the purchase, and agreed to do so with the public agreement of the elders and all concerned. Apparently the title to the land was not simply freehold ownership as we know it but also carried clear responsibilities for those folk who occupied it, even if they were not able to manage it properly for themselves.

Such transactions were highly public ones, closely governed by protocol, and carried out in the assembly of the elders of the people. The witnessed and sealed deeds of ownership (scrolls) were lodged with an official keeper for safekeeping. An unsealed deed was also made as a copy for everyday use.

The scene in the throne room is an enactment similar to both of these transactions. The sealed deed in God's hand is the title deed to his creation on earth, and God is the keeper of it, the one who oversees all transactions concerning it.

We know that originally God gave dominion of the earth to Adam and Eve (see Genesis 1:26). However, in accepting Satan's lying assurance that they could be independent of God if they partook of the Tree of the Knowledge of Good and Evil, Adam effectively handed over their dominion to him. But this was an illegal transaction. Satan was not of the family line. He had no rights in the matter, and so he could never take legal possession of the title deed. He is a liar, a thief and a usurper, and he must yield up his possession of the property if someone with a legal claim to the title turns up.

By means of his deception, Satan had won temporary power over the earth and its inhabitants. Adam, although apparently still in charge, had sold his family and his heirs into bondage; now they were enslaved to Satan and his angels (1 John 5:19), and blind as they were to their slavery they were without the possibility of release.

God's response to this tragedy was to set in motion the great spiritual battle that has lasted down through the ages, unseen and mostly unrecognised by unbelieving mankind. In cursing Satan (who had previously rebelled against him), God reduced him from his angelic form to that of a hideous monster. And by cursing the ground he ensured that man would not be idle in his reduced state, being always occupied with the need to sustain himself and his family by the sweat of his brow.

However, the curse came with a promise. Satan's dominion would end one day. A time would come when he would be defeated and destroyed by the seed of the woman he had deceived. One day one of her children would be the means of his end.

"Because you have done this, cursed are you above all cattle, and above all wild animals; on your belly you shall go, and dust you shall eat all the days of your life. I will put enmity between you and the woman, and between your seed and her seed; **he shall bruise your head** *and you shall bruise his heel"* (Genesis 3:14–15).

All these things are known to Satan because God had warned him from the beginning, but because he himself is a liar he believes he can yet defy God's Word concerning him and his angels.

The genealogies in Matthew 1 and Luke 3 take great care to accurately present Jesus' lineage. Jesus is humanly a direct descendent of Adam (see Luke 3:38), not as Joseph's son (Luke 3:23) but as a son of Eve (the woman's line). [It is important to recall that it is the iniquity of the fathers (not the mothers) that is visited upon the children throughout the generations (see Exodus 20:5)]. Because he was conceived by the Holy Spirit and not by a man, Jesus was born without iniquity (only the second such person in history), so he was a second Adam in this respect. Through the human bloodline of his mother, he had the right to redeem the property lost by his forebear thousands of years before. But there was a price set for the redemption of the property, and it was not cheap. We know that price. It is the unblemished lifeblood of a sinless man poured out for Adam's sin and all subsequent sins. What a cost! What a price to pay! Yes! Only the blood of the Lamb without blemish was sufficient to redeem the whole world. God himself would pay the price in his beloved Son. Surely that is love and grace.

By God's grace, Jesus has done it; when he took the scroll a paean of praise broke out in heaven confirming the result of his sacrifice, and the destiny of those saved.

> *"**Worthy art thou to take the scroll** and to open its seals, for thou wast slain and by thy blood didst ransom men for God from every tribe and tongue and people and nation, and hast made them a kingdom and priests to our God, and they shall reign on earth"* (Revelation 5:9–10).

No wonder the heavenly places rang with joy. The taking of the scroll from the hand of the Father signified that at last the whole process of dealing with the tragedy of Eden was in the hands of Jesus. He had the right to open the scroll, indicating his total authority to do with his property whatever he considered fit to do. Dominion rightfully belonged to the Lamb that was slain, and now he would exercise it.

Chapter 5 of John's account finishes with a very short but wonderful scene that is out of the time sequence we have been following so far. This scene projects far into the future, to a time when the full effects of this wonderful redemption will be seen, a time when all is reconciled to God at last and every living and created being delights to praise and worship the Lamb of God. Such a day will come, and once it arrives we have every expectation that we shall never, ever be moved from it.

> *"**To him who sits upon the throne and to the Lamb be blessing and honour for ever and ever!**"* (Revelation 5:13).

And the four living creatures said, "Amen!" and the elders fell down and worshipped. What a truly wonderful scene, and we shall be there to share it.

SUMMARY

❖ This unique vision of God in his throne room is a gift to the saints.

❖ This is our destiny as conquerors—we are to share the throne room with Jesus.

❖ This is accessible to the conqueror "in the spirit" by hearing with faith.

❖ We are seated together with Jesus, NOW!

❖ The Lion of Judah is the Lamb who takes away the sin of the world.

❖ The scroll is the legal deed to the creation.

❖ Jesus earned the legal right to ownership of creation.

❖ Once the scroll is in his hands, all created beings fall down to worship him.

❖ He begins to exercise his authority as he opens the scroll.

OPENING THE FIRST FOUR SEALS
OF THE SCROLL
REVELATION 6:1-8

**Act I, Scene 4—OPENING THE FIRST FOUR
SEALS OF THE SCROLL**

**Time: Begins before Pentecost
and Runs through Seal 5**

Place: On Earth

People: The Church, Israel, and the World

When Jesus took the scroll out of his Father's hand, it demonstrated one certainty: everything and everyone on this earth belongs to Jesus. Jesus already had the keys of the kingdom of heaven (Matthew 16:19), and then he took the keys of death and Hades (Revelation 1:18). Now, through this action we are to see that he has legally purchased the created world and its inhabitants. This entirely accords with the writer to the Hebrews, who says:

> *"Thou didst make him for a little while lower than the angels, thou hast crowned him with glory and honour, putting everything in subjection under his feet. Now in putting everything in subjection to him, he left nothing outside his control. As it is,* **we do not yet see everything in subjection to him.** *But we see Jesus, who for a little while was made lower than the angels, crowned with glory and honour because of the suffering of death, so that by the grace of God he might taste death for everyone"* (Hebrews 2:7–9).

Hebrews makes it clear that from the moment when Jesus took the scroll, he was legally entitled to absolute rights and authority in the world and the world legally owes total submission to him. Although this rule is not yet visible to the human eye, nothing can take place, or can happen that he does not permit. It is he who permits Satan and his angels to operate and is even permitting man's rebellion against him to continue for a season.

Because of the traumatic events that will follow, it is important to establish this truth for God's people. Because God accepted the price he paid, *Jesus, the Son of Man, is Lord of all right now, and he is King over everything!*

Jesus does not just take the scroll and rip the seals off as if he were opening a Christmas box. The taking of the scroll and the purposeful opening of each seal show us that Jesus is taking up his authority in a complex sequence of strategic activities that he initiates from heaven. Although the contents of the scroll are important, Jesus wants to use the process of removing the seals to teach us some profound truths about his objectives. His strategy will achieve a total and absolute recovery of the earth. We are shown the means by which he will accomplish God's plan.

The four horsemen that are sent forth at the opening of the first four seals share a common purpose. As Jesus breaks each seal, one the four living creatures attending God's throne is heard to speak. Each voice is like thunder, uttering one commanding and unmistakable word: *"Come!"* Most commentaries offer a tragically trivial explanation of this great cry issuing from God's throne. Many see this as being a word directed to the riders and their horses that are seen then to *go out* on their mission. But this is hardly an appropriate response to a command to "come." So it is that this explanation misses an incredible *revelation*. The voices of the living creatures present a heart cry. The command echoes right through the *Revelation* itself. It is the ongoing call of God to his creation. These commands repeat the words uttered by Jesus while he was still on earth:

> *"Come! Come to me all who labour and are heavy laden and I will give you rest"*
> (Matthew 11:28).

The new call of the four living creatures follows on the mediatory work of Christ that is now complete—all can be saved! But it means more than a call to be saved. In salvation we are immediately reconciled wholly and completely to our God; therefore as our response, we must take the steps to "come" to him! But where is he to be found? The rest and peace that he promises is not found in church membership or religious practices; it is found only in God's presence. God wants relationship with us. He wants to be with us, and he wants us to be with him. We saw that bringing people into God's presence was the intended ministry of the lampstand-churches. This is what the Holy Spirit has been saying to the churches through the ages, and it should be clear to us all. Consider these words from the last chapter of the *Revelation*:

> *"The Spirit and the Bride say, 'Come!' Let him who hears say, 'Come!' And let him*
> *who is thirsty come, let him who desires take the water of life without price"*
> (Revelation 22:17).

It is the same powerful command that is given each time Jesus opens a seal: "Come!" and the Spirit and the bride agree on it. *If a church does not have the same message and purpose as the Holy Spirit, then it is not part of the bride of Christ.* It is "apostate," for it is not saying what the Holy Spirit is saying to the churches and it has no effective ministry in the world. This heart cry "Come!" has to be the central ministry of the lampstand-church.

That this call to "come" is reemphasised at the end of the *Revelation* shows us the unchanging purpose of God in sending Jesus Christ. God wants his children to be fully reconciled to him now, and only as they are can they find the living water that flows from his throne. His church must be pointing his saved people to the only source of life-giving water so that they can drink themselves and minister to others.

> *"[Jesus said,] 'If any one thirst, let him come to me and drink. He who believes in me*
> *as the scripture has said, "Out of his heart shall flow rivers of living water."' Now this*
> *he said about the Spirit, which those who believed in him were to receive; for as yet the*
> *Spirit had not been given, because Jesus was not yet glorified"* (John 7:38–39).

For nearly two thousand years, the cry has gone out from the living creatures at God's throne. Throughout the whole earth and to all mankind, it still rings out today: "Come!" With patience and long-suffering, overlooking rejection, not punishing the provocations of those religious people who know the truth but live the lie (John 8:44), putting up with the injustices and wickedness of man's economy, God has continued to hold out his hands. Even today, when the turmoil and social upheaval in the world is so great, the call is there: "Come!"

But in all this, Jesus is no sentimentalist. He is a realist. He knows better than anyone what the heart of man is like. He knows well what Satan has in mind and desires to achieve. Jesus uses the opening of the seals to show us the disciplines he imposes on the earth to take account of these things. He is the one who dispatches each horse and rider to fulfil a specific role in order to achieve his purpose, which is not just to "save men and women" but to bring them to himself and his Father in a personal relationship and into spiritual maturity. We discover that these riders have momentous tasks to perform until he removes them.

The "four horsemen of the Apocalypse" as they are known, have been interpreted variously by commentators and scholars, but unless we understand the heart of God and his holy love for his creation, we can never penetrate the deliberate mystery they represent.

Throughout Scripture we find that animals, birds, and pests are used as representations of beings from the spiritual realm. We see that tame animals (for example, lambs or horses) are normally shown as being helpful to us; whereas the forces of darkness are represented by reptiles and carrion-eating birds (for example, vultures, snakes, and frogs) and mutant animals (for example, the beasts of Daniel and *Revelation*).

Here in the *Revelation*, we have four wonderful horses, domesticated, beautifully formed, reliable, willing creatures, each one of a symbolic colour. These are ridden by God's emissaries, who are not identified but are dressed and equipped in symbolic fashion. It is for us to interpret the symbolism in the pictures and be informed by them.

The opening of the first four seals reveals for the first time the strategy Jesus has adopted to restrain and thwart Satan in the exercise of his illegal dominion in the world. I believe the four horsemen are the spiritual response of King Jesus to the four demonic creatures Daniel saw coming up from the sea, who would attempt to rule the world on Satan's behalf. Despite appearances, in the battle for men's loyalty through the ages, Satan has never been able to have things all his own way. History shows us that he has never yet been able to achieve peace and well-being on the earth. Why is that? It is because without the Prince of Peace there is no peace.

The first horse Jesus sends out is white in colour. White always symbolises purity in Scripture (see also Revelation 19:11). Its rider is crowned and carries a bow, speaking of his supreme authority and his purpose to fire arrows at specific targets. He goes out "*conquering and in order that he might conquer*" (the clue to proper interpretation here lies in the use of the word "conquer"). The sending out of this rider is Jesus' first act once he has the scroll in his hands, and it recognises that man must die if he is to be resurrected to new life. It is the Holy Spirit alone who convicts the world of "sin, and righteousness, and judgement" (John 16:8). Without this conviction from God, none can come to him. It is the Holy Spirit alone who gives new life (John 3:1–16), and it is the Holy Spirit alone who fills us and empowers us once we are born again (Acts 2:38–39), and he alone is the one who leads us into all truth (John 16:13–14).

We know from Scripture that after his death and resurrection, the first act of Jesus' authority over the earth was the inauguration of his church at Pentecost. Thus, the symbolism of the white horse and its rider becomes clear. Jesus' followers could not become conquerors unless they were first conquered by the Holy Spirit. Those who were obediently waiting for the Spirit's coming were already born again, as Jesus breathed upon them in the upper room (John 20:22); now they were waiting to be filled with the Holy Spirit (the first outpouring of living water) so that they would be properly equipped to go and "make disciples of all nations" (Matthew 28:18–20).

It was only by means of this divine conquering that they are enabled to become conquerors. The language seems to be somewhat of a riddle, and so it is. It is a riddle to be unravelled by the conqueror so as to encourage Jesus' disciples to press on into maturity. This understanding is in perfect harmony with all that we learned from the first three chapters of *Revelation,* and it speaks to us once more of the great purpose of Jesus—that his people should be fitted for heaven by being conquerors during their lifetime. *We can conquer only as we allow the Holy Spirit to conquer us.*

In his Pentecost sermon, Peter said of the Holy Spirit:

> *"The promise is to you and to your children and to all who are far off, everyone whom the Lord calls to him"* (Acts 2:39).

Yes! From the very beginning, the Lord's call to all is, "Come!"

The rider of the white horse was to be the first part of Jesus' strategy to restrain the madness of Satan, his angels, and the corrupt leaders of the earth's empires as they try to eliminate the "conquerors" from the church and the earth. Thankfully, Satan and his henchmen are not free to do whatever they want in regard to God's people. They can act only by Jesus' permission. A time will come when, in a last period of special testing, that restraint on Satan's activities will be removed, but Jesus will determine when that will be (and it does not follow that the Holy Spirit's work in his people is removed at that time).

> *"He who restrains it will do so until he is taken out of the way"* (2 Thessalonians 2:7).

There is good reason why the second horseman does not present the difficulty of understanding the first one does. The work of the first rider is on behalf of the lampstand-churches, but the work of the second rider has to do with the world at large, and as such its meaning is clear and unequivocal.

> *"'There is no peace,' says the Lord, 'for the wicked'"* (Isaiah 48:22).

Isaiah reported this eternal principle many years before the Messiah came, and Jesus confirms it when he sends out the rider on the horse of red, the colour of blood. As a consequence of that rider's work, we have always an environment of insecurity and potential war, and thus a constant reminder to all the world of the consequences of rebellion against God and the inability of Satan to bring peace to the earth.

For many it is a great puzzle that wars erupt from nowhere, even among the most sophisticated nations. We know from James 4:1–2 what the source of this violence is, but Jesus establishes by the revelation of the red horse and its rider that there will be no peace on earth apart from that bestowed by the Prince of Peace. This sits uneasily with our assumptions that God must automatically affirm peace, even though the Old Testament contradicts the idea. We pray for peace in the world almost for its own sake, but Jesus knows that such peace in an unredeemed society will only give rise to even greater wickedness.

The great call from the throne in a voice of thunder crying, "Come!" reminds us once more of Jesus' overriding purpose in the opening of those four seals. It is surely true and well documented that where there is persecution and war, men and women are more ready to cry out to God than when there is peace and order in life. In those situations, the insecurity of our surroundings makes us all realise the fragility of man-made societies and the temporary nature of life itself. If it takes war to cause people to seek God, then surely that is a price that is worth paying (although it is true that the world will not think so).

The third rider, on a black horse, again presents a complex enigma for us to resolve, but if we look at it in the context of all that Jesus has shown us through John's visions so far in the *Revelation*, we will be able to see its amazing significance without having to strain for explanation.

It helps if we see that we are looking at an alternation of subject matter with the opening of each seal on the scroll. It seems that the complexity of the allegories of seals I, III, and V are there both to hide and reveal the spiritual destiny of the churches, whereas seals II, IV, and VI are more easily understood allegories that are not to be hidden because they have to do with the social destiny of the world at large.

If we use this insight with the third rider, we see that his horse is black, a sombre rather than threatening colour, denoting the sombre enterprise he is undertaking. The clue to this is found in the rider's hand, for he is holding a balance. In allegory, this balance is not for weighing material things but evidence, as in judgement. This picture shows us that throughout this age of the church, Jesus is constantly weighing the effectiveness of his churches as lampstands, just as we saw in Jesus' judgements of his churches in *Revelation* chapters 2 and 3. Peter wrote in the context of the suffering God's people were to endure:

> *"For the time has come for judgement to begin with the household of God"* (1 Peter 4:17).

His picture of the churches being judged is consistent with the work of Jesus the Priest ministering to his lampstands, and with the specific criticisms he delivers to each one in turn. We saw then the basis of his judgements, and it is shown to us here again. We must again pose the question, is my church an *effective lampstand?*

The rider of the black horse is shown to cause a severe shortage of wheat—the basic constituent of bread. As this is allegory, the lack of wheat points to a special kind of bread shortage in the churches. It is a famine even more dire than physical starvation. It is the loss of that word that changes both preacher and hearer: the utterance of the Word and words of God that the Holy Spirit uses to change us all. Without this bread we have no spiritual food or drink. We suffer spiritual starvation with all its symptoms, and we can never be conquerors.

The prophet Amos wrote of Israel:

> *"'Behold, the days are coming,' says the Lord God, 'when I will send a famine on the land; not a famine of bread, nor a thirst for water, but of hearing the words of the Lord.'"* (Amos 8:11)

The meaning is clear: *If God's Word is not producing conquerors in a church, then he will bring a famine of the Word in that church, both spoken and heard.* We have already seen that church leaders are to be stars in Jesus' hand; they have grave responsibilities to lead their flock to good pasture.

> *"But do not harm the oil and the wine!"* (Revelation 6:6).

This lovely instruction from heaven points us back to the work of the rider of the first horse. The judgement taking place is also an assessment of the churches' response to the work of the Holy Spirit. Where this is found to be in good order, it is to be left in place. But inevitably, *where there is no Holy Spirit ministry, there are no conquerors.* The oil and the wine is commonly used allegory for the Holy Spirit. Jesus wants us all to have a full measure of the anointing oil externally and the joy of the glorious heavenly wine internally. Without the oil there can be no fire on the lampstand.

A proper supply of God's Word and the presence of the Holy Spirit in God's people will always produce dynamic churches that are based not upon traditions from the past but upon what he is saying each day in each situation and to each individual. This is not to say that all traditions are wrong or that God may not use them; it is simply to say that tradition must not be a straitjacket that becomes a hindrance to the work of the Holy Spirit or stifles the revelation of truth. A lampstand-church can be built only when Jesus is its head. There can be no secondhand *revelation*: every individual and every generation must discover God for themselves. Of course there must be organisation and order, but if this controls rather than facilitates the work of the Holy Spirit, that work will soon die.

The work of the first horseman and the third horseman has been going on for nearly two thousand years, so we are in the privileged position of having an historic overview of its effects. Does not the history of the churches accord with the explanation we have advanced here? It seems that in every age churches rise up in power, zeal, and holy living only to decline within a generation or two into religious practices of lifeless formality.

Then we come to the fourth horseman and his pale green horse. This colour speaks of the bilious green of a decaying corpse. The call from heaven is still, "Come!" but the rider, by the deliberate instruction of Jesus, brings widespread death by means of the sword, famine, pestilence, and wild beasts. A "quarter of the earth" at any one time may be devastated. How are we to understand this terrible work that has been going on for two thousand years already?

Ezekiel helps us by revealing that these disastrous events represent God's judgements on recalcitrant and rebellious societies.

> *"[God's] four sore acts of judgment, sword, famine, evil beasts and pestilence . . .*
> *cut off . . . man and beast"* Ezekiel (14:21).

God's purpose in this is clear. These judgements are not punishment but consequences of the choices made by men and women. They are designed to get people's attention. If societies will not accept the lordship of Jesus, then they expose themselves to the work of the rider of the green horse.

How often we puzzle over the so-called "acts of God" that devastate entire populations: earthquakes, floods, famines, plagues, things that can sweep across the world. How often we pray to God for relief and help, or the ending of wars. But this revelation of Scripture shows us that Jesus is firmly and definitely in charge of all that is going on.

In fact, Jesus has placed limits on the death rate so that it is never more than one-fourth of the population at any given time. Neither man nor Satan has the power to wipe out mankind. Jesus is working everything out in accordance with his overall strategy. Terrorism, climate change, food and water shortages, epidemic diseases—our most modern fears—are all firmly within his control. That is good news for us.

The way out is still available: "Come!" says the voice from heaven. It is the churches' responsibility to make the call clear, but how confused we can be. Not knowing the Scripture, we seek to ameliorate famine, arbitrate in war, cure epidemics, and control natural disasters. Instead of calling people's attention to God's purposes, we substitute our deficient compassion for God's perfect love, and so people are condemned to eternal darkness. Every natural catastrophe brings suffering and death, and most often to the Third World nations. Why is this? These Scriptures leave us in no doubt as to the priorities of God. Is it not a wonder that Jesus' judgements are not more severe when we compare God's priorities with those of many of our churches today?

Death stalks the earth in its many forms: disease, abortion, starvation, war. In the Middle Ages, the terrible Black Death decimated the population of Europe. It is all but forgotten now, but today we have our own homemade "black death": AIDS. For so long, the cause of that earlier epidemic was unknown and could not be combated, but the cause of our own rampant epidemic is found in willful promiscuity and sexual immorality that reaches out to touch the innocent and guilty alike. But if much death is accidental, the aborting of babies is not. It is estimated that we deliberately abort approximately 50 million of our babies every year. It goes on all the time, everywhere and in all cultures.

Why does Jesus allow it to happen when it is such an offence to God? Because it is not yet his time to take up his rule. It is still a time of opportunity for men and women to "Come!"

> *'When people say, 'There is peace and security,' then sudden destruction will come*
> *upon them as travail comes upon a woman with child, and there will be no escape.*
> *But you are not in darkness for that day to overtake you like a thief in the night"*
> (1 Thessalonians 5:3–4).

We are living in the time when the work of all four riders is still going on around us, but we are approaching a climax. According to the signs, the end is in sight. It seems that there will be an increasing confrontation between the Christian way and the world's way, with people trying to ignore the effects of what they are producing on the earth by their lifestyle. The climax of the uninhibited iniquity in mankind is detailed in the *Revelation*; it will bring social disaster on a worldwide scale that we can hardly imagine.

The time from when Jesus took the scroll and opened the first seal to the opening of the fourth seal has been the great evangelistic phase of Jesus' reign. The Bible calls this, "the times of the Gentiles" (Luke 21:24), a period of time when God is not dealing with Israel. It is the age of the "lampstand-churches"; the age of the proclamation of God's call—"Come!" It is the time when the Spirit and the bride agree on a single, central message: "*Come!*"

But when the fifth seal is opened, something changes. At this point, there is no voice from heaven. There is no further call to "Come!" The darkness on earth is gathering for its darkest hour before the great dawn.

SUMMARY

In opening the seals of the scroll, Jesus reveals his strategy to obstruct Satan's dominion on earth. Down through the centuries, he has been ministering directly to his lampstand-churches and to the world.

❖ **Seal 1**—Churches

"COME!" The white horse goes forth.
The Holy Spirit empowers the conquerors in the lampstand-churches.

❖ **Seal 2**—World

"COME!" The red horse goes forth.
Peace is taken from the earth.

❖ **Seal 3**—Churches

"COME!" The black horse goes forth.
Judgement of the churches on the basis of the Word and the Holy Spirit

❖ **Seal 4**—World

"COME!" The green horse goes forth.
Judgement of society: death

THE FIFTH SEAL
REVELATION 6:9-11

Act I, Scene 5—THE FIFTH SEAL

Place: In Heaven

Time: 3 ½ Years before Christ's Return

People: The Last Faithful Witnesses

At the opening of the fifth seal, John sees under the altar the souls of many martyrs: those who had been slain *"for the word of God and for the witness they had borne"* (Revelation 6:9). They are those who having conquered in life, now sleep in death, awaiting the day of the Lord. Their appearance to him as being "under the altar" symbolises their special place of rest and protection as they await the Lord's coming. The altar is a reference to the altar of incense that is within the Holy Place, the antechamber to the Holy of Holies. It speaks of the lives of these souls as having been a fragrant offering acceptable to the Lord (see Exodus 30:1–10). The work of the priest was to dress the lamps and burn incense on the altar both morning and evening, thus providing a perpetual incense before the Lord through all generations. These precious souls are in a safe place of waiting and resting in heaven.

Among them is Stephen, the first Christian to lose his life for his witness to Jesus. The Acts account of his death gives us a vivid picture of Stephen's response to the work of the horsemen sent out by Jesus. He had responded to the call by the living creature from God's throne to "Come!" He had been filled with the Holy Spirit (Acts 6:5). His face shone as a result of the glory of the Lord within him (Acts 6:15; cf. 2 Corinthians 3:18). Being in the Spirit, he saw the glory of the Lord in the throne room of God (Acts 7:55). And because of the glory that was in him and because of the love of God shed abroad in his heart by the Holy Spirit (Romans 5:5), he was able to stand for Jesus even in the face of certain death. He became more than a conqueror (Romans 8:37). By the express design of Jesus, there are to be many such witnesses, both old covenant saints and new covenant saints, who are awaiting the opening of Seal 5.

John hears this group asking the most natural of questions. Perhaps it is the question of all martyrs: *"How long must we wait?"* Jesus deliberately uses his answer to the question to point us to a last great persecution, which is to come before he returns. There have been hints of such a time in other Scriptures, but in the *Revelation* Jesus makes it clear.

> *"They were . . . told to rest a little longer until the number of their fellow servants and their brethren should be complete, who were to be killed as they themselves had been"*
> (Revelation 6:11).

We saw earlier that Seals 1 and 3 were specifically concerned with Jesus' dealings with his church, and this is true also of Seal 5. The fifth seal's opening will lead to a time when death will face any would-be conqueror, bringing to the exact number those destined to die. This is the time of "tribulation" to which Jesus points (Matthew 24:9), a time when a relatively brief but severe pogrom from within the apostate churches will sweep huge numbers into the heavenly sanctuary.

> *"Many will fall away, and betray one another, and hate one another. And many false prophets will arise and lead many astray. And because wickedness [lit. iniquity] is multiplied most men's love will grow cold.* **But he who endures to the end will be saved**" (Matthew 24:10–13).

Few today understand that Christianity is not intended to be an easy ride in this world. Perseverance and endurance in the face of religious hostility are essential ingredients in the Christlike character we must acquire. The parallel passage in Revelation 13, which we will look at later, reveals that it is the Antichrist who triggers the persecution of those who refuse to accept him as a saviour, and there we are given a specific time for his reign, three and a half years, during which the persecution takes place:

> *"Also it was allowed to make war on the saints and conquer them. . . . here is a call* **for the endurance and faith of the saints**" (Revelation 13:7,10).

This awful time of tribulation for the saints is indicative of the final response by the world to "this gospel of the kingdom," which is to be preached in "all the world" before the "end" comes (Matthew 24:14). This phase will immediately precede the snatching up of the saints to glory of which Jesus spoke in the same passage (Matthew 24:36–44).

Today we are still able to proclaim Jesus freely in most of the world, although it seems that attitudes toward Christian evangelism are hardening in many countries that are specifically non-Christian, and the doors of Muslim countries are mostly shut already.

At the last, before Jesus comes, the faith of the witnesses of Jesus will be purified in the fires of persecution. Jesus wants us to know in advance that such a sacrifice is acceptable to the Father, and we are not to be dismayed by the prospect.

That the close of this time will come with the rapture of the saints we will find confirmed for us later on as we study Revelation 12 and 13. But the revelation of Seal 5 is given to us here so that we might understand fully that such seemingly tragic events are not only a part of Jesus' strategy for dealing with Satan, but they also prepare us to reign with him.

For those who persevere to the end, this period concludes on the day of the Lord. He comes in the clouds, and those saints who live through this time of testing but have not been slain for their witness to Jesus will be caught up to be with him in the clouds, and they will join there all those who were conquerors before them (1 Thessalonians 4:13–18). This is our great hope and the promise that will keep us through the darkest times, but for now we must postpone our joyful researches until we deduce further confirming evidence from chapter 12.

It is only *after this wonderful moment of the rapture* of the saints that the *"Great Tribulation"* spoken of by Jesus in Matthew 24:21 begins, with the opening of the Seal 6.

THE SIXTH SEAL
REVELATION 6:12-17

Act I, Scene 6—THE SIXTH SEAL

Time: After the Rapture

Place: On Earth

People: All Mankind

The opening of the sixth seal of the scroll (Revelation 6:12) introduces us to an extraordinary period of traumatic natural calamity on earth and in the sky. As with the opening of Seals 2 and 4, the sixth seal shows us Jesus once again dealing with the world at large rather than with his church. The *"lampstand-church of the conquerors"* is now gone from the earth. But there are many "left behind," non-conquering Christians who, wondering what is going on, face the crisis of the Great Tribulation Jesus warned of.

The words John uses to describe what he is seeing here are not difficult to understand, for he is describing shocking but literal events. There is always danger in spiritualizing prophecy when it is uncomfortable for us to receive it intellectually. In this case a literal interpretation is consistent with many other Scriptures. As we noted before, when the events John describes concern the fate of mankind in general, then the language he uses is clear for all to read if they will. Ignorance of what is written in God's Word is not going to be an excuse available to most people on the day of judgement.

The prophet Joel (2:30–31) wrote about this time, and the prophets Isaiah and Ezekiel also refer to a time of dramatic changes to the sun, moon, and stars in their writings of future events. Such are commonly referred to by Old Testament prophets as being the physical signs that will precede the day of the Lord's coming, so most Jews would be familiar with them as signs to look out for. It is important for us to realise that the opening of Seal 6 has significance to the modern nation of Israel, for it is the point in time when God begins to deal specifically with his "chosen" people once more. Jesus also referred to these events in his end-time prophecies (see Matthew 24:29–30).

Far from being totally ignorant of God as they have pretended to be for so long, it seems that when these things happen the terrified people of the world have some awareness of what they mean. Once the stars, sun, and moon are being physically moved and changed, the sheer terror of what is happening will cause people to cry out for help. Where else can they turn except to almighty God, whom they have already rejected? His coming to judge his creatures in wholly justifiable wrath (Revelation 6:15–17) is a truly terrifying prospect. God's coming down on the mountain to speak with Moses engendered terror in his chosen people; how much more terrifying will be his appearing to the generations who have consistently rejected the *revelation* that is printed in the creation itself? They have not only rebelled against his order for life but also have sought to deny his existence in a vain attempt to be God to themselves and avoid their responsibility to seek him.

If Seal 5 saw the tribulation visited on the saints by the apostate churches enthralled by the world, then Seal 6 can be seen as God's response: his Great Tribulation coming upon the world at large, as a direct consequence of what was done to the saints.

Man's complacency is first shattered by a great earthquake, accompanied by the darkening of the sun. A normal eclipse of the sun can only last for eight minutes in any one place. What John refers to is quite different; it will surely be a worldwide phenomenon lasting for some time, although we do not know how long. These two events, taken together with the blood-red colour of the full moon, will be a shocking and an unmistakable signal to those who know the Scriptures.

The brief description John gives of these events couples them together with stars falling to the earth. This phenomenon cannot be literally what is happening, even if John was referring to large meteors, but it signals something else of great importance. We remember how in the *Revelation* stars and angels are interchangeable. The understanding of the picture becomes clear later on in Revelation 12, where this use of allegory establishes an important point of timing.

The wording used by John, *"as the fig tree sheds its winter (lit. untimely) fruit when shaken by a gale"* (Revelation 6:13), is also intended to aid our understanding. For a fig tree to have winter fruit, or more literally, fruit out of time, is a description of a very unnatural crop. This figure of speech may be signifying the time when the fallen angels are finally cast down and restricted to the physical earth, and we will see the confirmation of this later.

The sky vanishing like a scroll being rolled up (Revelation 6:14) follows upon the fall of the stars, and these two signs point us to Isaiah's prophecy (Isaiah 34:4). There we read that these signs are to introduce a time of "vengeance." Thus there is a link here with the answer given to the souls under God's altar, that a time of avenging their shed blood was soon coming.

Not only are the sun, moon, and stars being affected, but the unseen spiritual realms also are being changed in anticipation of Jesus' coming. Space has always been a great mystery to man, a source of speculation concerning other possible life-forms and UFOs. Because of its infinite extent, man without understanding of the heavens is persuaded that there can be nothing beyond it.

As we know from the opening words of the Bible—*"In the beginning God made the heavens and the earth"*—it seems that he made two heavens at this time. When Satan was first thrown down from heaven, he was removed from the third heaven, that is, from the presence of God. On this basis, the first heaven is coexistent with our atmosphere: when Paul describes Satan as "the Prince of the power of the air" (Ephesians 2:2), he is speaking of the first heaven, where Satan has been actively ruling mankind with his spiritual forces in opposition to God's order.

What we call space is spatially and spiritually the second heaven, a kind of neutral arena where both God's angels and Satan's angels are able to operate (cf. Job 1:6–12) and even struggle with one another.

The third heaven is not created; it is outside of space and time. It is beyond and yet around everything. It was revealed to us in Revelation 4 as the dwelling place of God and his holy angels; it is a holy place where nothing unclean can ever enter. Until the time of the sixth seal, it seems that the second heaven provides a kind of buffer zone between our atmosphere (the first heaven) and the dwelling place of God and his angels (the third heaven). What John now describes is the removal of the second heaven, and with its removal Satan's sphere of activity is confined to the first heaven around earth. This is the next stage in his inevitable progress toward hell.

On earth itself John sees *"every mountain and island"* being removed from its place (Revelation 6:14). This is an unutterably terrifying experience for those on the earth; it will seem as if the whole planet is at the point of disintegration. The ground under our feet always seems to be stable and permanent. To see parts of the earth that supposedly have been in place for "millions of years" being moved violently by unexplained forces will shatter every sense of security that is in us. Where will people turn in this extremity of terror?

> *"Fall on us, and hide us from the face of him who is seated on the throne and from the wrath of the Lamb; for the great day of their wrath has come and who can stand before it?"* (Revelation 6:16–17).

This is the cry of desperate men and women who realize at last who they are dealing with— but is it too late for mercy? Many have been taught that one can compromise with God's order for life. Many others have thought that they can negotiate the terms of their salvation with God. But this is error. God is not a God of religion but a God of his Word. By God's grace, even now, in the face of open hostility and provocation, this time of the sixth seal is an opportunity for repentance and faith. God has not yet shut the door, but the cost is martyrdom.

We are given no indication here of the duration of the events described in the opening of this sixth seal. What we can see, and what those who are alive at the time will see, is that everything that has remained unchanged since the beginning of creation will now be changed. The sun and moon and stars will be changed. The sky itself will appear to be different. The mountains and hills will be removed. None of what I am writing can make any sense to those who do not believe the Scriptures, but there are many who say they believe the Scriptures without knowing what is written here.

When these things take place, it will be nearly too late for mankind, for the opening of the seventh seal is the time for the fulfilment of prophetic Scriptures that have been available for generations. It will be the cutting off point of the salvation offered us since Calvary.

> *"See that you do not refuse him who is speaking. For if they did not escape when they refused him who warned them on earth, much less shall we escape if we reject him who warns from heaven. God has promised,* **"Yet once more I will shake not only the earth but also (the) heaven.** *This phrase 'yet once more' indicates* **the removal of what has been shaken as of what has been made,** *in order that what cannot be shaken may remain. Therefore let us be grateful for receiving a kingdom that cannot be shaken, and thus let us offer to God acceptable worship, with reverence and with awe; for our God is a consuming fire"* (Hebrews 12:25–29).

We have been warned.

144,000
REVELATION 7:1-8

Act I, Scene 7—144,000　　　　　　　　**Time: Beginning of the Last Seven Years**

Place: Earth　　　　　　　　　　　　　　　　　　　**People: Israel**

John has been watching Jesus open the seals one by one, but after the opening of the sixth seal, the scene changes and some important details are added. The opening of the seventh seal does not take place until chapter 8, so we can surmise that chapter 7 recounts what happens on the earth after the rapture has taken place and Seal 6 is opened.

In chapter 7, we find two key groups of people separated out for special attention. The first of these is a throng of 144,000 people drawn equally from each of the twelve tribes of Israel. This is a significant group because it is the first time in *Revelation* that God's chosen people of Israel are specifically featured, and to understand what is happening we have to look back into relevant Old Testament prophecies.

Many years ago the prophet Daniel, when foretelling Israel's future as a nation, spoke of a period of seventy weeks of years (in prophetic language this means 70 x 7 = 490 years) that would pass to bring a full end to the suffering that the nation would undergo on account of its failure to keep covenant.

> ***"Seventy weeks of years*** *are decreed concerning your people and your holy city, to finish the transgression, to put an end to sin and to atone for iniquity, to bring in everlasting righteousness, to seal both vision and prophet and to anoint a most holy place"* (Daniel 9:24).

This key Old Testament prophecy predicts a coming time when the offence of Israel will have been purged and the nation's relationship with God will be restored (but under the terms of the new covenant). The period of *"seventy weeks of years"* before *"everlasting righteousness"* is established in the earth, foretells in prophetic language the second coming of the Messiah (the "Anointed One").

The prophecy goes on to make clear that a hiatus would occur in the time line at a certain point. Sixty-two weeks of years (62 x 7 = 434 years) from the beginning an *"anointed one is cut off"* (Daniel 9:26). The time that would pass before the hiatus ended is not indicated; but when it does end, the events covered by the prophecy will be concluded in a final seven-year period. We know now that that unspecified interval of time allowed for the "times of the Gentiles," during which the gospel has been preached (and largely rejected) in all nations of the world. In this time, Jesus has built his lampstand-church of conquerors. The time has stretched out for some two thousand years now and will end with the opening of the sixth seal.

When the people of Israel entered the land of Canaan, God ordained rest for them. This included a Sabbath rest on the seventh day of each week (Exodus 20:8–11), a one-year Sabbath rest for the land every seventh year (Leviticus 25:3–4), and after forty-nine years (i.e., after the seventh seven years), the Jubilee year was to be a special Sabbath year of restoration (see Leviticus 25:8–55). A prophetic "week" (lit. the word *shabua* means "sevens") is thus seven years long.

So in understanding Daniel's prophecy, we consider two different "sevens": first, 1 week = 7 literal days; second, 1 prophetic week = 7 years (so 69 weeks of years = 483 years)

Daniel's prophecy is designed to give precise timing to the key events in Israel's history. Seventy weeks of years will *"finish transgression, put an end to sin and atone for iniquity"* (Daniel 9:24). What a wonderful moment for all to anticipate. The sixty-nine-week promise was fulfilled exactly in the death of Jesus in AD 29.

The command Daniel refers to in Daniel 9:25 was issued by Artaxerxes in approx 454 BC (Nehemiah 2:4–8). It is hard to fix these historical times with any certainty of accuracy, but there is general agreement around the following, which shows how the 70 weeks (490 years), the 7 weeks (49 years), the 62 weeks (434 years) and the 1 week (7 years) are accounted for.

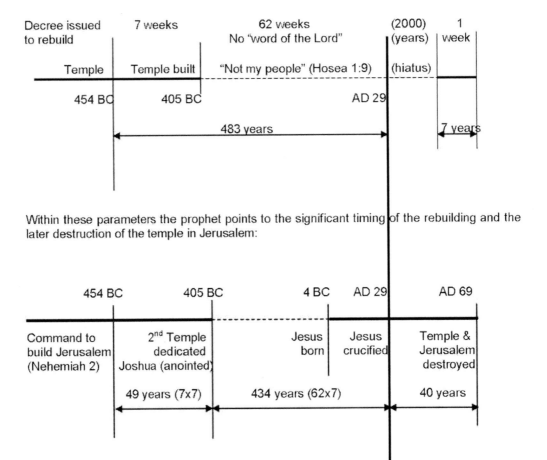

Within these parameters the prophet points to the significant timing of the rebuilding and the later destruction of the temple in Jerusalem:

*"Know therefore and understand that from the going forth of the word to restore and build Jerusalem to the coming of an anointed one, a prince, there shall be **seven weeks**. Then for **sixty-two weeks** it shall be built again with squares and moat, but in a troubled time. And after the sixty-two weeks, **an anointed one shall be cut off**, and shall have nothing; and the people of the prince who is to come shall destroy the sanctuary. Its end shall come with a flood, and to the end there shall be war; desolations are decreed. And he shall make a strong covenant with many for **one week**; and for half a week he shall cause sacrifice and offering to cease; and upon the wing of abominations shall come one who makes desolate, until the decreed end is poured out on the desolator"* (Daniel 9:25–27).

We know from history that Jerusalem and its temple were restored in line with the prophecy (Ezra 7:13–22). The anointed prince who then comes is Joshua (Zechariah 3) the high priest, who is presented as a prophetic type of Messiah who was to come and to whom Zechariah makes direct reference as the Branch (see Zechariah 3:8).

And we know that Jesus, the second "anointed one" of the prophecy, came to Israel right on time. He is "the anointed one who is cut off"—Israel's promised Messiah who was shockingly crucified by his own people. So it is the death of Jesus that concludes the period of the sixty-nine weeks referred to by Daniel. We know that this tragedy was followed by the destruction of both the temple and the city of Jerusalem itself, just as Jesus himself predicted, and since that time Jerusalem has been the most fought over city in the world.

So there is one last week (seven years) of the prophecy left to be fulfilled. Immediately upon its completion will follow the triumphant appearance of King Jesus (i.e., the second coming). It is this week that is initiated with the opening of Seal 6 and is concluded after Seal 7 has run its course.

Daniel divides the final week (seven years) into two periods of three and a half years within which God will complete all the work he has in mind. This would suggest that both the sixth seal and the seventh seal each cover a period of about three and a half years. We will be able to confirm this idea later on.

Daniel's prophecy makes no distinction between the prince who destroyed the city in AD 70 (the Roman general Titus) and the one who will make a "strong covenant" with many for one week in the last days. We are to know from this that although they are different people separated by thousands of years, they are of the same type (i.e., both are military representatives of a Roman government). A fuller understanding of this individual too will come later in the *Revelation*.

What we are now to understand is that at the opening of the sixth seal Jesus once more is ministering directly to his people Israel. It is the end of the very long time in which Israel has been *lo-ammi*, that is, "not my people" (Hosea 1:9). Importantly, *the opening of the sixth seal signals the beginning of the "last week" of Daniel's prophecy.*

John sees four angels (Revelation 7:1), perhaps like those "stars" that fell to earth when Seal 6 was opened. They have been waiting to carry out a task of further destruction on earth, but they are still restrained from beginning their work because there is important ministry that must first be completed.

The angel rising from the east where the sun rises is to seal a special group of God's people on their foreheads. This is the seal of the Holy Spirit by which believers in Jesus (Ephesians 1:13–14) are guaranteed their inheritance in heaven. Twelve thousand from each of the twelve tribes of Israel are to be sealed on their foreheads. Only God knows who and where these Israelites are in the world today because they are chosen from the so-called lost tribes. No doubt this is why the task of sealing them is committed to an angel. These then are believers in Jesus, and we will find them again in Revelation 14, where they are in heaven. Although the final destiny of these people is made clear, it is not clear whether they too are raptured or, perhaps more likely, will die for their faith during the time of the sixth seal.

It is an important part of understanding the *Revelation* that one does not confuse the different groups of people in *Revelation* with one another. This group of 144,000 has been claimed as being "the saved church" (especially by the Jehovah's Witnesses), but on its face value it is clear to us that it is Israel that is being dealt with here. It is certain that this is a special church that has been drawn from out of all the tribes of Israel, and it has a special place in God's plan in the last days. This church appears to be the fulfillment of Joel's prophecy that links the outpouring of God's Spirit with the events that follow from the opening of the sixth seal:

> *"And it shall come to pass afterward, that I will pour out my spirit on all flesh; your sons and daughters shall prophesy, your old men shall dream dreams, and your young men shall see visions. Even upon the menservants and maidservants in those days, I will pour out my spirit. And I will give portents in the heavens and on the earth, blood and fire and columns of smoke. The sun shall be turned to darkness, and the moon to blood, before the great and terrible day of the Lord comes"* (Joel 2:28–31).

It is also important that we do not go beyond the description John gives as we seek to establish the identity of this group. There is no indication here of where these tribes are to be found, in Israel or elsewhere, nor if they are together. As we study further in the *Revelation* more details emerge of events taking place in Israel that add to our insights.

WASHED ROBES
REVELATION 7:9-17

Act I, Scene 8—WASHED ROBES

Time: After the Opening of Seal 6 and Before the Opening of Seal 7

Place: Heaven

People: Those Who Come Out of the Great Tribulation

In the last scene, God is dealing with Israelites on the earth. In this new scene, John is once more in heaven. Here he sees a huge group of people standing in front of the throne and the Lamb (Revelation 7:9). Vast numbers of folk from *"every nation, all tribes and people and tongues"* (i.e., from all over the world) are standing there. The number of people is so huge and their origins are so universal that identifying them correctly is very important. One of the elders draws John's (and our) attention to this by asking him, *"Who are these, clothed in white robes, and from whence have they come?"* (Revelation 7:13).

Since any one of us could find ourselves among these people, we too really need to know why they are clothed like this. Although they are now in heaven, where were they before that? John declined to guess at the answers, and so the elder replies to his own question:

> *"These are they who **have come out of the Great Tribulation**; they have **washed their robes and made them white in the blood of the Lamb**"* (Revelation 7:14).

We must first understand that these people are not "conquerors" because the rapture of the conquerors occurred before the Great Tribulation. These multitudes of people have been through the "Great Tribulation" (that deeply troublesome time which begins with the opening of the sixth seal). They are different too from those martyred souls who were under God's altar, for they had been given a white robe (see 6:11). The conquerors of Sardis (3:4) had not *"soiled their robes"* and they are counted worthy to receive their white garments (3:5). It seems that this vast group of people had received white robes, but they were no longer clean. They have had to wash their dirty and stained robes in *"the blood of the Lamb."*

This is a serious issue that challenges every believer today. Why are these robes soiled? Of what does this need for the washing of robes speak? The immediate implication of what we have read is that numerous Christians, perhaps unwittingly, do not fulfil Jesus' requirements to be raptured as conquerors. How can this be? Is there any Scripture evidence for this? Yes, there is. Jude writes:

> *"Convince some, who doubt; save some, by snatching them out of the fire; on some have mercy with fear, hating even **the garment spotted by the flesh**"* (Jude 1:22–23).

In his brief letter that precedes the book of Revelation, Jude was warning of this very problem. A vast multitude of Christians will miss becoming conquerors because they were not properly taught, or perhaps they were not obedient to, the full revelation of God's Word. The shocking truth is that today there are vast numbers of people in our churches who are deceived. They are people who have compromised in their walk of faith, often without knowing it. They know intellectually the call of Jesus to a life-laying-down walk with him, yet they succumb to the temptation to hold back and compromise with the standards of the society in which they live. Unless we are disciples of Jesus, we will fail to deal fully with the world, the flesh, and the devil. We might have made a good beginning, but without sanctification, the iniquity that defiles us stays hidden within our hearts.

Zechariah wrote vividly of these dirty garments:

> *"Now Joshua was standing before the angel clothed in filthy garments. And the angel said to those who were standing before him, "Remove the filthy garments from him." And to him he said, "Behold, I have **taken your iniquity away from you,** and I will clothe you in rich apparel"* (Zechariah 3:3–4).

The iniquity in Joshua's heart is the same as that of all men and women. It is dealt with only by the process of sanctification. We have seen already how the *Revelation* churches, instead of being lampstand-churches, had settled for an easier path of good works and outward appearances. In the same way, apostate churches in the last days will leave multitudes of believers with stained and soiled robes. They will be left behind at the rapture to face the horrors of the Great Tribulation.

We are here observing a major issue that challenges much modern evangelical teaching. What John is seeing in Revelation 7, is undeniable. It makes clear that the epistle of James is no lightweight epistle as some have suggested. It effectively punctures the heresy that is rampant within the churches, that sees faith as primarily a matter of intellectual assent to a series of propositions concerning Jesus and God rather than a relationship with Father-God that requires our obedience to his revealed Word in all situations. James spells out what all the other epistles enshrine.

> *"But be doers of the word and not hearers only, **deceiving yourselves**"* (James 1:22).

And:

> *"So faith by itself, **if it has no works**, is dead"* (James 2:17).

And again:

> *"For as the body apart from the spirit is dead, so **faith apart. from works is dead**"* (James 2:26).

There can be no doubt that Jesus requires his people to be changed by the progressive work of the Holy Spirit within them and by a very practical obedience to his leading in their daily activities. We saw that the oil and the wine referred to in the opening of the fourth seal are symbolic of an internal anointing and an external anointing by the Holy Spirit, whereby the saints are empowered for such obedience. Without this double anointing, there is a famine of hearing the Word of God in the churches. That is, people habitually hear the Word but don't do it.

The changes of character and lifestyle wrought within the Christian must lead to service of the poorest and weakest in our society, not just by patronising the works of others but by the personal involvement of each one. Thus, James makes the theory quite clear:

> *"Religion that is pure and undefiled before God and the Father is this: to visit orphans and widows in their affliction, and to keep oneself unstained from the world"* (James 1:27).

In Revelation 7:9–17 we are looking at a supreme example of God's grace and mercy, for many people who have failed the Lord in their lives nevertheless are given a way back to him. They failed to become conquerors and so have missed being taken up with the saints in the rapture, but by their knowledge of God's Word they now recognise what has happened. Their eyes are opened by the Holy Spirit and, at last, the true nature of the Antichrist world ruler who has deceived them is revealed to them, and they realise the serious predicament they are in.

Jesus had never abandoned them, but bringing them face-to-face with the truth now at the opening of Seal 6, they are given a last opportunity. In the face of direct persecution, which will cost them everything they hold dear, they must stand for Jesus and refuse to accept the "*mark of the beast*" that is being universally imposed. By so doing they will choose almost certain death, but at the last they are saved. Their faithfulness, now proven in the fire, is accepted by God as a washing away of all the compromise and uncleanness that had been staining their robes.

Their destiny is to stand before the throne as his servants in the temple of God (Revelation 7:9, 15). They do not share the throne of Jesus as conquerors, for they have a different destiny now. The hunger and thirst they have suffered and the great weeping and pain that has been their experience in this time of the sixth seal is over. They are with the Lord who loves them so much. What a picture of tenderness and caring John sees as God himself ministers to them to comfort and relieve them.

The fate of these believers points to that Great Tribulation Jesus spoke of (see Matthew 24:21). This is a last, worldwide persecution of his followers. It is similar to that persecution suffered by the early church under the Romans and by countless unknown saints since in a world that has been orchestrated by the demonic powers. But God knows each one of us, and each martyr is precious to him.

We see that by the end of the three and a half years of the Great Tribulation the true church is gone from the earth. They have reached their destiny. It may be that many others, previously unbelievers, also will be saved by the witness of these martyrs. Who is left? Well, unbelieving Israel is still left, and the rest of unbelieving mankind is left. What they must face is revealed to us next, in the opening of Seal 7.

THE SEVENTH SEAL
REVELATION 8 AND 9

Act I, Scene 9—THE SEVENTH SEAL

Time: Last 3 ½ Years

Place: Heaven, with Consequences on Earth

People: All

> *"When the Lamb opened the seventh seal, there was silence in heaven for about half an hour"* (Revelation 8:1).

This is an awesome moment. Suddenly in heaven, all becomes still. The music, the bustle, the great sounds, even the worship is stilled. An air of expectancy, or perhaps it is apprehensive anticipation, falls upon everyone. All eyes are on Jesus, awaiting his next action. It seems as if the heavenly hosts are in no doubt as to what is to come. They know the implications of the seventh seal, and so should we. Half an hour can be a long time, but this pause is pregnant with meaning. It is the prelude to the outpouring of God's wrath on what remains of his handiwork in creation. Had there ever been such stillness in heaven before?

The long-suffering patience of God is at an end. The prayers of the saints, crying, "How long Lord?" have risen up to God as incense for many centuries. Now his answer comes; now the earth will be purged with the fire from the altar of God, as has been long promised.

Just as when one of the seraphs attending God's throne took a coal from the fire to purge the lips of Isaiah (Isaiah 6:6–7), so now a censer full of holy fire is cast onto the earth by the angel of God to accomplish the same purpose on a comprehensive scale. As each of the seven angels blows his trumpet in turn, so a disaster is initiated on earth. How could John find words to describe these fearful and amazing calamities following one after another?

It must be said that the interpretations of these events are many and various. As with other parts of the *Revelation,* students often view what they see through the lens of their own understanding of apocalyptic prophecy and then seek to fit the pieces into that mould. It is inevitable that every generation will develop its own understanding of these things in the light of current happenings in the world. However, as with the prophecies concerning the first advent of Jesus, there will be a single moment of time when all the conditions for the fulfillment of the prophecies will come together. This seems to be near now, but still, in God's grace, at the time of this writing (2010) there is a little time left; we too, must be asking, "How long Lord?"

Jesus gave us the *Revelation* to enlighten us at the proper time. He did not intend to put before us an unsolvable mystery. We were warned at the outset of the book to make ourselves thoroughly familiar with all the words of the prophecy and to keep them (i.e., treasure them) in our hearts so that we would be prepared when the time comes to act. We are not called upon to make fanciful and ingenious theories. All the words of the prophecy of the events that follow the opening of the seventh seal should first be regarded at their face value as they are written, with the expectation that other parts of Scripture will help us discern any allegorical or spiritual interpretation that may be appropriate.

There is always purpose, order, and logic in God's work, even in the expression of his wrath. It is remarkable that in the early years of the twenty-first century the world has at last awakened to the damage that has been done to the environment by the industrial processes of society. It might be asked whether God cares about this. We shall find a clear answer to the question later on, but it is for consideration whether or not the events that follow the blowing of these seven trumpets are, at least in part, the direct consequence of man's misrule of his environment. It seems as if man, having done his worst, is now to endure the extension of his efforts under God's hand.

> *"Now the seven angels who had the seven trumpets made ready to blow them"* (Revelation 8:6).

This activity is not a covert one. When Jesus opened the first four seals of the scroll, only those who understood the Scripture could recognise what was going on. But the blowing of these trumpets is a battle call. It is a proclamation from heaven to earth that the Lord is now taking action. John tells us of seven angels with seven trumpets, followed later by seven vials of wrath, which bring into effect an ascending order of terror and devastation.

These events are the complete measure and fullness of God's response to the society created by man and lived out over thousands of years of rebellion against him. These agonizing events are written here for us. We do need to have comprehension of them because it will help us to realise just what outrage the holiness of our God has suffered, and is still suffering, at the hands of proud men. What have we done to his beautiful creation, the earth itself, the creatures on the earth who were made subject to man, and to one another? Our achievements can be measured by the expression of God's wrath set out for us here.

That his righteous wrath is compressed into a mere three and a half years is itself merciful, for during this time man's continuing hostility to his Creator and his determination not to bend the knee to Jesus are accompanied by cursing.

First, John saw "hail, and fire, mixed with blood" (Revelation 8:7) fall on the earth, burning up the vegetation. This is a lethal cocktail and seems to speak of chemical fallout. Perhaps the acid rain that is now destroying our forests is a forewarning of it.

Second, he saw "something like a great mountain, burning with fire" (Revelation 8:8) thrown into the sea, poisoning it and affecting the ships in its vicinity. Was this a failed spaceship or a nuclear missile? The possibility for deadly contamination of the waters is already proven by our own pollution of the oceans with unsafe effluent.

Third, John saw a great star fall from heaven, poisoning the water sources and watercourses. The star is given a name: Wormwood. It will poison much of the drinking water so that many actually die because they are unable to find pure water to drink. This too sounds very much like severe pollution. When a star falls, it is not an involuntary act; it is *caused* to fall. This star with the unpleasant name of Wormwood would seem to be one of Satan's hosts, thrown down for the express purpose of this act.

It is illuminating for us that when the nuclear power station disaster occurred at Chernobyl (the name meaning *Wormwood*) in the USSR in 1986, its connection with Revelation terminology was quickly recognised. So it will be with many of these events—people will recognise where they come from but will be quite unwilling to acknowledge any personal liability before God.

As these first three events follow relentlessly one after another, the earth's inhabitants will grow increasingly anxious. But when the fourth angel sounds his trumpet (Revelation 8:12) and the sun, moon, and stars begin again to falter in their light-giving role, what will people think then?

But this is not the end; even worse things will come. An eagle (a divine messenger) flies in midheaven, warning of the terror of the next three trumpet calls, which he describes as "woes" (Revelation 8:13). And terrors indeed they are. Chapter 9 carries John's account of the first two of them. There seems to be little point in trying to spiritualise these events. Far-fetched allegorical interpretations have been proposed, but they carry little conviction, whereas a literal understanding is consistent with all that is taking place.

An angel (Revelation 9:1) takes the key to the bottomless pit and releases a great horde of horrific, demonic creatures whose effect can be compared with that of an immense plague of locusts/scorpions, except that their target is human. The "bottomless pit" features often in the *Revelation* and is always a prison that is kept locked. It seems to be the secure place where certain fallen angels and unclean spirits are kept by God. In Luke's account of the deliverance of the demoniac by Jesus (Luke 8:31), we read that the demon, Legion, pleaded not to be sent to this pit *(abyss)*. Later, we shall see that this is the place where Satan himself is confined for a thousand years.

John says that these creatures "torture" men for five months (Revelation 9:5). The word he uses here in the original is often translated as "torment," a word that is typically used in Scripture to describe the work of demons. That they are real is evident from their power to bring pain, though not death. Such a monstrous plague would be quite disgusting to endure—even worse than the plagues in Egypt. The naming of the king (Abaddon/Apollyon, or "Destroyer") who is "angel of the bottomless pit" is an indication that this is a fallen angel, a part of the governmental structure instituted by Satan to rule his kingdom.

The second woe is called a plague. Now John sees creatures even more terrible than before appearing, so that he has difficulty describing them (Revelation 9:17). He speaks of seeing them in a "vision." The description of "fire and smoke and sulphur issuing from their mouths" and the sting in their tails (v. 19) conjures up a picture of dragonlike creatures. And there are two hundred million of them!

We are left to conjecture at their source, knowing only that they have arisen to terrorise mankind. They are brought into action by four angels who have been bound at the great River Euphrates, presumably since the first rebellion of the angels, awaiting this moment.

These four angels are a party to Satan's original rebellion but are now being used by God for a work of destruction in the world. It is interesting and instructive that this hour, day, month, and year were known to God back in the day in which they were bound (Revelation 9:15). We have seen that nothing takes God by surprise; he always knows the end from the beginning.

At this stage, one-third of mankind is killed by these awful things (vv. 18–19). Just as the nation of Egypt groaned at the communal loss of all the firstborn sons when the angel of death passed over their land, so there will be such a groan going up from the earth at this terrible carnage. Death will reach into every home and family.

What is the response of the population of the earth to these stupendous horrors? Do they turn to the living God and cry out for mercy? Do they at last recognise the error of their ways? Do they remember that the fear of the Lord is the beginning of wisdom? We read a very sobering answer to these questions in the last two verses of this chapter.

If at this point the reader feels that he is surfeited with the horror of these events he or she is having to consider, then spare a thought for John, who was having to record all the details as he saw them unfolding before him. He had no escape. He could not put the book down and walk away. He had to see it through, sharing the broken heart of God. No doubt he already realised just how corrupt people are, and how stubborn; he was under no illusions about this. But now he had to watch the visitation of God's just wrath expressed in vengeance. He was seeing the judgments of a holy God, judgments that human beings had decided in their own wisdom could not possibly come from a God of love. So, by making God in their own image, they had deceived themselves. These events are uncomfortable to contemplate when set against our notions of the just desserts of fallen man, and they give the lie to our own tolerance of iniquity and sin.

It is clear that these events have been taking place in sequence, and each phase must have a time span. Revelation 9:10 gives this as five months for the fifth trumpet. If each of the first six trumpets has a similar time span, then the total time for these would be two and a half years. If the duration of the opened Seal 7 is three and a half years, then there would be a final period of at least one year for the cataclysmic events of the seventh trumpet, but we must wait for seven chapters of important *revelation* before we learn more of this.

SUMMARY

❖ The opening of Seal 5 signifies the beginning of the countdown to Jesus' return.

Seal 5—No call to "COME!"
Time of tribulation on conquerors
End-times gospel preached in the world (Matthew 24:9–14)
The Antichrist is revealed

❖ The rapture occurs

Seal 6—Great Tribulation begins
Natural disasters occur
144,000 Israeli conquerors sealed and taken to glory
Believers wash their robes, resisting the 666 mark of the Beast

Seal 7—The wrath of God
The first six trumpets are blown in heaven
God's creation is devastated
The first two "woes" are enacted
The four bound angels at the Euphrates River are released

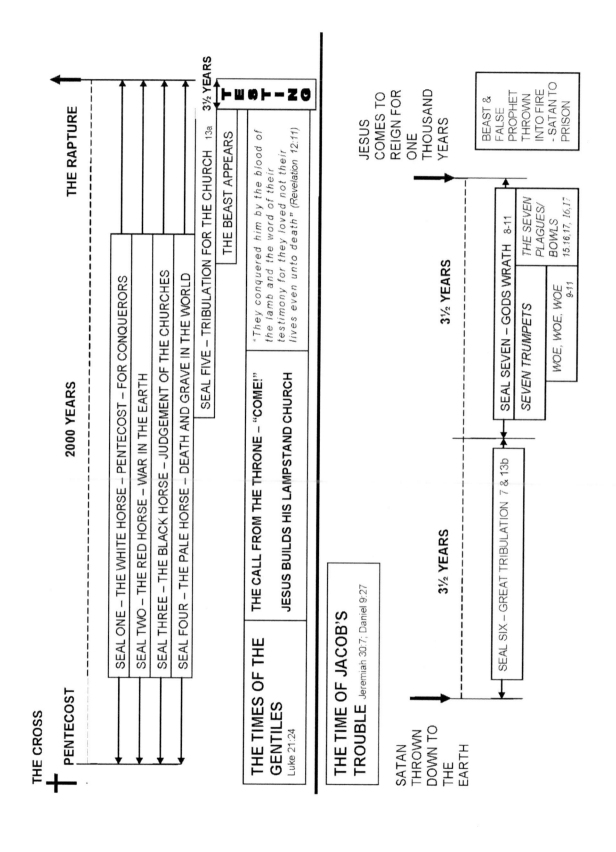

THE CROSS

PENTECOST

2000 YEARS

THE RAPTURE

3½ YEARS

TESTING

SEAL ONE – THE WHITE HORSE – PENTECOST – FOR CONQUERORS

SEAL TWO – THE RED HORSE – WAR IN THE EARTH

SEAL THREE – THE BLACK HORSE – JUDGEMENT OF THE CHURCHES

SEAL FOUR – THE PALE HORSE – DEATH AND GRAVE IN THE WORLD

SEAL FIVE – TRIBULATION FOR THE CHURCH 13a

THE BEAST APPEARS

"They conquered him by the blood of the lamb and the word of their testimony for they loved not their lives even unto death" (Revelation 12:11)

| THE TIMES OF THE GENTILES Luke 21:24 | THE CALL FROM THE THRONE – "COME!" |
| | JESUS BUILDS HIS LAMPSTAND CHURCH |

THE TIME OF JACOB'S TROUBLE Jeremiah 30:7; Daniel 9:27

SATAN THROWN DOWN TO THE EARTH

3½ YEARS

SEAL SIX – GREAT TRIBULATION 7 & 13b

JESUS COMES TO REIGN FOR ONE THOUSAND YEARS

3½ YEARS

SEAL SEVEN – GODS WRATH 8-11

SEVEN TRUMPETS

THE SEVEN PLAGUES/ BOWLS 15.16.17, 16.17.

WOE, WOE, WOE 9-11

BEAST & FALSE PROPHET THROWN INTO FIRE - SATAN TO PRISON

MORE WORK FOR JOHN TO DO
REVELATION 10

Act I, Scene 10—MORE WORK FOR JOHN TO DO　　　　**Time: After the Sixth Trumpet**

Place: Earth　　　　　　　　　　　　　　　　　　　　　**People: Israel**

Quite suddenly, with one trumpet still to be blown, the unrolling catalogue of disaster that John has been watching stops and the scene changes. In order to comprehend fully what John recounts in the next scenes, it is important that we hold in mind the phenomenal events that have taken place since Jesus opened the fifth seal. In that phase of Jesus' strategy, we saw the appointing of the Antichrist world ruler and his persecution of Christian "conquerors." This was followed by the rapture of the church and the opening of the sixth seal.

This new phase, the first half-week of Daniel's prophecy concerning Israel, brought fearful signs in the heavens and natural disasters on earth. Thus, the first step of destabilising the rule of the Antichrist began. His reaction was to initiate the Great Tribulation in which countless numbers of Christian believers died as they refused to accept the "*666 mark of the Beast.*" At this time too, 144,000 Spirit-filled Israelites were giving powerful testimony to their nation, only to meet with the same fate as the other Christian martyrs. After three and a half years, the whole world is in economic and social turmoil. The hopes that people had put in their world ruler are beginning to fade.

When Jesus opened the seventh seal, he initiated the phase in which God would visibly visit his wrath on the earth and its inhabitants. As each of the seven angels blew his trumpet in heaven, a new disaster was heralded on earth. In ascending degrees of awfulness, six trumpets had been blown. The world was holding its breath in fearful anticipation of what was still to come.

Now it is that John sees a "*mighty angel*" come down from heaven to bestride the earth (Revelation 10:1). The glorious appearance of this angel is not unlike that of the Lord himself, and his voice too takes us back to John's first meeting with Jesus (1:15). On that occasion, John had been told to write down what he heard, but now, for some unexplained reason, he is forbidden to record it (10:4).

Instead, John reports the angel's solemn pronouncement: "*that there should be no more delay, but that in the days of the trumpet call to be sounded by the seventh angel,* **the mystery of God**, *as announced to his servants the prophets, should be fulfilled*" (Revelation 10:6–7). The end of this painful phase of God's plan is in sight.

Inevitably we are drawn to ask, what is this "*mystery of God, as announced to his servants the prophets*" of which he speaks? Time and time again, the Old Testament prophets warned the people of Israel of God's impending judgements. Their warnings pointed to a time when God would be so exasperated with their apostasy that he would reject them altogether, just as history has shown. However, they also foresaw a time when Israel's status as God's chosen people in the world would be restored to them. Paul writes about this in his letter to the Romans in chapters 9, 10, and 11.

> *"Lest you be wise in your own conceits, I want you to understand this* **mystery,** *brethren: a hardening has come upon part of Israel* **until the full number of the Gentiles come in,** *and so all Israel will be saved; as it is written,* **"The Deliverer will come from Zion, he will banish ungodliness from Jacob;** *and this will be my covenant with them when I take away their sins"* (Romans 11:25–27).

For centuries they have been blind and deaf to God's revelation, so that the Gentile nations might believe; but by this announcement the great angel tells us that the time spoken of by the prophets and by Paul has now come. God has achieved his objective with the Gentile nations; *"the full number of the Gentiles has come in."* The "true" church was removed from the earth at the rapture and is together with God. The multitude of believers from out of the Great Tribulation stands before God's throne in heaven, and the 144,000 believers from Israel are also in heaven (see Revelation 14:1).

Jesus is now preparing to deal with the reluctant and rebellious remnant of Israel that has refused to accept the opportunities he has given them. The solemnity of the statement the angel makes, and the authoritative nature of the pronouncement, is warranted by the importance of this moment. *"There will be no more delay"* (Revelation 10:6). It is time for the fulfilling of all the Old Testament prophecies that promised a cleansing of the people of Israel and the city of Jerusalem, thus clearing the way for the seventh angel to blow his trumpet.

John is given a *"little scroll"* to eat (Revelation 10:9). Written in it is detailed prophecy of the events to come pertaining to Israel. Before John can speak them, he must eat them. Ezekiel had a similar experience (see Ezekiel 2:8, 3:3). When he ate the scroll of the Lord, he too found that it tasted as sweet as honey in his mouth, although it did not leave the same bitterness in his stomach that John experienced. The prophetic Word of God that is *revelation* must come from within the prophet, not just from his head.

One of the techniques used in the Bible to link together prophecies given at different times is the use of a common phrase or picture. In this case, our attention is drawn to Ezekiel's experience quite deliberately. The words on the scroll he had to eat were words of *"lamentation and mourning and woe"* (Ezekiel 2:10) to be spoken to *"the house of Israel"* (3:1). We are to see that as Ezekiel was chosen to prophesy concerning a rebellious and disobedient Israel, even so John now is fitted to speak to a rebellious and disobedient Israel prophetic words that would affect *"many peoples and nations and tongues and kings"* (Revelation 10:11). The effect of his words would be similar to the effect Ezekiel's words had on Israel in his day.

God had no illusions about Israel, even as he sent Ezekiel to speak to them (see Ezekiel 3:7–11), nor does he entertain illusions about Israel and the nations he is dealing with in the last days. How many peoples and nations and tongues and kings have read these prophecies of John during the last two thousand years? How many have desired to comprehend them so that they might alter their lives and please God? It really must be very few indeed. No wonder the words are bitter in his stomach!

THE LAST CHANCE
REVELATION 11:1-14

Act I, Scene 11—THE LAST CHANCE · **Time: Last 3 ½ Years**

Place: Jerusalem · **People: Israel**

Revelation 11 records three and a half years of extraordinary spiritual activity in Jerusalem. These events are the outworking of the scroll John had eaten. It is as if the director making a film of God's plan has chosen at this point to cut away from the sweeping events Jesus is instituting on the earth through the opening of Seals 6 and 7 to focus on a single significant story. We are to take a close look at the one-time city of God—Jerusalem—that over the centuries had been the focal point of so much human hatred, anger, and violence.

Whereas previously he has only been an observer of events, John now becomes a participant in the action. He is given a measuring rod like a staff and the instruction to *"measure the temple of God and the altar and those who worship there"* (Revelation 11:1). "The rod" John is given is described by the same word used in 2:27 for the "rod of iron"; the implication is that the act of measuring is for purposes of judgement or destruction, rather than for construction.

Our attention is drawn by this means to what is physically built on the Temple Mount in Jerusalem, the site where God's temple once stood. John is to be the one who measures it because he knew the temple as it was in Jesus' time, when it was still operating as God's temple and before it was destroyed. He will have understanding of what he has found once his survey is complete.

Although God is going to deal directly with the people of Israel once more, it will not be on the basis of the old covenant, for that covenant no longer exists and cannot be resurrected. *"God does not dwell in buildings made with hands,"* said Stephen in his impassioned defence to the Sanhedrin (see Acts 7:48, cf. 17:24). Any supposed temple built in Jerusalem will be a temple to another God, and God draws our attention to it because it plays a crucial role at this stage in Israel's history. Any such building (whether in Jerusalem or elsewhere) is an abomination to God.

So the temple building John is to measure is not a temple to the Lord as was Solomon's temple or even Herod's temple, for all temple worship ceased with the end of the old covenant when the great temple curtain was rent in two at the moment of Jesus' crucifixion. Since the destruction of the temple by the Romans in AD 70, there has been no Jewish temple and no temple worship.

Currently, there is a building on the site of the temple. It is the Dome of the Rock, a Muslim shrine occupying the approximate site of the old temple and honouring the god of Islam. Erected in the seventh century, it is the third holiest site of Islam and stands as a deliberate challenge to the tenets of Judaism and Christianity. On its frieze are the words: "God is one and has no son."

We know that in the last days, the Antichrist will *take his seat in the temple of God proclaiming himself to be God*" (2 Thessalonians 2:4). This means that a special building on the mount (either the current one or a new building altogether) will be used by the Antichrist to present himself to all peoples and religions as God.

From the earliest time of his rebellion, Satan has yearned to be "*as God.*" He yearns to be worshipped. Now he knows that his days are numbered. This terrible deceit is a last, desperate endeavour on his part to fulfil his heart's desire. Through his surrogate "king," he will commit the ultimate blasphemy. People will indeed worship him, but they do not know that these are the last days of his seeming triumph in ruling the world.

A Muslim Mosque   or   **a Jewish Temple**

or a Christian Cathedral

John is specifically told that the court outside the temple is not to be measured: *"the nations will trample over the holy city for forty-two months"* (Revelation 11:2), the duration of the seventh seal. The words used are not dissimilar from those of Jesus when he described the future of Jerusalem: *"And Jerusalem will be trodden down by the Gentiles until the times of the Gentiles are fulfilled"* (Luke 21:24). Although Israel has had sovereignty over Jerusalem since 1967, the word "trampling" speaks of political and military authority having been given over to the nations. In other words, the Gentiles may do as they please in the city.

Today Jerusalem is seldom out of the world news. The religious, political, and historic divisions that exist between the peoples in the land seem to be intractable. The words spoken to John here reveal how that problem will be temporarily resolved in the future. They imply that the city will become an "international city." The militarily all-powerful Antichrist will broker a "peace" deal between the Muslim Arabs and the Jews to which all the nations of the world will be party. It will be a momentary political triumph, appearing to bring peace and greater security to the world—but it will not last.

> *"When people say, 'There is peace and security,' then sudden destruction will come upon them as travail comes upon a woman with child and there will be no escape"* (1 Thessalonians 5:3).

Jerusalem, the capital city of Israel that we know today, is never named in *Revelation*. Considering its central place in end-times prophecy, this is remarkable, but there is good reason for it. In Revelation 11:8, we find an important key to understanding and interpreting what John was told to do. Jerusalem, here called the *"great city,"* far from being *"holy,"* is identified by name as *"Sodom and Egypt, where their Lord was crucified."*

This is spiritual *revelation* concerning the spiritual state of the inhabitants of Jerusalem at the time of the end. It is a heartbreaking description. It is the ultimate fulfillment of Ezekiel's tragic prophecy concerning God's city (see Ezekiel 16). Of course any capital city is simply a centre where people work and live together, but normally the king would have his palace there, and it would be the centre of commerce and government. So, in the Bible, the capital city of a nation is often used to represent the nation.

The name given here to Jerusalem reveals the state of the nation by the time of the opening of the seventh seal. Is it any wonder that Jesus cannot bring himself to speak the name "Jerusalem" in this *Revelation*? *"The city of God"* has become a byword for corruption, sin, and wickedness of the most extreme kind. Both Sodom and Egypt are notorious in the Bible; they are places that God has judged and punished in the past as an example to us all. Now Jesus shows us that the modern, secular city of Jerusalem is in the same category and will reap a similar judgement.

In verses 3–13, we see that John is again a spectator, watching what is going on in the city. He sees *"two witnesses"*—men with amazing powers—ministering to the people. The reference to the two olive trees takes us back once more to the Old Testament, where a similar scene was witnessed by Zechariah (Zechariah 4). In Zechariah's case he saw not only a lampstand but also two olive trees standing beside it, thus forging a link between these two prophecies. It is in Zechariah too that we discover the significant status of the witnesses: *"These are the two anointed who stand by the Lord of the whole earth"* (v. 14).

The two men have not featured before in *Revelation,* but they were not new to John. With Peter and James, he was present at the transfiguration and saw and heard Moses and Elijah talking with Jesus (Matthew 17:3). At that time, Jesus referred to the expectation of the scribes that Elijah would come as a forerunner to prepare the way for the Messiah. Thus John is seeing here a second and final fulfillment of that prophecy—a testimony that would be very well understood by all Jews. Elijah and Moses are forerunners of the Messiah, preparing Israel for his appearing. Malachi too spoke of Elijah's coming *"before the great and terrible day of the Lord"* (Malachi 4:5).

God makes his point very clear to Israel. These are divine missionaries. They are protected from harm for the duration of their ministry (Revelation 11:5). The miracles the two witnesses perform relate back to their earlier work. Specifically, Elijah caused a three-and-a-half-year drought in Israel (1 Kings 17:1, 18:1; Luke 4:24; James 5:17), and Moses brought plagues upon Egypt (Exodus 7–10). The Lord's intention is clear: by these mighty miracles the ministry of each of the witnesses is authenticated before the people, making their witness to Jesus, the soon-coming Messiah, entirely trustworthy. Indeed, who, knowing the Scriptures, could possibly entertain doubts about them?

The dramatic events go on for three and a half years before a most sinister character appears. John sees an individual—identified only as "*the beast that ascends from the bottomless pit*" (Revelation 11:7)—who is permitted to attack the two witnesses. For now, we can surmise that this man is the leader of Israel and like all the other world leaders has made an accommodation with the Antichrist in order to gain his position.

A devastating turn of events takes place. The two men of God are publicly executed, and both the local populace and the world at large, having rejected their miraculous ministry, will actually celebrate their demise. The world will be stunned, however, when the two are resurrected in full view of the public. The spoken witness of these two men is simply that Jesus Christ is the Messiah and they bring a call to national repentance! "*Repent for the kingdom of heaven is at hand*" – it is not a new message. The nation is given one more opportunity to accept the truth, and they refuse it.

This then is the fulfillment of the first part of the "mystery of God, as he announced to his servants the prophets" (Revelation 10:7). Israel is to have the gospel preached to them by God's anointed messengers from heaven, with attendant miracles and signs that accord entirely with Scripture prophecy. Although Israel will finally reject them, kill them, and scorn them, just as they did Jesus, it seems that there will be some who receive their gospel. This is the group who are identified in heaven as singing "*the song of Moses, the servant of God, and of the Lamb*" (15:2–3).

Television will be the means of beaming the scenes from Jerusalem all around the world for the entertainment of millions. When it is over, an earthquake shatters Jerusalem. Then, and only then, in great fear (but no faith) will men and women give "glory to God" (11:13).

John then realises that this disastrous event in Jerusalem, the second "*woe*," takes place at the blowing of the sixth trumpet (9:13). The second "*woe*" does not refer to the whole three-and-a-half-year period of the witnesses' ministry but just to the time when their testimony is finished (11:7). The third and final "*woe*" is still to come.

THE SEVENTH TRUMPET BLOWN
REVELATION 11:15-19

Act I, Scene 12—THE SEVENTH TRUMPET BLOWN

Time: When Jesus Initiates the Outpouring of God's Wrath

Place: Heaven

People: Those Around God's Throne

"*The third woe is soon to come*," says Revelation 11:14, but in fact the account of its effects on earth do not begin until chapter 16. First, further information is provided to John; this is another key moment in time.

With the blowing of the seventh trumpet, John is once more back in the throne room in heaven. There are two important announcements to be made. First, he hears the loud voices:

> "*The kingdom of the world has become the kingdom of our Lord and of his Christ,*
> *and he shall reign for ever and ever*" (Revelation 11:15).

At last the terrible consequences of the fall in Eden are about to be universally reversed. This is the moment! This is the point in time when Jesus is *seen* to reign, even by those who do not accept him. The different phases of the seals that show us Jesus' strategy is nearly complete. Now the King is ready to come into his inheritance.

Second, John hears the wonderful song of the twenty-four elders who are seated on their thrones. They seem to be quite familiar with Jesus' plans, and they delight to declare them.

> "*We give thanks to thee, Lord God Almighty, who art and who wast, thou that hast taken thy great power, and begun to reign. The nations raged, but thy wrath came, and the time for the dead to be judged, for rewarding thy servants, the prophets and the saints, and those that fear thy name, both small and great, and for destroying the destroyers of the earth*" (Revelation 11:17–18).

These words, "*thou hast . . . begun to reign,*" mean that his activity is now by personal intervention, not by angelic intermediary. This is the most wonderful moment, for it is the vindication of the cross. The seeming defeat of Calvary is seen for what it was: the beginning of a triumphant ending.

Everyone, from Adam and Eve onward, will now be dealt with by Jesus, with the exception only of those who are already received into heaven. He will implement the following programme in due season:

1. wrath to be delivered
2. the dead to be judged
3. servants to be rewarded
4. the destroyers of the earth to be destroyed

In an age where "green" issues have become politically fashionable and we have belatedly recognised our responsibility for the pollution and exploitation of our environment, it is interesting to discover in *Revelation* that from the beginning, God has taken great exception to the careless way in which his beautiful and perfect creation has been treated. The original *"dominion"* given to mankind (Genesis 1:26) carried with it a privilege and a responsibility for which we are answerable to the Creator himself.

The opening of God's temple in heaven (Revelation 11:19) is accompanied by a violent reaction of the natural elements on earth. These signs, which John sees here from his heavenly vantage point, he describes again in 16:18 at the conclusion of the pouring out of the seven bowls of wrath. On this basis, as we saw in the last chapter, it seems likely that the time for the final expression of God's wrath (fully described in chapter 16) is, mercifully, a very short one—one last year.

SUMMARY

❖ The angel signals that he has important and difficult revelation for John to understand and deliver.

❖ No more delay: the great mystery concerning his people Israel and his city Jerusalem is to be revealed at last.

❖ God's two witnesses have been preaching from the opening of the seventh seal. They are finally killed by the "king"—the beast who ascends from the bottomless pit—and they ascend to glory.

❖ The final phase of God's wrath is at hand—the seventh trumpet in heaven brings the third "woe" on earth.

JESUS' STRATEGY

JESUS OPENS SEAL 5
Ch 6:9-11 – tribulation of church

JESUS OPENS SEAL 6
Ch 6:12-17 – Great Tribulation
Sun, moon, and stars
Ch 7:1-8 – sealing 144,000 (Israelites)
Ch 7:9-17 – saints washing robes

JESUS OPENS SEAL 7
Chs 8 & 9 – 6 trumpets; 2 woes

INTERLUDE – Ch 10 – FURTHER DETAILS OF BITTER THINGS
Ch 11:1-14 - 2 prophets (holy city);
Ch 11:15-19 – the 7th trumpet in heaven

SATAN'S STRATEGY

Ch 12:1-6 - Great sign: mother & child
The conquerors go (rapture)
Ch 12:7-12 – The dragon thrown down

2nd woe complete

Ch 12:13-17 – dragon persecutes saints left behind
Ch 13:11-18 – false prophet imposes 666 mark of Beast
Ch 14:1-5 – 144,000 in heaven

Ch 13:1-10 – Antichrist world leader is appointed, martyrs the saints

GOD'S WRATH

INTERLUDE – Ch 14:6-13 – LAST WARNINGS TO ALL

Ch 14:14-20 – harvest time in earth
harvest time in Israel
Chs 15 & 16 – 7 golden bowls of wrath poured out
Chs 17 & 18 – Babylon destroyed
Ch 19:1-10 – Lamb's marriage supper In heaven
Ch 19:11-20:6 – King Jesus comes

Rightly dividing Revelation

PERIOD ABOUT 3½ YEARS (Rev:13:5)

PERIOD ABOUT 3½ YEARS (Rev:12:6,14)

PERIOD ABOUT 3½ YEARS (Rev:11:2,3)

THE WOMAN AND THE CHILD—
A GREAT PORTENT
REVELATION 12

**Act II, Scene 1—THE WOMAN AND THE CHILD
—A GREAT PORTENT**

**Time: Following the Seventh
Trumpet**

Place: The Sky

People: A Woman and a Beast

Until this stage of the *Revelation*, John has been dealing with real situations. He has been led through the events that follow the opening of the seven seals of the scroll up to the point when the seventh trumpet has been blown in heaven. Now, immediately following the blowing of the seventh trumpet, there is a pause in the procession of events that are being shown to him. At this key moment, a new and disturbing riddle is interposed.

Quite suddenly John is presented with a vast tableau in the sky. It is a picture he calls a "great portent" (Revelation 12:1): a phrase used to describe the foretelling of ominous events to come. The picture he is confronted with presents a very different experience from all that has gone before. He is not required to interpret it or even to comment on it; his task is to record exactly what he sees and hears. The responsibility for interpretation lies with those who will read it in the future, but this will not be a purely academic exercise. The interpreter must see and feel what John saw and felt, for this *revelation* is intended to challenge us to the roots of our faith.

John sees two "portents." The first is a woman, and the second is a monster. Although they are shown as interactive together in one picture, they are presented separately in order to make a clear distinction between the interests and purposes of the different spiritual authorities that they each represent.

We are all fascinated by stories like *Beauty and the Beast*. The idea has its roots in the interaction between the "good" and "evil" that is manifested in every individual and the way in which one ultimately triumphs over the other. As Christians we understand it to be a picture of the very real spiritual battle in which we are all engaged.

The first character John sees is a beautiful *"woman clothed with the sun, and with the moon under her feet, and on her head a crown of twelve stars"*. She is about to deliver a baby; in fact, so real is the picture that she is crying out and groaning as the labour pains of birth grip her.

The second character is a shocking and even disgusting sight—intentionally obscene! It is a monstrous, seven-headed dragon, blood red in colour and having ten horns. It is slavering and panting before the woman, intending to eat her baby as soon as it is born. This is truly the stuff of nightmares, and many are put off from grappling with its meaning because they do not care to picture it and discern its implications for themselves. But the horror of the picture is neither gratuitous nor accidental; it is *revelation* of God's view of the situation he depicts. Jesus wants us to realize just how gross and offensive to him is the monster and his intention.

Dramatically, the woman delivers her baby; a male child is brought forth. What a moment of drama! Most of us are familiar with the joy and wonder that accompany the birth of a child, and there is no accident in God's using this as a model to teach us deep lessons. Will the monster prevail? What can possibly save the child from its awful fate? Thankfully, before the dragon can effect his terrible purpose, God intervenes. The child is literally snatched to safety from the jaws of death. He is taken to be with God on his throne in heaven.

John then sees how the woman herself is saved from harm for a short period. She flees for her life from the menacing dragon to a place of safety in the wilderness, where she will be nourished for 1,260 days.

Although it is very briefly recounted, we must not be tempted to put this incredible drama to one side as something that is unlikely to have much significance for us. In fact, Jesus uses this means to deliver to us profound, eternal truths without which we can never know God as he wants us to.

Every part of the *Revelation* is essential to the rest of God's Word. It is coherent within itself as a prophetic book, but it is integrated with all Scripture from Genesis onward, including its history, doctrine, and prophecy. The truth to be revealed by this wonderful vision is central to, and therefore coherent with, all the prophetic mysteries in the Bible from beginning to end. Purposely set in the heart of the *Revelation*, **it is the key that unlocks the door to insight and understanding of the whole book, and thus of the whole Bible.**

Our task is to use the detailed evidence that has been supplied within the pictures in order to identify the characters and discern the truth portrayed by what takes place. We need to understand the woman and her role, the child and his role, and the dragon and his role.

The woman, unnamed in the vision, is simply presented as a pregnant mother without explanation. The central purpose of her existence is to be the mother of a child whose destiny is to reign and rule with God. The only other clues we have by which to establish her identity are her distinctive clothing, her footstool, her crown, and, perhaps most tellingly, the activity of the dragon.

If we look for Scripture passages employing the allegory of a woman giving birth, we find two in the New Testament. The first is Jesus' comparison of the different phases of the approaching "end times" to the birth pains of a woman in labour (see Matthew 24:4–14). He is teaching that as a mother experiences an escalating amount of pain as the moment of birth approaches, so nature itself will show signs of increasing stress before the day of the Lord.

The second is Paul's use of this figure of speech when he writes of the end times:

> *"For the* **creation** *waits with eager longing for the revealing of the sons of God; for the* **creation** *was subjected to futility, not of its own will but by the will of him who subjected it in hope; because* **creation** *itself will be set free from its bondage to decay and obtain the glorious liberty of the children of God. We know that the whole* **creation has been groaning in travail** *[lit. birth pangs] together until now; and not only the* **creation,** *but we ourselves, who have the first fruits of the Spirit, groan inwardly as we wait for adoption as sons, the redemption of our bodies. For in this hope we were saved"* (Romans 8:19–24).

Paul here pictures God's "creation" as an expectant mother carrying a child, and it is the pain that must come before the birth that he draws attention to. That pain is inescapable; creation is in travail until she at last gives birth to the "*sons of God*": the rapture of the conquerors.

These two remarkable parallel passages, taken together with John's picture of the woman with child, lead us to consider that **the central purpose of God's creation is the birth of this child.**

If this is correct, then the *"great portent"* causes us to reconsider what we can learn from the creation account in Genesis. We know that *"in the beginning God created the heavens and the earth."* The planet Earth was the first part of God's physical-material creation. In the first verse of the Bible, we are introduced to an earth floating in space, dark, empty, and lifeless, although covered with water. Yet God had not forgotten her, for the Holy Spirit *"was moving over the face of the waters."*

We have no knowledge of how long the earth was in this lifeless state, but when the right time came, God stepped in. Beginning by turning her darkness to light, in six days he brought her fully to life and clothed her. The sun, moon, and stars, created on day 4, provided her clothing, footstool, and crown. What we have seen in this final instalment of God's *revelation* of himself is God's created earth pictured as a pure, beautiful, virginal woman who is clothed with the sun, with the moon under her feet, and on her head a crown of twelve stars.

Now we can see that her integrity and innocence are not marred by her pregnancy, for, being without a husband, she was created with the seed of her child already in her. In other words, *she is the revelation of the purpose God had in making his creation.*

Once we understand God's purpose in making his creation—and not before then—we can begin to gain insight into the plan of action by which he will achieve that purpose.

This astonishing vision in the *Revelation* reveals to us the Father-heart of God as never before. God loves his creation because she came out of him; and in this love he gave her life by his Word, and she was made perfectly beautiful and wonderfully complete. Her purpose is to bring forth a male child who is a true *"son"* for God, and in this sense we can think of her as the *"wife"* of God brought forth out of himself. She is created by the Word of God for the specific purpose of bringing forth a child for God. It was in this sense also that Adam *"was made in the image of God,"* for just as God brought forth the "mother" earth from himself, so God brought forth Eve from within Adam.

God did not speak Adam into existence as he did everything else that he created. Instead, he took the pre-created dust of the ground and formed man from it. The man God formed had woman (his wife) in him. When God breathed his Spirit into that man, the man became a living soul.

Here is a mystery; the first man, a created son who was made in the image of God, could not conceive or give birth to children. He needed a wife so that children could be born to them. God miraculously brought woman out of man so that children might be born to them, for him. Why did God choose to create Adam and Eve in this manner, so differently from the rest of creation? The *Revelation* gives us the answer: *it is so that we understand that the whole of history with all its complexity, even unto today, is a necessary part of God's plan to bring his original purpose to fruition. The creation is still carrying her child today; the child is not yet born, but creation waits eagerly for that day to come. Until it comes, God's creation is a work in progress.*

Throughout the Bible, marriage (leading to the birth of children) has prophetic symbolism that helps us to know and understand God. He intended marriage to be a profound and sublime love relationship between a spiritual man and woman. When God populated the earth with creatures, he did so by making vast numbers of them and establishing a procreative activity among them. But these are creatures of instinct, having only a functional relationship with one another. They were created with gender, and the conception of their offspring is mechanical. God's creatures are not creative; they are there to serve, for they are not God's central purpose. The

Bible is careful to tell us that when God *made man* **in his own image**, *male and female (but together as one) created he them,* they were different.

This statement has less to do with man's physical attributes than it does with his spiritual capacity to have a relationship with both God and his wife. The great mystery that is the church is fully realised only in the spiritual unity of its members, both together and with Jesus.

> *"For this reason a man shall leave his mother and father and be joined to his wife; and the two shall become one flesh.* **This mystery is a profound one,** *and I am saying it refers to Christ and his church"* (Ephesians 5:31–32).

When we have this insight, we can see how the process of man's creation paralleled the process by which God created the earth. Despite the use of gender terms that we understand, God (Father, Son, and Holy Spirit) is without gender. In the creation process, he shows us that he embodies all the attributes of mother and father within himself. Adam could not bring forth children by himself. He needed a partner fit for him, and none was found. So God took Eve out of him and caused her to live. Similarly, God had prepared the earth (as a "mother"), and in the six-day creation he caused her to live. What was her purpose? It was to bring forth Adam (and Eve) made out of her substance—the dust—and all the children who would follow from them.

No matter what racial, physical, or social differences exist between individuals, every human being is made by God from that original dust and is directly descended from Adam and Eve. Since Adam and Eve were God's first family, all are born members of God's family because *the purpose of the creation of the earth was for mankind to become a family for God.*

> *"Thus says the Lord, the holy One of Israel, and his Maker: 'Will you question me about* **my children**, *or command me concerning the work of my hands?* **I made the earth, and created man upon it:** *it was my hand that stretched out the heavens, and I commanded all their host'"* (Isaiah 45:11–12).

> *"Thus says the Lord,* **who created the heavens (he is God), who formed the earth** *and made it* **(he established it; he did not create it a chaos, he formed it to be inhabited!)**: *'I am the Lord and there is no other'"* (Isaiah 45:18).

Isaiah prophetically states here that God expressly created the earth to be inhabited by mankind, as his children. God, Spirit as he surely is, reassuringly reveals to us that he has a physical "appearance." Jesus, who is the Son of Man, in his appearances in the *Revelation* is a glorified man. Because we are to identify with God in personal relationship now, it is important that we do not see him as some monstrous, otherworldly creature. As we are in Christ, he is unequivocally our Daddy! When the whole process of salvation has at last changed us into his likeness (1 John 3:2), we shall see him as he is. Our character is being changed into his likeness now; on that day our physical appearance will changed also to be like him. How wonderful.

> *"Thus it is written, 'The first man Adam became a living being': the last Adam became a life-giving spirit. But it is not the spiritual which is first but the physical, and then the spiritual. The first man was from the earth, a man of dust; the second man is from heaven. As was the man of dust, so are those who are of the dust; and as is the man of heaven, so are those who are of heaven. Just as we have borne the image of the man of dust, we shall also bear the image of the man of heaven"*
> (1 Corinthians 15:45–49).

We know well the story of the fall and Satan's part in it. However, our new insights reveal the secret of Satan's apparent success. It was the unity of marriage and family that Satan attacked in Eden because he knew that if he could break it, the understanding of God's purpose in family would be lost to man. *The whole of creation is predicated upon God's desire for a family for himself.*

We know well the effects of that terrible fall in Eden. Satan succeeded in driving a wedge between husband and wife, and as a consequence they could no longer exercise their joint dominion over creation. Dominion effectively passed to Satan, and the consequences have reached down through the ages, indelibly staining and spoiling the life of every child. Sinning became inevitable because iniquity replaced God's love in us.

For thousands of years, this dark situation has existed in the world. But what we are looking at in this vision of "creation" in the *Revelation* is a wonderful, if little-recognised, truth that the complication of iniquity introduced by Satan into the paradise of Eden is not the terrible hindrance to God's master plan that it first seems. The *"great portent"* reveals that the fall in Eden (and its consequences) is the very means God is using to achieve his heart's desire. Satan and his angels are essential players on God's stage, and they significantly contribute to the achievement of God's purpose.

By breaking the unity of the first marriage, Satan has managed to fog the meaning and practical significance of spiritual oneness down through the ages. But in doing so he has also signed his own death warrant. Let us now consider this as we examine the second portent: the Beast waiting to devour the child of "creation."

In Revelation 12:9, we are told distinctly that the great dragon is Satan, the devil. In verse 4, we see the dragon sweeping a third of the stars down from heaven and casting them to the earth. This is a dramatic *revelation* of Satan's rebellion together with one-third of the angels in heaven. Since the Bible gives us no account of the creation of the angels, we must assume that this traumatic event took place before Eden was created but at a time when the planet Earth existed, for the angels are cast down to a preexisting earth.

Satan and his followers had been trusted servants of God, serving at his throne. They were not automatons, however. Their rebellion and fall demonstrate that they had freedom and liberty in heaven. We can only conjecture as to what was going on, but the time came when they chose to use their freedom to turn against their Creator, and he had permitted them to do so.

Apparently the earth was the one place that the angels could go and establish their own kingdom, so Satan colonised the earth prior to the six-day creation. Of course, knowing all things, God's plan took full account of this situation. In making his creation on the earth, God was invading Satan's space. Thus Satan, identified here as the *"ancient serpent"* (Revelation 12:9), could come to Eve in the garden with God's full knowledge. He thought he knew God's plan and was determined to frustrate it. *Satan knew from the beginning that God had purposed in his heart to give to this child of creation the very place on his throne that he himself had so wickedly aspired to* (see Isaiah 14:12–14).

Because he was a spirit, Satan could not physically assault Adam. But he knew that if he could subvert Adam and or Eve, according to God's warning they would die.

We know the story. The *"great portent"* of *Revelation* dramatically portrays the final outcome resulting from that first confrontation in Eden. God revealed the consequences for all mankind of Eve's actions: *"I will put enmity between her seed and your seed"* (Genesis 3:15). The promised seed of the woman is not all mankind but Jesus.

> *"Since therefore the children share in flesh and blood, he himself likewise partook of the same nature, that through death **he might destroy him who has the power of death, that is the devil,** and deliver all those who through fear of death were subject to lifelong bondage. For surely it is not with angels that he is concerned, but with the descendants of Abraham"* (Hebrews 2:14–16).

In the plan of God, Jesus came to destroy the devil, but he was not going to do it in an instant. He was going to use this monster to achieve his purposes. The monster and his hordes would endeavour to consume the followers of Jesus by any means, but they are empowered to overcome him in every test and trial. Before a believer is fit to reign with Christ, he must be trained and proved. Our Father is our trainer, Jesus is our companion, and the Holy Spirit is our power in every circumstance. We have seen from the beginning of this work that Christians are called to be conquerors. Satan and his forces are the enemies we are to conquer.

So now we must address the all-important question: Who is this child snatched up to God's throne? Is it Jesus, as many affirm? Is it Israel? Is it the church? The answer is not whimsical, nor is it conjecture. We must review the evidence given to us. We know that the child is, *"one who is to rule all the nations with a rod of iron"* (Revelation 12:5). When interpreted correctly, this single clue intentionally allows no room for error in our understanding of the child's identity. It is special in Scripture, for it is found only in Psalms (2:9), speaking of the coming Messiah of Israel; in Revelation 2:27, speaking of the one in the church who conquers; and in Revelation 19:15, speaking of Jesus, the Word of God, the King of Kings and Lord of Lords, during his millennial reign.

It is life-changing *revelation* for us to realise that *ruling the nations with a rod of iron* is the intended destiny of those who are conquerors. Jesus makes the promise to the *conquerors* in the Thyatira church (Revelation 2:26–27). This is the future task they will share in their joint reign with Jesus. This understanding is further confirmed by Jesus' wonderful promise to the saints of Laodicea who also *conquer as he conquered* (Revelation 3:21). Those who follow his example will share his throne, which is his Father's throne (cf. Ephesians 2:6).

It is now a simple step of logic to deduce that the child brought forth by the woman is a picture of the corporate body of all those Christians who *conquer* in this lifetime, of whom Jesus is the first. John sees the child caught up to the throne of God (Revelation 12:5). The Greek word he uses for this action is *harpazo*, which has an element of force in it. It describes a snatching away or taking by force. It is the same word Paul uses in 1 Thessalonians 4:17, where he describes how the saints will be caught up to meet the Lord in the air.

One day soon, the last conqueror will be adjudged by God to have completed his walk of faith. At that moment of time, all those conquerors remaining on earth will be snatched up *as one*, joining with those conquerors who are already dead (but asleep), to be with Christ. This is the only place in the *Revelation* that refers to this wondrous, instantaneous event. This "snatching up" graphically describes the "rapture" spoken of by Jesus (Matthew 24:40–41; Luke 17:34–36), which will take place at the coming *(Gr. parousia)* of the Lord.

This picture of the child of God snatched up to God's throne is not about the destiny of a single human being, not even of Jesus. It is the Father's wonderful answer to Jesus' prayer in John 17. It is a picture of the one true church that Jesus said he would build. The visible churches down through the ages have been fractured constantly by divisions and disputes, and yet out of them Jesus has been secretly and patiently forming his own church of those he calls conquerors.

> *"For it was fitting that he, for whom and by whom all things exist, in bringing **many sons to glory**, should make the pioneer of their salvation perfect through suffering. For he who sanctifies and those who are sanctified have one origin. That is why he is not ashamed to call them brethren"* (Hebrews 2:10–11).

> *"**He who conquers** shall have this heritage, and I will be his God and he shall be my son"* (Revelation 21:7).

Surely these are some of the most wonderful and encouraging words of Scripture, and they fit perfectly with the picture of the child snatched up to God's throne. What a moment that will be!

We find that the snatching up of the child to God's throne really stirs things up in the second heaven. Of all unimaginable things, a battle between the angels of God and Satan's angels then ensues. It seems as if this must be a wrestling match, for no weapons appear, and there are no casualties. But the result is that Satan and his followers are thrown down and are now totally and finally excluded from (the second) heaven. There being nowhere else to go, they are now confined to the earth's atmosphere (the first heaven). John hears the voice declaring this very good news for those in heaven, but it means serious trouble on earth.

> *"Woe to you, O earth and sea, for the devil has come down to you in great wrath, for he knows his time is short!"* (Revelation 12:12).

In verses 10 and 11 we have important confirmation of our analysis of the allegorical language of the vision. Here is a parenthetical statement that is another key to understanding the meaning. The critical element in the epic battle to throw Satan and his angels down from heaven is that Jesus' followers on the earth have completed their work in the face of all Satan's efforts.

The faithful work of the conqueror may not bring applause or approval from the world. It does not depend upon visible success. It is not necessarily religious or churchy. It is all-day, everyday, obedience to the leading of the Holy Spirit within our circumstances. It is going on now in countless unsung situations, and it is leading to the permanent downfall of man's age-old enemy. The victory we win over Satan may be unrecognised on earth by other people, or even by ourselves, but it is clearly recorded and established in heaven, and it is preparing us for a glory we cannot imagine.

> *"And I heard a loud voice in heaven saying, '**Now the salvation and the power and the kingdom of our God and the authority of his Christ have come,** for the accuser of our brethren has been thrown down, who accuses them day and night before our God. And **they have conquered him** by the blood of the lamb and the word of their testimony, **for they loved not their lives even unto death**'"* (Revelation 12:10–11).

This *revelation* makes it clear that *we are required by God to conquer Satan and his forces while we are alive on this earth.*

The two main parts of this work are shown here. The first is God's gift to us: *"the blood of the Lamb"* upon which we all depend. The second is our response to that gift: *"the word of our testimony,"* that is, the witness to Jesus that is to motivate everything we do and say in our lives—even at the cost of our natural life itself, as revealed at the opening of Seal 5. Conquerors must speak for Jesus. A silent witness is not enough; the world can hear only if the name of Jesus, Creator, Saviour, Lord, and King, is spoken out by his people as they testify to what he has done in them.

We have here, then, a beautiful confirmation of our earlier hypothesis. Without the victories achieved by those who conquer amid pain, disaster, and suffering, Satan could not be finally excluded from the heavens. Is it then any wonder that he makes it his purpose to eliminate the sources of his own downfall? We have so misunderstood the heart of God. He does not want great churches or great reputations. He wants people who are faithful even to death.

This great, central, mystical vision of "the woman who is a mother" fulfils a wonderful purpose. It combines all the elements that make up the sweeping events of God's plan through eternity. For this reason, the task of interpretation is difficult to contain in one's mind. First, the purposes of God himself are revealed. Then the strategy of Satan in hostile opposition is shown. Then is revealed the continuing work of Jesus in his people, both Gentiles and Jews, that enables us all to be conquerors whatever our circumstances.

John takes up his story again in verse 13. The woman flies away from the serpent into the wilderness *"for a time, and times, and a half a time"* (v. 14). Here she is to be nourished, as Elijah was nourished by the ravens when he fled to Cherith (1 Kings 17:3–4). James 5:17 tells us that this period of drought, during which Elijah was nourished miraculously by God, was for a similar period of three and a half years. This is a time coinciding with the Seal 6 period. For these three and a half years, creation itself is protected from Satan's worst aggression as in his pent-up hatred, frustration, and rage, he attempts to sweep the woman away by a flood of water out of his mouth. Having failed to destroy the child, Satan now seeks to destroy the mother. But somehow the earth is able to absorb the outpouring so that created life is preserved for what lies ahead. The use of a flood in prophecy is not new. It is used in the Old Testament to describe the effect of an overwhelming military conquest that the Lord permits to come upon a nation as judgement (e.g., Jeremiah 47). This description may refer to the time of Great Tribulation, which follows the opening of Seal 6.

We are told that Satan goes off in a rage to make war on *"the rest of her offspring"* (Revelation 12:17). Now he knows that the end is very near. Who are the woman's other offspring? That they are not simply the rest of mankind is clear, because it is certain that these offspring referred to are somehow followers of Jesus. We see them identified, not as conquerors, but put in a different category. They are *"those who keep the commandments of God and the faith of Jesus"* (*Revelation* 14:12). These are the 144,000 believing Israelites, and perhaps the multitude who pass through the Great Tribulation and so "wash their robes" during the three-and-a-half-year period of Seal 6.

Our study of the great portent cannot be concluded without reference to the time measurements that are detailed here. The woman, we are told, is to be protected for "one thousand two hundred and sixty days" (v. 6), and this is referred to again as "a time and times, and half a time" (v. 14). Revelation 11:2–3 speaks of a similar period of time (forty-two months and one thousand two hundred and sixty days) during which God's two witnesses in Jerusalem are prophesying and the nations are trampling over the Holy City. These two periods are probably contemporaneous with the three-and-a-half-year term of Seal 7.

Thus, it seems that similar periods of time cover Seals 5, 6, and 7. Each period is to last for about three and a half years, thereby identifying the last two terms with the last seven-year period of Daniel's prophecy (Daniel 9:27).

In the first eleven chapters, John has been given a *revelation* of Jesus' rule in the world once he had the scroll and opened the first four seals. The scenes cover all that has been going on since the day of Pentecost until now. They reveal Jesus' strategy being worked out in the history of the world. In our brief lives, we too have been observers of the strategy by which *Jesus, as the ruler of all creation, is fulfilling his Father's purpose of getting a special child for himself from out of the creation.*

Now, and with that in mind, we must be taught new lessons. In the following passages, we will see all things from a different perspective; we will see Satan's strategy revealed in the desolate future that faces our world before Jesus returns. Already we know how Satan has sought to destroy would-be conquerors through the generations. This new *revelation* will also cover the time period encompassed by the last three seals of the scroll.

THE ANTICHRIST'S COUNTERATTACK
REVELATION 13:1-10

Act III, Scene 1—THE ANTICHRIST'S COUNTERATTACK **Time: Seal 5**

Place: Earth **People: The Nations**

Revelation 13 introduces a new perspective on world events. Up to this point we have been observers of Jesus' strategic management of the world since he took the scroll from God the Father. In Revelation 12, Satan was revealed as a grotesque and monstrous spirit, hostile to God and man, whose sole endeavour is to frustrate God's purpose and plan to make men and women joint heirs with Jesus Christ. He has been allowed to operate under restriction down through the centuries, and Christians have had to battle with him and his demons in the process of their sanctification.

When we come to chapter 13, we are taken back in time to when Jesus opens the fifth seal. This is when Jesus is going to remove his restraint from Satan. For a brief and predetermined period, he will have free reign in the world.

John finds himself standing on a vast, sandy beach looking at the sea. As he watches, the waves part and a great upheaval of the waters takes place as out of them emerges a most hideous and frightening creature. The detailed description we are given is important in each particular, because it is there to help us identity the Beast.

Obviously such a monster is unnatural. Because of its *seven* heads, it might be said to be "perfectly" unnatural, but this is not intended as a comic book caricature that God is depicting for us. This is *revelation* of a very significant individual who will appear on the world stage in the last days. In fact, it reveals to us just what the Antichrist will be like when he comes. This is not a picture of his outward appearance that we are seeing but of the inward man. He is the spitting image of his master, the devil. Just as we shall be like Christ when the work of sanctification is complete in us, so this man is the image of Satan because the work of iniquity is complete in him.

Originally God had declared that all his creation, including man, was *"very good."* This unnatural creature is representative of the thousands of years of cumulative corruption that have taken place since the day of the fall. He is an iniquity-filled mutation of Adam, the perfect original. The seven heads identify him with the Beast of chapter 12, and the ten crowns show the comprehensive nature of his rule through the world's rulers who are in willing subjection to him.

Modern man takes an optimistic view of his development since Eden. Physically and intellectually, he may appear to have progressed and become more sophisticated, but inside, without salvation, he is still a corrupted and dying corpse. In this picture, a man so beautifully created in the image of God is spiritually an obscene, multiheaded beast in the image of Satan. Satan has at last got himself a man made in his own image—*the Antichrist who is to come is the devil incarnate!*

This individual even seeks to present himself as the "saviour of the world," a messiah who will bring peace and prosperity on earth. Indeed, in verse 3 we read that he, or one of his associates, will have been brought back from the dead in such a way that all around the world people will marvel at the miracle that has taken place. (Supposing, for example, he caused Ariel Sharon to be restored to life in Israel). *"Only God could do such a thing!"* people will say, and unless we know the Scriptures, we will probably agree with them. But those who know what is written here will recognise this event as a satanic counterfeit. They will understand that God has permitted this very thing to happen so that those who have refused to *"love the truth and so be saved"* (2 Thessalonians 2:10) will be given over to believing a lie (v. 11). The whole world will be enthusiastically swept away with the events portrayed here, and *unless the lessons of the Revelation have been received, God's people will be deceived and follow the Beast like everyone else.*

> *"One of its heads seemed to have a mortal wound, but its mortal wound was healed,*
> *and the whole earth followed the beast with wonder. Men worshipped the dragon, for*
> *he had given his authority to the beast, and they worshiped the beast saying, 'Who is*
> *like the beast and who can fight against it?'"* (Revelation 13:3–4).

At last Satan, by the apparent miraculous raising of a dead man to life, will achieve his heart's desire: he will pose as God and seek to be worshipped as God. Shocking as this will be for many, it is the sign the one who knows and respects the prophecies in the Word of God has been waiting for: the revealing of the Man of Iniquity (or Lawlessness, or Sin), whom we know as the Antichrist.

> *"Let no one deceive you in any way, for that day will not come unless the rebellion [or*
> *apostasy] comes first, and the man of lawlessness [or iniquity] is revealed, the son of*
> *perdition, who opposes and exalts himself against every so-called god or object of*
> *worship, so that he takes his seat in the temple of God, proclaiming himself to be*
> *God"* (2 Thessalonians 2:3–4).

God has shown us that these things must happen; we are not to be surprised or upset when they occur, because this is our time. The rule of Antichrist is the last test for the conqueror. It will separate the sheep from the goats in the churches. The Christian conquerors will be persecuted, and many will die because they identify this ruler for who he is and refuse to worship him along with the rest of the world. Who will be able to resist the pressure to conform to the general acceptance of this creature? Who will have faith to endure the hostility of society in those terrible times? Without this *revelation*, it will be impossible, and most churches will be deceived into following him.

With understanding gained from the prophecies of Daniel, we know that this leader will be a sophisticated and able liar, a con man living by deceit and flattery, manipulating for his own devilish ends sycophantic men and women, including even church leaders. His brand of spiritual poison will engulf all his entourage. He will know how to play the deep chords of man's unspoken lusts: *"I will give you the desires of your heart, provided only that you follow me unconditionally!"* It will be as if Adam's original rebellion has, at last, found vindication. The Antichrist is *"like God,"* apparently able to bring peace, prosperity, and security to the world; and man, it seems, is finally in charge of his own destiny without the God of the Bible. After all the anxiety and terror produced by the opening of the fourth seal, it will seem that man has been able to recover his grip on his circumstances through this "great leader."

But God has permitted this to happen; and we know that Jesus initiated this phase as he opened the fifth seal, thus setting in motion the extraordinary events we have been studying. It is a clear signal that we are coming to the climax of the ages.

John's description of *"the beast rising out of the sea"* (Revelation 13:1) causes us to refer to a much earlier prophecy on the same subject, where similar images are used. In Daniel's dream (Daniel 7), he sees four great beasts that rise up out of the sea. The bizarre descriptions are given us so that we can identify the nation or empire to which they each refer. A detailed explanation of Daniel's vision is outside the scope of what we are doing here, but it is clear from his description that the "beast from the sea" of Revelation 13 and the "little horn" of Daniel's vision are the same individual.

The "little horn" arises out of the collapse of the terrible empire represented by the fourth beast. That great empire collapses and breaks into ten nations, and a new leader rises to power, pulling down three of the other leaders. This is the Antichrist we are to look out for as described by Daniel.

From its description, the beast that John sees appears to be a composite of the four beasts of Daniel 7. We derive from this that the leader who first established himself as the "little horn" has now furthered his career by combining all four empires that preceded him. This is in effect a worldwide conspiracy of all the nations of the world brought together and orchestrated by the unseen, ruling, demonic powers under the direction of their master.

In Daniel 2, we read the account of Nebuchadnezzar's dream of the great, golden statue and of Daniel's interpretation of its meaning. This imagery showed the four earthly kingdoms (empires) that would dominate the world in turn until the coming of Christ, followed by a later, fifth empire. In Daniel 7, we are shown a further four kingdoms (empires) in the earth, which will dominate the world from Christ's first appearance until his second coming.

There have been many powerful political empires that have come and gone in the last two thousand years, but none of them fits the detailed specification of Daniel's dream. As there are no obvious candidates, this tells us that we must look for empires of a different nature. The *Revelation* has shown us that all during this time, behind the scenes, the unseen prince of darkness has been at work, pursuing his agenda to "consume the child of God." In other words, his intention has been focused upon the elimination of Christian conquerors.

The four empires of Daniel's dream are not empires as we conventionally think of them, for they have a longevity going far beyond that of the great empires of history, and they never disappear totally. At the last, all four empires exist together (Daniel 7:12); they have not obliterated one another, as is usually the case. We have the enormous benefit of hindsight by which to examine these prophecies.

Also, as we have seen in the *Revelation*, once Jesus had taken the scroll, he instituted a strategy in the world to counteract the empires of Satan. He sent the four horsemen to patrol the earth. In contrast, in Daniel 7 we are shown Satan's emissaries from the pit (Daniel 7:17). They are represented by the four deformed creatures coming out of the sea in stark contrast to the beautiful horses of Jesus. These demon-led empires, then, have the sole purpose of thwarting the strategy of Jesus to bring men and women to himself. Thus, we see the great spiritual battle of the ages between the four horsemen of Jesus and the four beasts of Satan, culminating with a fifth beast, the little horn, who will resist Jesus in person—the Antichrist.

A study of Daniel's beasts can be made to deduce their individual characteristics and the precise meanings and implications of the way their deceptive philosophy dominates and deceives each particular society. Although this exegesis is beyond our scope here, we can see all four of these "kingdoms" in existence today. All four represent powerful systems of alternative governments that seek to order the political, economic, and social existence of mankind apart from any recognition of the lordship of Jesus or the authority of God's Word.

There are four anti-Christian empires in history as described by Daniel which have served this end.

Beast I—as in Daniel 7:4: **THE ROMAN CHURCH**

(Apostate Christianity; type: the Holy Roman Empire; governed by a man in Christ's place, e.g., the pope, who calls himself "Holy Father")

Beast II—as in Daniel 7:5: **ISLAM**

(False religion led by false prophet denying Jesus as God's son [see 1 John 2:22]; denying the Bible; original conversions by the sword; religion of law; arising from Ishmael)

Beast III—as in Daniel 7:6: **CAPITALISM**

(Materialistic idolatry; type: British Empire; worldwide trading system dominated by money lending)

Beast IV—as in Daniel 7:7–8: **ATHEISTIC HUMANISM/SOCIALISM**

(Communism/socialism; "there is no God"; type: USSR and China)

Before Jesus returns, we can expect to see a grand coalition of apostate Christianity, Islamic nations, capitalism and humanism/socialism that will come together under one ruler. Such a grouping of the world's economic, military, and religious powers would leave very little opportunity for opposition. No nation could opt out of the new political organisation and still sustain itself. The central spiritual "glue" for such a group will be the golden calf of money and the persuasion of supreme military power. Together they will capture all the elements of the world's religions in a political-spiritual harmony.

It is unlikely that the nations of the world will easily give up their sovereignty without some powerful external, coercive act. According to *Revelation* this will be provided by the dreadful final events of that time initiated by the opening of Seal 4. The rider on the "pale" horse, who goes forth at the opening of the fourth seal, brings sword, famine, pestilence, and wild beasts upon the earth, causing death on a worldwide scale, destroying approximately a quarter of the earth's population (Revelation 6:8)—some one and a quarter billion people could die. In the face of such a crisis, the Antichrist will be able to draw together the world's great empires in a final conspiracy against God.

The call of God that accompanies the opening of the fourth seal is to "Come!"—to come and seek forgiveness in Jesus, to come and drink the water of life. Rather than respond to that gracious call, mankind will once again seek salvation in a saviour of their own making. This is the beginning of a final act of rebellion against God, and Satan already has just the candidate to take centre stage when Jesus opens the fifth seal.

Now will come the persecution of the saints, and those who are to join the souls under God's altar (Revelation 6:9) will face their last challenge. One of the telltale flaws of the Antichrist is that he cannot but blaspheme (13:5). Out of his mouth will flow words against Jesus and his people. This characteristic stands out clearly in both Daniel's account and the *Revelation* account. He will never be able to conceal his paranoia. After the imposition of initial, petty restrictions and pressures on believers, outright persecution will come. Just as Herod found his attacks on the early Christians earned him popularity with the Jews (Acts 12:3), so the Antichrist will find that his attacks on the nonconforming "fundamentalist" (therefore extremist) Christians will earn him popularity with the people at large.

Conquering Christians will be seen generally to be self-righteous, ungrateful kill-joys who ought to be thankfully supporting the great man who is leading the world out of its problems instead of indulging in carping criticism of him and calling him "offensive" names (i.e., Antichrist). The irony of their position will be that everyone else, even the formal churches, will be against them. They will be the sole irritant in an otherwise homogeneous acceptance of this ruler, who will be accepted by all faiths and all political systems as he preaches a message of universal brotherhood, peace, and justice. Their faithfulness will cost conquerors everything, even their lives (Revelation 13:7–10).

If this is true, then we have the answer to the question posed by the saints under the altar (Revelation 6:10): "How long?" By the blood of the Lamb, and by this last act of faithful witness, after three and a half years of persecution, the corporate brothers of Jesus will be snatched up to the throne of God in the twinkling of an eye.

THE FALSE PROPHET
REVELATION 13:11-18

Act III, Scene 2—THE FALSE PROPHET   **Time: Seal 6**

Place: The World   **People: The Nations and Israel**

The general upheaval that ensues on earth when Jesus opens Seal 6 heralds the arrival of Satan and his angels on earth. *"The stars of the sky fell to the earth as the fig tree sheds its winter fruit when shaken by a gale"*—so John describes the fall of these wretched rebel spirits from the heavens (Revelation 6:13). Now they are confined to the atmosphere of this planet. There are terrible days of physical and spiritual darkness ahead as the world begins to comprehend that the wrath of almighty God is imminent.

It is clear from chapter 12 that the rapture of the saints (after forty-two months of persecution [13:5]) leads instantly to the casting down from heaven of Satan and his angels. Once these saints have been removed to heaven, and coincident with Satan's confinement to the earth, a new horror appears. John writes:

> *"Then I saw another beast which rose out of the earth; it had two horns like a lamb and it spoke like a dragon"* (Revelation 13:11).

The demonic nature of this new individual is clearly signalled by the description of his origin (i.e., *out of the earth*) and by the satanic words he uses. He is clearly there to deceive, presenting a lamblike figure in appearance, calculated to be Christlike to the onlooker. His purpose is to enhance the "godlikeness" of the Antichrist. This is the False Prophet, who is determined to promote the Antichrist to the status of God on earth. Many tyrants who have ruled on the earth have ended up as megalomaniacs with delusions of divinity, and the Antichrist will be no different. The initial adulation of the people will utterly corrupt him.

The original pretence to suave, political ambition will be replaced by a longing for worship. He will not be able to hide the desires of his heart, longings that exactly mirror the iniquity in the heart of his master. Satan had aspired to be God and to receive the worship that is due to God alone (see Isaiah 14:13–14). He had once tried his best to confuse Jesus into falling down and worshipping him. Now, in this last desperate attempt, he seeks the direct worship of mankind through his surrogate, and the False Prophet is there to orchestrate the proceedings.

Such is the travesty of the Antichrist's counterfeit dominion that with the help of the False Prophet he actually institutes a marking of the worshippers, which is an attempt to emulate the seal of the Holy Spirit in the lives of the believers. By decree, all are to be marked on the right hand or the forehead with the number 666. Although it is pathetic, God uses this work of the Antichrist to establish a final and permanent dividing line between those who are Satan's and any who would even now be his. All are to know that there is a choice to be made. To refuse the mark of the beast is to lose one's livelihood, to face persecution and death, and, perhaps even worse, to see one's loved ones starve.

This is the situation that faces the people described in Revelation 7:9–17, who found that they had to "wash their robes in the blood of the Lamb." It seems that there will be a huge number of people, from every nation of the world, who had thought that they were true Christians. These are people who knew at least something of Scripture but never entered into God's rest. They had been deceived into adopting a way of life that was less than that Christ called for. They never knew what it was to take up their cross on behalf of Jesus. They never knew what it meant to lay down their life on his behalf. They were never a witness in a hostile world. They were never conquerors. At this point in the proceedings, the awful truth of their situation will begin to dawn on them. In the face of the demands now being made upon them, they will no longer be able to ignore the challenge to their faith.

When the False Prophet begins to call for the Antichrist to be worshipped, they will smell a rat, and with good reason. When the call goes out for every individual to be marked with the special mark of the Antichrist, the dreadful truth will dawn upon them for sure. This is the end. The *Revelation* shows us that at this point there will be no pretence. The "mark of the beast" will be the watershed for eternity. Many who have sought to prevaricate, to trim their sails to the wind, to avoid the issues, will now have their final choice to make. Resist and starve, resist and see your children and loved ones die, or give way and be damned for eternity.

This is the "flood" referred to in Revelation 12:15. And these people are "the rest of her offspring" (12:17). Many will find a new boldness. Many will refuse the temptation of Satan and his henchmen. They will die and in so doing inherit eternal life, taking their place before the throne of God, as we saw in Act 1, Scene 9. No wonder chapter 7 carries the wonderful promises of Jesus made to those who do not yield.

> *"They shall hunger no more, neither thirst any more; the sun shall not strike them,*
> *nor shall any scorching heat. . . . and God will wipe away every tear from their eyes"*
> (Revelation 7:16–17).

Finally, John tells us the "number of the beast"—six hundred and sixty-six (666). The number six in Scripture speaks prophetically of man. Used in this configuration, it speaks of man in his defiance to God. It is perhaps the most famous number in the world, known to multitudes who know nothing else of Scripture. Over the years, various interpretations of this number have been used ingeniously to identify many contenders for the title of Antichrist, from Caesar to Hitler and many others beside. But this is no game: it is not about making exciting predictions to tease our imagination or sell books. Those who possess the necessary wisdom will be in no doubt about its implications when that terrible number begins to be imposed upon all people.

GATHERING DARKNESS
REVELATION 14:1-5

Act III, Scene 3—GATHERING DARKNESS

Time: Seal 6

Place: Heaven

People: Israel

In chapter 14 of the *Revelation,* the attention, once again, switches to what is going on in heaven itself. In chapter 7, we met an extraordinary group of Christians, the 144,000 people drawn from among the twelve tribes of Israel and sealed upon their foreheads. Here, John sees them standing on Mount Zion with the Lamb.

We know that the believers on earth are especially hated by Satan when he is thrown down to the earth, and the 144,000 thousand in Israel are no exception. Satan sets out to make war on those left behind after the rapture. The seal on the foreheads of these believers is clearly in direct contrast to the 666 mark of the Beast, which is being universally imposed during the three-and-a-half-year Seal 6 period. Perhaps, because of the special nature of Israel, they will have been exempt from the necessity to receive the mark of the Beast at first. But when this requirement is imposed on them, they will reject the claims of the Antichrist and the False Prophet and will refuse the mark. This will produce public opposition, outrage, and resentment leading to severe persecution by the authorities. The 144,000 too will have to face death for their faith in Jesus.

These ones are "redeemed" we are told, but we do not know how they get to heaven. Have they been raptured, or are they martyred for their faith? We do not know the answer, for John is not invited to enquire about them as he was about the second group in Revelation 7. In some ways this 144,000 is a puzzling group because their chastity is shown to be a significant factor. It seems that such is the crisis of the times they face that marriage and family become less of a priority and these men devote themselves totally to the ministry they were called to. Because of this, they are declared to be *"spotless."*

The 144,000 are a unique group in heaven, for they are *"before the throne"* (i.e., they are not sharing the throne with Jesus) singing a wonderful worship song that only they can know. For them, there are no more questions or problems; they have a wonderful destiny:

> *"They sing a new song before the throne and before the four living creatures and before the elders. No one could learn that song except the one hundred and forty-four thousand who had been redeemed from the earth. It is these who have not defiled themselves with women, for they are chaste [virgins]; it is these who follow the Lamb wherever he goes; these have been redeemed from mankind as first fruits*

for God and the Lamb, and in their mouth no lie was found for they are spotless"
(Revelation 14:3–5).

Their spotlessness (clean white robes) is established by their faith in Jesus. Their behaviour during the crisis of the times was impeccable. Their unique destiny is *"to follow the Lamb wherever he goes"*—a kind of royal bodyguard. This is not the position or the role of those who are conquerors; their destiny is to sit on the throne with Jesus. Also the role of the 144,000 differs from that of those who were saved out of the Great Tribulation, whose destiny is to *"serve him day and night within his temple"* (7:15).

Before the opening of Seal 6, the *Revelation* has been about Jesus' strategy for building His church, but with the opening of Seal 6 we see that Jesus begins to deal with the nation of Israel in fulfillment of the "one week" referred to in Daniel 9:27. The seven years of trial for Israel has now commenced, and the first three and a half years is characterised by the salvation of 144,000 Israelites.

THE LAST CHANCE
REVELATION 14:6-13

Act III, Scene 4—THE LAST CHANCE   **Time: Prior to Seal 7**

Place: Midheaven   **People: All**

The three-and-a-half-year period of Seal 6 is over. At this point, there are no Christian people left on earth. The conquerors have been taken in the rapture; the multitudes that passed through the Great Tribulation have gone to glory; the 144,000 believers from Israel have also gone. Now Seal 7 is due to be opened.

In truth, the love of our Father for his creation is beyond our comprehension. Because that love is not separate from his holiness, there exists a tension between his desire to save his creation from the effects of man's rebellion and the necessity to allow iniquity to produce its inevitable harvest in the world. In allowing mankind to exercise the independence Adam chose in Eden, God must carry the terrible burden of the resulting pain, anguish, and suffering, knowing that through it all some at least will choose to come to him.

We have seen in the *Revelation* that for the last two thousand years God has made his churches to be lampstand witnesses to his great grace and love expressed in the death of his Son Jesus on the cross. All during this time, he has been calling individual men and women to "Come!" It is the simple message of a loving Father who has carefully made a way for his lost children to come home to him. Tragically, it seems that from the very beginning the visible church failed in its calling, substituting religious exercises and good works for the truth, thereby failing to challenge the hostility of the world to its Creator. However, through the *Revelation*, we know that despite appearances to the contrary, Jesus is achieving his objective.

In his mercy, therefore, God sent Moses and Elijah to Jerusalem again, just as he promised, to call Israel to receive their Messiah by faith. We have already seen the reception they are given by most of God's chosen people, so that folk are delighted when the two are killed and their bodies like those of stray dogs are publicly exposed to contempt. From any point of view, God has gone well beyond the bounds of patience and long-suffering in the face of such provocation. But that grace is not yet exhausted. The inevitable expression of the fearsome wrath of a holy God is conditioned by his desire to save mankind.

At this stage, Jesus causes three proclamations to be made to the entire world. Hundreds of millions of people—people of every religious persuasion and none, people of every nation and subgroup, people of every language and dialect—will hear for themselves. It is interesting to consider that of all the people who have ever been born, more than 50 percent will be living at this time. Everyone who is alive on earth at this last time hears in his or her own language *a command from God*, broadcast by supernatural means. The question is often asked, what will happen to those who have never heard the gospel? Here, that question is answered by the first angel flying in midheaven.

> "*Fear God and give him the glory, for the hour of his judgment has come; and worship him who made heaven and earth, the sea and the fountains of water*" (Revelation 14:7).

The angel commands all people to bow the knee to the Creator. This is called the *"eternal gospel"* because it has always been the obligation of men and women to recognise God in creation and so to worship him. There can never be an acceptable excuse for not doing so, and judgement is certain for those who disobey the proclamation.

Immediately following this, John sees another angel flying in midheaven, making a brief proclamation. This is explained in detail at a later point in *Revelation*, but the announcement here serves to fix the timing of the events taking place.

> "*Fallen, fallen is Babylon the great, she who made all the nations drink the wine of her impure passion*" (Revelation 14:8).

The second message signals the imminent end of Satan's major strategy. Babylon, the city that is synonymous with man's rebellion against God, is to be wiped out.

The third angel's announcement is a strongly worded warning that speaks not only to the population then living but also to all of us who live in the last days. We must be in no doubt as to the issues that are involved in taking on the mark of the Beast. If we are not properly informed before such a demand comes, it is unlikely that we will have the stomach to refuse it. However, when we are faced with such a choice, this prophetic announcement makes the consequences of capitulation quite clear.

> "*If anyone worships the beast and its image, and receives a mark on his forehead or on his hand, he shall drink the wine of God's wrath, poured unmixed into the cup of his anger, and he shall be tormented with fire and sulphur in the presence of the holy angels and in the presence of the Lamb. And the smoke of their torment goes up for ever and ever; and they have no rest, day or night, these worshippers of the beast and its image, and whoever receives the mark of its name*" (Revelation 14:9–11).

At this point in the unfolding panorama of God's plan, those many millions left on earth who hear the preaching of the "eternal gospel" and the warnings of the two angels fall into two groups. The first vast group is made up of the Gentile nations of the world, and the second is that unbelieving remnant people of Israel to whom the "two witnesses" in Jerusalem preached unsuccessfully. Even at this late stage, it seems that God is unwilling to finally close the door upon mankind, and so both groups are given a final opportunity to respond to his mercy. Although we are not given any indication of it, it is likely that as a result of the angels' intervention, many will respond and be "saved," but this is not the salvation of the new covenant that we know, for that chapter is closed at this time. In our study, we have seen that countless numbers of people have lived on earth without hearing God's Word or the new covenant gospel. Nevertheless, they are without excuse for unbelief because all are able, and have the responsibility to seek God on the basis of the evidence that he has provided in creation itself. Now such people cannot be born again, but they can be justified by living in faith-obedience to the lesser gospel that they have access to (see Romans 2:13–16).

Here, John tells us, it is a call "for the endurance of the saints, those who keep the commands of God and the faith of Jesus" (Revelation 14:12). The same preaching of the angels from heaven that arouses fury and hatred in determined unbelievers will enable many to believe. They must do so in the context of a desperately hostile, "antichrist" society around them. Once again, "believers" are tested; they must endure tribulation and even die for their faith.

Those believers who live through this terrible time until Jesus comes in glory will be vindicated at the great tribunals that he will conduct to try all mankind (see Matthew 25:31–46). They are the "sheep," whose actions during the time of their tribulation demonstrate their faith. They are accounted as "*righteous*" and, being placed at the Lord's right hand, will continue to live on under the new regime.

The unbelievers too will be judged by their actions at the same tribunals. Their lack of response to the "eternal gospel" that they have heard from such an authoritative source constitutes culpable rebellion against God's direct command. This will have been amply demonstrated by their active hostility to their believing neighbours during the last days, and they reap the reward of the "goats." They have chosen "*eternal punishment*" rather than obedience to God.

> "*Blessed are the dead who die in the Lord henceforth.*" '*Blessed indeed*,' says the Spirit, '*that they may rest from their labours, for their deeds follow them!*'" (Revelation 14:13).

The use of the word "henceforth" might speak directly of that time, which we have been discussing above, but equally it may take us back to the beginning of the *Revelation*. Jesus knew the challenges and difficulties that would confront his people through the years. He knew that men and women would be despised, tortured, and often killed for their faith. The conquering of Satan is through faith, even unto death, in every age. John gives further assurance that experiencing suffering and disaster is not a mark of God's disapproval but is our preparation for glory and a test of our faith. These who persevere in the Lord even to death are indeed blessed.

All this instruction from heaven is the prelude to the last great act of mercy—the harvest of the last believers.

SUMMARY

❖ The conspiracy of the nations against God in the last days will be led by Satan's man, the Antichrist.

❖ The world will cede total political and military power to him.

❖ He will have spiritual power from his demonic mentor, Satan, such that he will do amazing signs and wonders.

❖ He will persecute the conquerors until they are taken away before the opening of Seal 6.

❖ The False Prophet appears and proclaims the Antichrist to be God.

❖ He persecutes the remaining believers and introduces the 666 mark.

❖ Worship of the Beast becomes mandatory.

❖ Then the Great Tribulation begins.

❖ Those left behind "wash their robes."

❖ The 144,000 Israelites are now seen in heaven.

❖ A phenomenal warning is broadcast from heaven directly to those who face these desperate times.

❖ The two prophets appear in Jerusalem.

❖ The eternal gospel is preached by angels.

❖ Many are "saved" and die for their faith.

THE HARVEST TIME
REVELATION 14:14-20

Act IV, Scene 1—THE HARVEST TIME

Place: The Clouds

Time: Seal 7, Trumpet 7

People: All

John was not given the *Revelation* with chapter breaks and verse numbers as we find in our Bibles. As far as we know he wrote it down verbatim, from beginning to end, allowing the changes of scene to provide its only punctuation. The necessity of breaking his written account into chapters and verses so that it can be studied in detail can lead to inappropriate breaks in the narrative. Revelation 14:14 is one such example. There is an important change of scene signalled here by the text, but it is easily lost because of the lack of a chapter break.

John sees a wonderful sight:

> *"Lo, a white cloud, and seated on the cloud one like a son of man, with a golden crown on his head, and a sharp sickle in his hand"* (Revelation 14:14).

This moment opens a new act in our unfolding drama. John sees Jesus in glory, seated on the clouds. This vision speaks to the promise in Revelation 1:7 that Jesus will come in the clouds and every eye will see him come. It also gives the long-awaited answer to the rather plaintive question of the souls under the altar: *"Lord . . . how long?"* (Revelation 6:10). We know that Jesus will come first in the clouds on the day of the rapture, but his actual return to the earth will not take place until the wrath of God is ended. In the time line of the *Revelation*, the great moment of the rapture has taken place some seven years previously. This scene is taking place toward the end of the seventh-seal phase, immediately before the pouring out of the seven bowls of God's wrath.

From the second heaven, Jesus has been orchestrating the gathering in of his people. In this vision, John sees Jesus equipped for the final reaping, the harvest to which he referred in Matthew 13 (vv. 30, 41–42, 49–50), which must take place at the close of the age. The prophet Joel had used exactly this terminology many years before (see Joel 3:13). In his prophecy, this harvest was the prelude to the gathering together of the nations for judgement for the treatment they had accorded the Jews during their long banishment from the land. The picture of the wheat being reaped is symbolic of the ingathering of those faithful souls who are God's by virtue of their refusal to accept the mark of the Beast, and their endeavour to keep God's law.

Only when this harvest is completed can the second harvest—a grape harvest—begin. This is quite different in nature. The language used identifies these events as the fulfillment of the prophecies of Isaiah 34 and 63:1–6. In this harvest, the gathering in is followed immediately by the pressing of the grapes to extract their juice, and it takes place on earth. This symbolises God's judgement and vengeance on a recalcitrant population. It is a graphic description of terrible bloodshed, and its location, specified as being outside "the city," is given to us in Revelation 14:20 (again Jerusalem is not mentioned by name). It is evident that this is God's judgement of the Gentile nations as they join together to attack Jerusalem. Further details will be forthcoming.

It is a remarkable feature of the *Revelation* that John does not convey any sense of personal weariness or strain as a result of all he has seen. The awesome events he witnesses would be incredible if they were not so specifically designed as the conclusion of God's Word. Nowhere else in the Bible do we find such panoramic views of history past linked directly to the upheavals and traumas that will certainly soon come upon the world. We who read John's writings and seek insight into their significance need a perseverance in our studies that can come only from the Holy Spirit, for we are called to be witnesses to the truth, and the end is surely nearer now than ever before.

SEVEN BOWLS OF WRATH
REVELATION 15

Act IV, Scene 2—SEVEN BOWLS OF WRATH   **Time: The End of Seal 7**

Place: Heaven

People: Multitude before the Throne

At this point, John sees another *"portent in heaven, great and wonderful"*: seven angels carrying seven plagues that will bring the wrath of God to a conclusion. Before the angels begin their work, however, John is shown what has happened to those who heard and responded to the preaching of the two witnesses in Jerusalem. They have died for their newfound faith rather than submit to the Antichrist's rule, and now they have their reward.

> *"And I saw what appeared to be a sea of glass mingled with fire, and* **those who had conquered the beast and its image and the number of its name,** *standing beside the sea of glass with harps of God in their hands, and they sing the song of Moses the servant of God, and the song of the Lamb"* (Revelation 15:2–3).

This multitude are standing beside the sea of glass (i.e., *"before the throne"*), as were the saints from the time of the Great Tribulation and the 144,000 Israelites (cf. 4:6, 7:9,11, 14:3), and they *"sing the song of Moses, the servant of God, and the song of the Lamb."* This is the fourth group of believers we have identified in heaven, each one distinguished by a different activity in God's throne room. The harvest is safely gathered in.

Then, in Revelation 15:5, the temple in heaven is opened once more to John for him to witness a remarkable scene that relates directly back to his account in 11:19. At this point, the seventh trumpet of the seventh seal has been sounded; it is a prelude to the third and final "woe." Between 15:5 and 16:1 the narrative stops to allow further insight to be given so that we do not see the terrible events that are taking place on earth in isolation from their cause. God wants us to understand that the prophecies contained in his Word, even dating back to the Garden of Eden, are being fulfilled at last. Thus, there is no room for doubt concerning the source of the events that are to follow. The bowls containing the plagues are actually handed out by one of the four living creatures at God's throne (15:7). The long-promised, righteous wrath of God will be poured out. Seven angels have the task of initiating this last phase and will bring it to a dramatic conclusion in a series of escalating terrors.

THE SEVEN BOWLS POURED OUT
REVELATION 16

Act IV, Scene 3—THE SEVEN BOWLS POURED OUT　　　　　**Time: The End**

Place: On Earth　　　　　**People: All Mankind**

The events that began with the opening of Seal 7 were initiated by angels blowing seven trumpets; and as they did so, demonic powers were released on the earth to do their work. Now things are quite different. The seventh trumpet of the seventh seal has brought us at last to the end of God's patience. He has done everything in his power to redeem men and women, to tell them, to call them; now he will deal with those who have rejected him. Now there is no more mercy. Mercy went before but was rejected. These people have made their choice. Everyone who heard the proclamation of the eternal gospel by the angelic messengers and refused to obey it will have to live through the visitation of God's wrath on earth—wrath brought by his angels directly from his temple in heaven.

It is important to see that the nature of God's wrath is quite different from that of man. This is no blind fury. It is not a lashing out in uncontrollable anger. It is neither mindless, nor without purpose. God is still working out his purposes through the visitation of his wrath upon the earth. In fact, this expression of his wrath gives us understanding of him and the balance between his holiness and his grace; otherwise, why would he not simply wipe out the remainder of mankind at this time? By this stage of the *Revelation*, it is surely clear to us that God will never compromise with iniquity. Man may continue to insist on his right to rebel against God in the face of his mercy right to the end, but it is his choice, and he must accept his responsibility for it and ultimately face God's wrath and judgement without further opportunity for redemption. God recognises the source of that rebellion. He will always respond to it and prevent it from corrupting his heaven.

Each of these plagues produces extreme unpleasantness. It is as if every aspect of ordinary life that we have taken for granted for generations begins to fall apart. Life on earth has been sustained for all people, whether good or evil, by the Word of God. Of course, the godless have never recognised their total dependence upon the Creator and his Word. They have decided, against the evidence, that the creation is an accident in time. They like to suppose that over millions of years, we have evolved to where we are today. We are even in control of our environment. Now, with the advent of these plagues, they begin to see what happens when God removes his favour and how futile are their pretensions to manage their environment.

The plagues do not produce death as the earlier judgements of the first six trumpets did. Those were operating at a time when the *"eternal gospel"* of God was still available to mankind. Now the judgements are calculated to reveal the corrupt character of those who are left on earth and the state of their hearts. The response is consistent. Rather than repent, people curse God. They curse him openly in defiance and hatred. Their response is their own condemnation. What further evidence of the effects of the willful rebellion of unredeemed mankind against God is required? The visitation of God's wrath is vindicated by the response of mankind.

It is a part of God's purpose in all of this that his own people—we who are living today—see and comprehend this truly terrible result of Adam's sin when it has come to full maturity. God has done everything possible to bring people to submit to him, but unless they come to him of their own volition, he can do nothing more for them. For generation after generation, he has demonstrated his own preparedness to accept continued rejection and hostility and still to offer one further chance; but there has to be an end.

In Revelation 16:12, John tells us quite explicitly that the River Euphrates is dried up as a result of the sixth bowl being poured out. This opens up the way for the army of the East to come through to Israel. Whether this army is comprised of the non-Arab Muslim nations that lie to the East of Israel or the hordes of the vast nations of the Far East we cannot be sure, but it will inevitably be a part of that great Antichrist conspiracy that focuses the hatred in human hearts on Israel. Indeed, for all generations past, the desire to destroy Israel, the people of God, and Jerusalem—the city of God—has been in men's hearts.

Then, at the pouring out of the sixth bowl, John sees the extraordinary phenomenon of the demonic spirits going forth from the mouths of the dragon, the Beast, and the False Prophet. These spirits, we are told, perform signs, thereby convincing the world's rulers of their authority and power so that they are all deceived into assembling their armies together at Armageddon.

Whom do they think they are going to fight? Do they think this is some invader from outer space? Is this perhaps some final call to eliminate Israel as the source of all the troubles of the world so that man-made peace and order can be restored? Whatever these leaders think they are doing, the awful truth is that they are combining their resources to fight against King Jesus, God himself.

John calls this the *"great day of God the Almighty"* (v. 14) and couples it with another warning to us, his people who read of these things, that we should not be caught unprepared, because he will come without further warning to mankind in general, *"like a thief,"* stealthily, and when the world is at its most unsuspecting.

The account of the actual battle occurs a little further on in the Revelation, but it seems that as the armies gather together, Jesus unleashes the last of the seven plagues to bring about the final devastation of Babylon, the city of man. This is a time when the very earth will seem to be about to disintegrate. Earthquakes have always been terrifying occurrences, but now comes the climactic shaking of the earth (v. 18), which will simply terrify everyone. This will be worldwide, and the most obvious result will be the total devastation of all towns and cities. Just as Jesus had said of the temple, *"There will not be left here one stone upon another"* (Matthew 24:2), so it will be of the cities of all the nations. The countless temples of mammon will all be laid low. Once the destruction has occurred, the ruins will be "bombed" by gigantic hailstones from the skies.

The dislocation of the Antichrist's empire will be complete. All communications will be disrupted. Power stations and the complex infrastructures of our society will all be desolated in a few moments of time. Satan and his minions will be powerless to resist it or to cope with it. The normal patterns of social life will be ended. As a consequence of all these things happening, John tells us once more, people will respond by *cursing God!*

THE WHORE REVEALED
REVELATION 17:1-6

Act IV, Scene 4—THE WHORE REVEALED

Place: On Earth

Time: General

People: All

Having witnessed the terrible events recounted in chapter 16, John is taken by one of the angels and whisked away into a wilderness. There, John is to learn about the judgement of this great city Babylon, which has been destroyed along with all the cities of the world. *This is revelation* we desperately need to heed before the day of the Lord is here.

In two of the most significant visions in *Revelation*, God combines the images of an uncouth, hideous beast and a beautiful woman. However, these *two women of Revelation* could not be more different. One is God's creature, a faithful "wife" carrying a child in innocence, the servant of God (chapter 12); the other is Satan's creature, a "whore," sexually provocative and totally complicit with the dragon she rides (chapter 17). To make his points, God uses human symbols that we all understand. We have seen already that the first woman symbolises the strategy of God in the world, and we shall now see how the second woman is used to reveal the opposing strategy of Satan.

First, we need to "see" what John saw. God intends this to be a gross and offensive picture because that is how he views what it portrays. John is shown a voluptuous woman riding on a monstrous beast; they are together. The creature is carrying her, and we are told that he is *"full of blasphemous names"* (Revelation 17:3), so identifying him with the Beast out of the sea in chapter 13. He is a similar (but not the same) son of Satan, spawned by the one who is the source of all lies and blasphemy. Despite the similarities of the description, this beast does not depict the Antichrist (the man of iniquity), but a remarkable contemporary of his, as we shall discover. The woman symbolises that seductive spirit of iniquity by which Satan has ruled over human hearts. She is designed to facilitate her father's purposes of blinding mankind to the spiritual realities of creation. By focusing on the sensual, the material, and the physical, she is able to seduce them from their duty to God, and so reign over them by appealing to their uncontrollable lusts.

"Babylon the Great, the mother of harlots and of earth's abominations" (17:5) is a startling name that aptly describes this woman. Responsibility is laid at her feet for much of what we generally attribute to Satan, so it is clear from both the picture and her name that she is his creature. She is the evil counterfeit of the woman of chapter 12. *She is Satan's alternative creation on earth.* She is the means by which he deceives mankind.

The imagery of sexual seduction is familiar to us all. In this case, it speaks of spiritual seduction, that is, idolatry, which is the worship of anything or anyone other than the God of creation. In the first vision of a woman, we saw a picture of the mother of all those who are faithful to God through the trials and challenges of life; in this one, we see a picture of all those who are seduced by the false promises of our godless society.

Who or what is this mysterious Babylon? The Greek name "Babylon" is derived from the Hebrew word, "Babel." It is the well-known successor to the original Babel that is featured in Genesis. It has not existed as a physical reality for thousands of years, although we have seen in our day some attempt to restore it as a tourist attraction in Iraq.

At the end of chapter 16, John sees the seventh angel pour out his bowl of wrath on the great city of Babylon, as if it is a real city. Verse 19 tells us that when he did this, *"the cities of the nations fell,"* and so we are to understand that Babylon is used prophetically as a type of all the world's cities. All the cities of the world share the same character and spirit as their mother Babylon, and God will destroy them all at the same time. Our challenge is to unravel the mystery of Babylon's identity so that we can gain insight into what God is showing us through this vision.

In the same way that Jerusalem has always been identified as the city of God, the Bible always identifies Babylon as the city of Satan, even when he used its power for his own purposes. In Isaiah 14:1–23, the fallen Lucifer is identified with the king of Babylon as the epitome of iniquity in that time. They are both marked by overweening pride and arrogance, and their punishment is the same. Isaiah was well aware of what this would lead to.

> *"May the descendants of evildoers nevermore be named! Prepare slaughter for his sons because of the guilt [iniquity] of their fathers, lest they rise and possess the earth, and fill the face of the world with cities"* (Isaiah 14:20–21).

We begin to see that Babylon is not judged simply because of her geographical position but for the way of life she represents. Today, more than ever in history, we live in a "city-age." Everything in life is geared to it. The peoples flock to the cities for work. It is the cities of the world that dominate society. Nations are proud of their wealth and display their magnificent city buildings as a testimony to the gods they serve. They stand as a public demonstration of the power and wealth of both the city and the country.

In this extraordinary vision, that which is respectable, admired, and acceptable in men's eyes is revealed as being anathema to God. *And we are to understand that all the world's leaders have fallen for the woman's suggestive charms!* Under their leadership, the cities are identified as having a single goal, and that is to gain as much wealth as possible by trade (we call it the GNP). This prophetic vision reveals that the underlying motivation of trade is *the lust of the soul* (18:14). No matter how we dress up society in respectable clothes of democracy or justice or social equality, we are quite unable to escape the inherent nature of fallen man. All are driven by the self-serving lusts of the flesh, and there is not one redeeming feature of our society that is acceptable to God.

Our justice is exposed by the gratuitous cruelty that denies help to countless refugees and basic accommodations to homeless families. Our supposed altruism is exposed by the numerous people who are starving while the wealthy live in fatness. Our gentleness is refuted by the ruthless repression of the militarily weak, and our mercy does not blink at the countless millions of unborn babies murdered before and even after birth. It is all unclean in God's eyes. It is the system of Satan. It found its first organised form under the leadership of Nimrod, and it has flourished ever since. People may do their best to bring change, but the *Revelation* shows us that the problem is unsolvable and our society is doomed. The Creator God requires righteousness, and that comes only by the *"obedience of faith"* (see Romans 1:3–6, 16–17).

Just as Nimrod's Babel needed to have one language in order to hold itself together, so Satan has needed the wonders of modern communications to bring his empire into being once again. For the first time since Nimrod's rule, by our technical competence we are able to overcome the confusion of language that God then brought upon the earth to frustrate the conspiracy of men against himself; now the new conspiracy can take place.

John introduces the woman as being dressed in purple and scarlet (Revelation 17:4). These have traditionally been the colours of royalty, and in this case they convey that this woman is of royal status, a device calculated to add to the image of desirability and respectability that she portrays. The woman is dressed, as we say, *"to kill."* The description of her appearance, with all her magnificent jewellery and holding a golden cup, is sexually explicit for good reason. She is called a *"great harlot,"* that is, a woman who deliberately seeks to attract men for sex, for payment. Those who do business with her become part of the satanic process by surrendering themselves to her—mind, body, and soul—as they seek to gain unlawful satisfaction from her. But they pay a terrible price.

There are two groups of people who are identified as the harlot's clients. The first group is *"the kings of the earth."* They have committed *"fornication"* with her (v. 2). All the leaders of our nations are here identified as having entered into an illicit liaison with this exotic, seductive creature. They have succumbed to her charms and have become one flesh with her. They have been willing to pay the price. They have sold their souls for what they think they can get. They trust her rewards rather than the provision of God.

The nature of this intercourse becomes clear to us in chapter 18. The leaders of the earth have made the pursuit of wealth the be-all and end-all of their aims. National strategies are fashioned by economic circumstances. Financiers and bankers are the gurus of the marketplace, in which profit takes precedence over people. It is in the last days that Babylon reaches its apotheosis. Naked materialism will be the order of the day. People may pay lip service to other causes, but the great harlot has them in total bondage.

God wanted a society of love, holy love. But he reveals that the underlying nature of our society is lust, the "Me first!" and the "Me most!" attitude. Every political philosophy is tainted with it. In fact, each competes on the basis of outdoing its opponents in its economic achievements. Meanwhile, *the poor are always with us* (Deuteronomy 15:11). Are our leaders alone to blame for this? It has been said somewhere that we get the leaders we deserve, and it is true because we appoint them to serve our lusts.

The second group that does business with this whore is trapped by her in a different manner. She is represented as holding a golden cup in her hand. This she offers to men to drink as a special favour. With a smile of assurance, and a wriggle of suggestion, she proffers the cup as a drink that will bring them stimulation and excitement. This is a drink that all unbelievers, and, sadly, many believers, imbibe each day if they can get it. Today, it seems, men do not so much need to be seduced as restrained. They line up for her drink; they clamour to be given it. Wealth, achievement, and personal indulgence in our society are considered to be justified by themselves; they constitute their own morality for us.

"Are you able to drink the cup that I drink?" Jesus asked James and John (Mark 10:38), indicating the path of self-denial and suffering the world would impose on those who would be his followers. Satan is always ready to offer an easier way, and here it is: drink from the harlot's cup. Why not? Everyone else is doing it. It conjures up a picture for us of gross sensuality and immorality, and that is what it is. The contents of the golden cup are revealed as being so obscene that we hardly dare describe it.

Who will look into the cup before they drink and consider its contents? Are we not dazzled by the appearance and subtle suggestions of the woman who offers it? We have become cognizant only of her promise of mysterious delights. *"Just look into my eyes. Just listen to my voice. Have no regard for God's Word; that is old-fashioned, out of date. Have fun now, while you can. This is free!"* And so we drink. And we are hooked.

122

That foul concoction is like a drug. We can never be satisfied with enough. Like all addicts before us, we will drive ourselves to exhaustion, we will sacrifice our loved ones, we will defy God, and we will never, ever be satisfied. Money, power, possessions, drink, drugs, success, anger, resentment, bitterness, public acclaim, personal isolation, hopelessness, despair—they are all there. The great harlot never delivers on her promises. How can she? All she wants is your soul. Once she has that, she needs nothing more from you.

Oh, foolish man! Have you never heard the words of Jesus?

> *"Come unto me all who labour and are heavy laden, and I will give you rest"*
> (Matthew 11:28).

Jesus alone can meet our needs. He alone can deliver us from the icy grip of iniquity in our hearts and so free us from our addiction to the cup of the woman. Do you not know that we have all drunk of that cup? Do you know now that it is a cup brimming with the juices of her sexual activity, the excretions of spiritually fornicating bodies? It is so presented to our view in the *Revelation* that we might see what an accursed and abominable concoction it is and recoil from it. It is the outworking of this filthy liquor in our lives that prevents so many of us from becoming conquerors who are to inherit God's promises. Many have turned to Jesus, but they have not understood the "cold turkey" process of getting rid of their inherited iniquity. The materialism and prosperity offered by the world and demanded by our flesh must die, and we need Jesus' help to do it. It is called sanctification.

Teachings abound today in our churches that we can have both Jesus and the cup of the harlot. We cannot.

> *"You cannot serve God and Mammon"* (Matthew 6:24).

Jesus said it, and it is clear. No one could do it when he said it, and no one can do it today. Brother and sister, you who read these words, whom do you serve: God or mammon? You cannot serve both. Do we really believe the first verses of James 5?

THE MYSTERY OF THE NAME REVEALED
REVELATION 17:7-18

Act IV, Scene 5—THE MYSTERY OF THE NAME REVEALED   **Time: General**

Place: Jerusalem   **People: Jerusalem**

John marvelled at the sight of the woman sitting on the beast (17:6). The beauty and the beast is the stuff of fairy tales for children, but these characters are all too real. The angel undertakes to explain the picture to John and tells us a complex riddle by which we are to solve the mystery of the woman's identity under the guidance of the Holy Spirit. Like those other mysteries that God has hidden carefully from the eyes of the merely curious or the unbelieving, the solving of this riddle is of great importance to his people.

Just as with the beasts we encountered in chapter 13, every feature of this picture is of significance to us. We have two characters here interacting with each other. We have understood the woman's character and purpose in the last scene; now we are to give her a particular identity. But first the angel draws John's attention to the beast. *"The beast that you saw was, and is not, and is to ascend from the bottomless pit and go to perdition"* (17:8). This is clearly a different beast from the beast in chapter 13 that rose out of the sea: the Antichrist. This one comes up from the pit. Thus, he will have had a previous existence, and from that we can identify him.

Although a replica of the red-coloured beast described in chapter 13, this beast is a different colour. It is *scarlet*, and it does not have the ten diadems on his horns. The disguise this second son of Satan uses to camouflage himself, rather like a chameleon, is to have a colour indicating his royal status: he is a pretend king; we are to look for an individual national leader. We have previously had a clue as to the identity of this beast in Revelation 11:7. There we briefly considered a description where *"the beast that ascends from the bottomless pit"* made war on the two witnesses in the Holy City.

This new beast is further identified, as was the Antichrist figure previously, by its seven heads; but the interpretation of those heads differs from that of the earlier beast. The meaning of this mystery is not easily discerned. John is told quite specifically that the seven heads are seven mountains. It is often pointed out that Rome is built upon seven hills, and for this reason alone it is tempting to make an identification of Babylon with the city of Rome, as many have done; but there is more to it than that. Other cities have been built upon multiple hills, including Jerusalem, so by this clue alone we cannot identify the city.

Let us consider Jerusalem: the unnamed Holy City of Revelation 11. When Jerusalem came under Israeli rule in 1967, one of the first acts of the government was to extend the existing boundaries of the city so that it covered an area of approximately fifty square miles and included many hills. On this basis we should consider Jerusalem as a candidate to be the city that God identifies as Babylon. On its own this clue is insufficient. The accurate interpretation of this mystery demands that the separate parts of the riddle point to the same conclusion.

We are given a further key clue. Each of these heads also represents a king. In verses 10 and 11, we are told that this beast is the last in a dynasty of eight kings: *"he was and is not and is to come"* (v. 8). Since *Revelation* was written at approximately AD 90–100, this would mean that at that time five of the kings in the dynastic line were dead, one was existing, and there was a seventh who would then appear briefly. After this (i.e., at the time of the end), an eighth king, or leader, *of the same line* would come. Although this is a seemingly complex statement, its very complexity greatly reduces the possibilities for misinterpretation. The fulfillment of the terms of the prophecy set out here requires these individuals to have been rulers in a city built on seven hills (where in prophetic language the number seven may indicate many hills).

As before, we must look into Scripture for further insight. Throughout the gospel accounts and in Acts, there is one ruling family that figures more prominently than any other: the Herod family, who were surrogate rulers of Israel for the Romans. The dynasty of the Herod family is quite remarkable for its obscure origins and its rapid climb to power in Israel under Roman patronage and for the role it played through the first seventy years of the first century. Their dubious lineage was one of the reasons why Herod the Great (whose father was an Edomite and thus descended from Esau) was so little trusted by his own people and especially by the priestly classes. He was not strictly a Jew, so he was not legally entitled to be king of Israel.

History reveals that the Herods were a consistently dysfunctional and sexually promiscuous family, always feuding, constantly immoral, and demonically led. The various members of the family play important bit parts throughout the gospels and Acts and are invariably unreliable, dishonest, and villainous.

In the diagram that follows, there are five Herods starred and shown by name in the family tree, plus Herod Agrippa II, who was alive in Rome at the time of John's writing. Whether or not there was another of the same line who lasted for a short time after him we cannot say with certainty. If this interpretation is correct, however, then the Herod dynasty fits the angel's words precisely, and we can expect to see a leader arise in Israel in the last days who will be one of the Herod family. Just as the Herod family then was dependent upon their Roman patrons, so this beast, the ruler of Israel, will be dependent upon the patronage of the Antichrist.

There can be no other families in history that have come so close to the proclamation of the greatest message the world has ever heard. One after another the Herods either met with or knew of Jesus and his followers. One after another they killed or tried to kill those connected to him. How anyone could be so close and yet so far away is hard to understand. Ironically, the Herods, who were descended from Esau, or Edom (Genesis 36:1), were fulfilling the long-standing prophecies concerning them (see Genesis 3:15, 25:23). They have been tools of Satan in the great battle of the ages, and we are to understand from the *Revelation* that once the Times of the Gentiles are over, they will once more rule in Jerusalem.

The most powerful political family Israel had known for many years had the opportunity to meet and serve the King of the universe. Instead, they lived only for themselves and never knew that the Messiah had come to Israel. The pattern is due to repeat itself in the last member of the infamous family, who will be raised from the pit for this purpose. Even now, a strong, charismatic leader is needed in Israel; where is he to be found?

[Ariel Sharon was born Ariel Scheinermann, on 26 February 1928 in Israel, to Lithuanian Jewish parents from Belarus. An Israeli statesman and retired general, he served as Israel's eleventh prime minister. He is currently in a permanent vegetative state after suffering a stroke on 4 January 2006. *The Jerusalem Post* (02.01.11) carried an article by a former Kadima minister that included the following paragraph:

"It is not yet time to share all the details of these and many more personal moments and national events that I was privileged to experience with him. In the meantime, all I can do is pray for a medical miracle that will improve his condition—and, mainly, miss him, like very many Israelis who, for the fifth year now, feel the enormous leadership void he left behind."

Is it time for that miracle to take place? Will the Antichrist provide the answer to that prayer?]

THE GENERATIONS OF THE HEROD DYNASTY

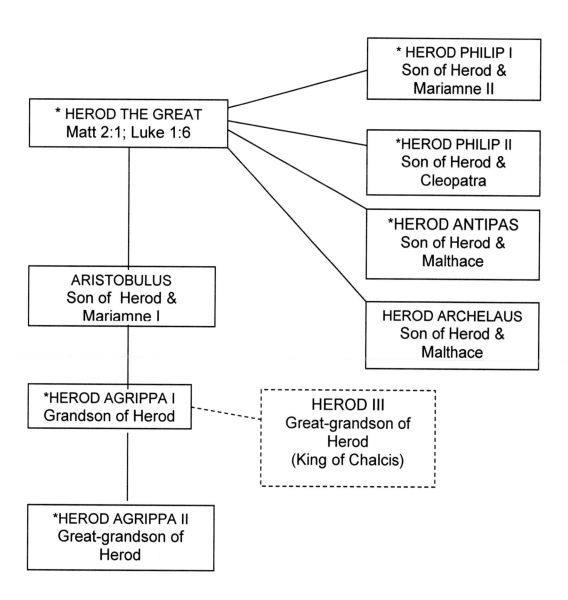

- Herod the Great (c. 74–4 BC), king of Judea, reconstructed the Second Temple in Jerusalem; the Gospel of Matthew says he ordered the massacre of the innocents (2:16–18).
- Herod Archelaus (23 BC-c. AD 18) was ethnarch of Samaria, Judea, and Idumea.
- Herod Antipas (20 BC-c. AD 40), tetrarch of Galilee and Peraea, is described in the New Testament as ordering John the Baptist's death and as mocking Jesus.
- Herod Agrippa I (c. 10 BC–AD 44), king of Judea, is called "Herod" in the Acts of the Apostles.

- Herod Philip I, was the father of Salome.
- Herod Philip II (4 BC–AD 34) was tetrarch of Ituraea and Trachonitis.
- Herod of Chalcis, also known as Herod III, was king of Chalcis (AD 41–48).
- Herod Agrippa II (AD 27–100), tetrarch of Chalcis, is called "King Agrippa" in Acts of the Apostles; it was before him that Paul of Tarsus defended himself (Acts 25–26).

The solving of this prophetic riddle leads to a staggering discovery:

Present-day Jerusalem, the City of God, the once Holy City, is a masquerade.

The city that was pictured in the Old Testament as the beloved wife of God has become in these last days, "Babylon the great, mother of harlots." She is the "mother" of all the world's great harlot-cities.

Is it any wonder that we find no mention of Jerusalem by name in the whole of the *Revelation*? In the forty plus years since Jerusalem was restored to her, Israel has had the opportunity to receive her Saviour Jesus. The gospel has been preached and witnessed to her, and many have been saved; but as a nation-state she and her capital have preferred to be the harlot. Today, Jerusalem is a secular society and an international centre of Freemasonry. Her aims and objectives are the same as every other city and nation in the world. The prophetic record is before us. Far from changing in the future as many hope, she will reject the witness of both the 144,000 Israeli believers, and the two prophets (Moses and Elijah) whom Jesus will send to her. In Revelation 11, Jerusalem is called the Holy City at the commencement, but she is called Sodom and Egypt at the conclusion. Did not Jesus himself lament?

> *"O Jerusalem, Jerusalem, killing the prophets and stoning those who are sent to you!*
> *How often I would have gathered your children together as a hen gathers her brood*
> *under her wings, and you would not! Behold your house is forsaken. And I tell you,*
> *you will not see me until you say, 'Blessed is he who comes in the name of the Lord!'"*
> (Luke 13:34–35).

The mystery of chapter 11, which we were not able to understand fully at the first reading, is now available to us. The dastardly murder of the two witnesses of Jesus is perpetrated by *the beast that ascends from the bottomless pit*. In the last days, there will again be a Herod-type ruling in Jerusalem. He will be Satan's man, a third beast, colluding with the Antichrist and the False Prophet.

What, then, of the understanding of the ten horns (17:12)? Who are the kings that these represent? It seems likely that this fragile alliance for "one hour" only is constructed between the beast-leader of Israel and the Arab nations around him. For this one hour, there will be agreement and peace between Israel and her neighbours after all the years of conflict. They find common cause at last. Their pact is put together for the purpose of resisting the coming of King Jesus, the Lamb (v. 14).

By this means, the final worldwide conspiracy will be complete. The Gentile nations, Israel itself, and the Arabs will be at one for a moment. The Antichrist, together with his very own false prophet, will hold himself out to be God. He will seat himself in the temple building in Jerusalem, with the endorsement of the Herod-ruler of Israel and the Arab nations round about, to be worshipped by all mankind.

His final vain heresy will remove any remaining doubts. Like so many dictators before him, he is revealed as a mad megalomaniac. But, his master has overreached himself. The end is at hand. In the final explosion of anger, hatred, and desire for vengeance, we see this beast (v. 16) now turn upon his own city, along with his Arab allies, to put her to the torch.

COME OUT OF HER
REVELATION 18

Act IV, Scene 6—COME OUT OF HER   **Time: Now**

Place: The World at Large   **People: God's People**

Now comes another pause in the story. The important lesson of Babylon is not yet completed. The discovery of her identity and her role in Satan's strategy is not only about future events. She touches all our lives. God wants us to understand the profound significance she has for each one of us.

The word "Babylon" is the Greek mode of spelling the Hebrew *Babel*. Names in Scripture have always had a far greater significance than we attach to names today. It is thought that when Nimrod founded his city in about 2230 BC, he called it *Babil*, meaning "gate of God." After the "confusion of tongues" instituted by God, some scholars think that its root meaning was connected to the Hebrew word *balal*, meaning "to confound."

By contrast Jerusalem, meaning "possession of peace," was built on four hills. (It covers many more hills now). It was captured by David soon after he was made king over all Israel. Ironically, despite its name, the city is probably the most fought over city in the world. Today it features in the news of world events to a degree far outstripping either its geographical or its economic significance. It features throughout Old Testament prophecy and, of course, in the New Testament it is the scene of the trial and death of Jesus.

Jerusalem was pictured in the Old Testament as the city of the living God, a place of his particular blessing, and an earthly picture of the heavenly city. It was to be an example to the nations. It was because of this important role that any wickedness or corruption associated with it was so profoundly objectionable to God.

We should not think that God's dealings with Jerusalem are simply a matter of governmental and moral order. As with all else to which we have been introduced in the *Revelation*, we are to know something of God's heart in all this. We are to comprehend his feelings. The harlotry of Jerusalem is not new in Scripture. To read Ezekiel's words in Ezekiel 16, and again in chapter 23, is to realise how God's own life is invested in his city. A city stands for the people in it, but it also stands for the people of the nation of which it is the capital city. We read in Ezekiel 16 a description of God's feelings about his people Israel, as addressed to Jerusalem.

> *"You grew exceedingly beautiful, and came to regal estate. And your renown went forth among the nations because of your beauty, for it was perfect through the splendour which I had bestowed upon you, says the Lord God. But you trusted in*

> *your beauty, and played the harlot because of your renown and lavished your harlotries on every passer-by"* (Ezekiel 16:13–15).

What a tragedy is revealed here. God's great love for this virgin bride was spurned for the sake of brazen harlotry. Can there be a more powerful picture of unfaithfulness than the gross sexual promiscuity of a pampered and adored virgin bride? It is this same spirit that is active in a restored Jerusalem today. The situation was tragic throughout Old Testament times, but now, after many generations of terrible punishment, what do we see? In 1967, Jerusalem once more became the capital of a sovereign Israel. The gospel has been preached for two thousand years. Has she learned the lessons of those years? Has she sought for God in repentance? In the modern, resurrected Jerusalem, we see the commercialism of her old ways in her commitment to capitalism. So much so, in his wondrous *Revelation*, Jesus can no longer call her by her real name but uses the name that speaks of confusion. The city of God has become the city of man.

As we look at her today, do we see a city of God's peace, order, and justice? Do we see a city devoted to the service of the Lord Jesus? Do we see a city that is a living example of what it means to walk in the way of the living God, enjoying his blessing and glory? God had always intended that Jerusalem would be different from the other cities of the world. Is she any different from them today? Sadly, it is the same; only, because of its apostasy, it is considered by God to be the ringleader and therefore especially culpable.

In chapter 18 of the *Revelation,* an angel with great authority and presence brings John to view this same city and its dramatic fall. This divine commentary speaks of all cities—London, New York, Tokyo, Moscow, Peking, Paris, Berlin, Mexico, Johannesburg, and Buenos Aires. Every city of every nation is included. They are all daughters of Babylon. There are no exceptions. For centuries we have viewed the backward people of the world as being plagued by demonic spirits, mainly because of their superstitions, ignorance, and fears. We like to think that by virtue of our own sophistication and scientific advancement, we can discount these things in our society. But the truth is, *every one of our cities is a dwelling place of demons, and our society is haunted and dominated by unclean fiends and foul spirits* (cf. Revelation 18:2).

This *revelation* from God shows us how we are snared and brought into bondage by spirits who easily take different guises to deceive us. Just as any alcoholic or drug addict is a desperate picture of what goes wrong when an individual is taken over by his lusts, so Jesus shows us that the nations, that is, all men and women, are in a similarly degraded state of addiction to materialism. The smartly dressed operator, the successful whiz kid, the city mogul, the sportsman, and the personality we so much admire are all vulnerable to these demons, operating legitimately at the level of man's unspoken lusts. Even respectable Christians in our prosperous, ordered churches are deceived. As we seek compromise with the world, its standards, morals, and lifestyles, we become vulnerable to our enemy. Is true Christianity ever respectable by the world's standards? Is my church a "lampstand-church" today? The question for us all is, "Do I believe this *revelation*?"

Can we believe this angel, whose glory is such that he makes the earth bright with his appearance? Can we accept the assessment from God concerning the leaders of the nations, that they are sold out, body and soul, to the harlot that they might have what she promises? It is a hard thing for us to do. The received wisdom of the day is that we are not far from God. Much teaching today suggests that the church is able to influence society so that it can improve to the point of becoming acceptable to God. This is a travesty of truth. It is the lie of the devil and does not accord with Scripture.

John hears a voice from heaven speaking.

> *"Come out of her, my people, lest you take part in her sins, lest you share in her plagues; for her sins are heaped as high as heaven and God has remembered her iniquities"* (Revelation 18:4–5).

Surely, that is clear enough. It is *"my people"* who are to come out of her. It is the lampstand-churches of Jesus that the angel is speaking to. This shows us that the visible church today is tarred with the same brush that Israel was tarred with all those years ago. Unless we receive the *revelation*, we do not understand what we are to come out of or how we are to do it. It is the same problem Jesus addressed in his messages to the seven churches at the beginning of the *Revelation*. Our structures, organisations, hierarchies, methods, aims, and objectives are corrupted by the world around us. We are ruled by our iniquitous culture and our feelings rather than by the *revelation* of God's truth.

Laziness, allied to comfortable complacency, denies us access to the living Word. Jesus calls each individual to be a conqueror on his own account, living by faith, which is daily, active obedience to his Word revealed by the Holy Spirit in us.

The truth has never changed. If you are to be a conqueror, you must *"come out"* of Babylon. This teaching is given here so that God's people will understand very clearly what they are dealing with. This is no academic exercise. It is God showing us exactly what he thinks about our society today and what its inevitable end is. There is no room for fudging the issue. We must receive it. We must discover what it means. And we must act on it. It is a call for immediate action in our lives.

It is inevitable that a society that believes it can be God to itself will reckon that it can go on forever. With mantras of fairness, human rights, tolerance, and equal opportunities, we dress up the nature of our lost society with well-meaning words. But it is all a sham, and the angel reveals the secret heart of the harlot.

> *"A queen I sit, I am no widow, mourning I shall never see"* (Revelation 18:7).

That is the proud attitude of our successful, godless city-cultures. But their judgement will come in a single day! With the arrogance of ignorance, she lulls her lovers into a continuation of their corrupted way of life, and her children are educated in her spirit.

Is our modern capitalist-democratic way of life really so offensive to God? The answer is found at the cross of Calvary, *"by which,"* Paul says, *"the world has been crucified to me and I to the world"* (Galatians 6:14). That which is not of God's Spirit is not acceptable to God. Jesus came to make it possible for people to put the flesh to death by the Spirit through the obedience of faith. There is no way in which the life of the flesh can be dressed up and presented as acceptable to God. Materialism and humanism are the plausible demons that dominate our godless rebellion.

This life of the flesh is revealed by the angel when he says:

> *"The fruit for which thy soul longed has gone from thee, and all thy dainties and thy splendour are lost to thee, never to be found again!"* (Revelation 18:14).

This fruit for which the soul longs is that which comes from the Tree of the Knowledge of Good and Evil. Adam and Eve, thinking that by it they could become God to themselves, gave up their relationship with their Creator in Eden. The tree and its fruit are available to us still, even today. John describes it in his first letter:

> *"Do not love the world or the things in the world. If anyone loves the world, love for the Father is not in him. For all that is in the world, the lust of the flesh, and the lust of the eyes and the pride of life, is not of the Father but is of the world. And the world passes away, and the lust of it; but he who does the will of God abides for ever"* (1 John 2:15–17).

The injunction *"Come out of her, my people!"* cannot be a physical removal of oneself from the city to the countryside because Babylon is within us—in our hearts, minds, and souls. This coming out is part of our sanctification; it is a deliberate separation from the accepted attitudes of society because we are looking for the city in heaven. We see it illustrated consistently in Scripture, beginning with Abraham.

> *"He went out, not knowing where he was to go . . . For he looked forward to the city which has foundations, and whose builder and maker is God"* (Hebrews 11:8, 10).

Jesus' call to his disciples to be conquerors can be accomplished only as we have insight into the world and society in which we live. With all its temptations and testings, it is the context within which our sanctification takes place. Satan and his princes may rule the world, but they certainly do not rule God's people. Satan and the world governed by him are but the proving ground of our growth toward spiritual maturity.

It was necessary for Israel to "come out" from Egypt in order to "come in" to the Promised Land. It was even necessary for them to "come out" of the wilderness before they could enter into their full inheritance in the Promised Land. But the people always resisted God's instructions. Their reluctance to leave behind what was familiar in order to seek something better but as yet unknown exactly mirrors the foot-dragging reluctance of the flesh to leave Babylon's delights.

These feelings afflict us all. We know well that this "coming out" will not bring any popular acclaim because it will be discerned as a rejection of those who stay behind. Yet Christians endure a great deal of discomfort and doubt because they have not understood the necessity of obeying the leading of the Holy Spirit. So it is that many who "stay in" seek a missing spirituality in their lives and follow all sorts of deceptive mystical paths in order to find it, when the only legitimate spirituality is in a new life of obedience lived outside of "Babylon."

Many of us Western Christians live in situations where our service is unwanted because everyone is so well off. Prosperity has given us the privilege of choosing how and where we live. Perhaps we choose to live where we do our work, or perhaps we choose the best place we could afford or perhaps the place where the education system is best. Is this the life we still live today? Do we live and work in accordance with God's leading, or are we living to work as the world dictates?

It is a hard saying, *"If anyone loves the world, love for my Father is not in him"* (1 John 2:15). It is not easy, but once the situation is recognised in our hearts, the Holy Spirit will give us guidance as to where we can go and what we can do. There is to be no fanfare and no red carpets laid out for us. We simply go and be. The pain of not having our service recognised is mortifying indeed, but that is part of the price to be paid if we are not to become just part of a tide of do-gooders who are ultimately self-serving.

Jesus is challenging our lifestyle, our expectations, and our ambitions. We have all been miseducated by the social systems of the harlot. Now we have the truth revealed to us, and we have the power of the Spirit within us. Now we have an opportunity for a new obedience. Now we can find a deeper relationship with our Father, for one cannot *"come in"* to the Holy of Holies without first *"coming out"* of Babylon. If we do not "come out" of her, we must stay in and share her plagues. Three times the angel emphasises the point that Babylon must perish and her people with her.

> *"In one hour has thy judgement come"* (Revelation 18:10).

> *"In one hour all this wealth has been laid waste"* (Revelation 18:17).

> *"In one hour she has been laid waste"* (Revelation 18:19).

There is no way back for Babylon, no redemption. The Word of God shows us that she is doomed and already judged; we are simply awaiting the time. It is the end of our prized civilisation. It is the end of two thousand years of man's achievements in civic government, science, and social engineering. In *one hour* God will bring it all to nothing.

No wonder the merchants weep and the traders cry out. Without all this, what is left? The angel throws down a great millstone into the sea (v. 21). One big splash, and then it is gone forever. His words read like poetry: "no more . . . no more . . . no more . . . no more . . . no more . . . no more." It is gone! It is over!

The angel reveals that *"the merchants were the great men of the earth"* (v. 23). We see it clearly today; the news is full of reports of financiers manipulating markets to their advantage; multinational corporations making megadeals; round-the-globe trading of anything and everything, twenty-four hours a day; the International Monetary Fund and World Bank reaching into every "Third World" country. It seems that every home is at the mercy of business monopolies reaping outrageous profits.

In verse 23, the angel says that all nations are deceived by *"her sorcery."* The Greek word used here is *pharmakeia* (as in the English "pharmacy"), meaning a drug with magic power. This is the demonic "love potion" of the harlot. It has the same grip on the individual as any hard drug addiction does, and it requires a similar "cold turkey" experience to come off it.

Although this way of life in the end times is epitomised by our consumerist society, it is not just a money thing. This same spirit of the harlot is responsible for the *"blood of the prophets and saints, and of all who have been slain on earth"* (18:24; cf. 17:6). This is a startling statement. All killing began with the death of Abel, killed by his brother in a fit of rage. In his first letter John wrote, *"Anyone who hates his brother is a murderer"* (1 John 3:15). Today in our world, amid natural calamities, starvation, epidemic sickness, and wars, mass murder is commonplace and goes unreported. I speak of the abortion industry. The murderous Babylonian spirit is active in almost every land and society, polluting the earth. Over 50 million babies are killed each year, either in the womb or as they are born, and God cares about each one of them.

> *"They served their idols, which became a snare to them. They sacrificed their sons and their daughters to demons; they poured out innocent blood, the blood of their sons and daughters, whom they sacrificed to the idols of Canaan; and the land was polluted with blood. Thus they became unclean by their acts, and played the harlot in their doings. Then the anger of the Lord was kindled against his people, and he abhorred his heritage"* (Psalm 106:36–40).

What we have here is deeper revelation of the incorrigible human spirit and soul, and it is not a pretty picture to look at. It includes an insatiable sensual appetite, a natural tendency to lie, and a willingness to kill. Such is the hidden nature of the humblest, gentlest creature without the saving grace of Jesus Christ. We can recognise Satan for who he is, but will we recognise ourselves? Are you still surprised at the coming wrath of God?

Are we prepared to face up to the true nature of our own world without Christ? God sees it clearly, as he always has, but will we see it now? Most of us like to think that we are not all bad, that we have at least some redeeming features. But this is not the record of history when measured against God's standard. Is it any wonder, then, that Jesus said, *"You must be born anew"* (John 3:7)?

The *Revelation* not only reveals the heart of almighty God to us. It not only reveals the purpose of Jesus to make it possible for people to be conquerors. It not only reveals Satan in all his ugliness, as well as his strategy in the world. It also reveals to us who we are and the condition of our souls. All nations are joined to the harlot, not just the Jews. All our political/religious/social structures and organisations, our churches and governments together, make up this terrible city of modern times: Jerusalem-Babylon. So again, *"Come out of her, my people"*; for by now it is obvious to us all that her sins are indeed heaped as high as heaven.

SUMMARY

❖ Seventh trumpet is sounded in heaven—THE WRATH OF GOD IS POURED OUT ON AN UNREPENTANT WORLD BY SEVEN ANGELS IN TURN.

❖ Jesus is in the clouds, the second heaven, supervising the destruction of the Antichrist empire.

❖ This the time of harvesting the fruit of the world.

❖ Babylon, the great whore, the city system of Satan, is cited as responsible for deceiving the whole world and shedding all blood.

❖ The mystery of Babylon today is revealed as modern Jerusalem, ruled by a latter-day Herod, and her judgement follows in a single day.

❖ All the cities of the world, daughters of Babylon, are finally and completely destroyed by earthquake and hailstones.

THE TIME HAS COME
REVELATION 19:1-10

Act V, Scene 1—THE TIME HAS COME   **Time: General**

Place: Heaven   **People: All**

From the beginning of chapter 19 to the end of the *Revelation*, all that John sees is of God's doing. Just as the sudden warmth of a spring day brings a promise of summer and a release from the chills and darkness of winter, so this new scene brings relief from the sombre events we have been studying.

> *"Hallelujah!"*
>> *"Hallelujah!"*
>>> *"Amen. Hallelujah!"*
>>>> *"Praise our God!"*
>>>>> *"Hallelujah!"*

So begin the next five passages of speech that John hears. There is nothing halfhearted about these hallelujahs. I suppose the nearest we can imagine is a marvellous performance of the "Hallelujah Chorus" from Handel's *Messiah*. But the performers in the heavenlies are masters of the art. First, there is a multitudinous chorale:

> *"Hallelujah! Salvation and glory and power belong to our God, for his judgements are true and just; he has judged the great harlot who corrupted the earth with her fornication, and he has avenged on her the blood of his servants"* (Revelation 19:1–2).

Then, like an echo:

> *"Hallelujah! The smoke from her goes up for ever and ever"* (Revelation 19:3).

At last Babylon, the anti-God system of Satan, has been judged and eliminated. For centuries it has seduced and trapped men and women in unhappiness and despair. A cataclysmic cleansing of the earth has been accomplished. Now those around God's throne are moved to a response of worship; the four living creatures and the elders too, fall down before him, saying:

> *"Amen. Hallelujah!"* (Revelation 19:4).

And from the throne comes a great voice, echoing through all heaven, through space and through time, crying:

"Praise our God, all you his servants, and you who fear him small and great"
(Revelation 19:5).

The voices that had proclaimed the great call from God's throne to all the earth to "Come!" as Jesus opened the scroll (Revelation 6) have spoken again with this great call to worship. The multitude who heard that first call, delight to obey this new call, and so they praise the one to whom all praise and honour is due.

"Hallelujah! For the Lord our God, the Almighty, reigns. Let us rejoice and exult and give him the glory, for the marriage of the Lamb has come, and his Bride has made herself ready; it was granted her to be clothed in fine linen bright and pure"—
for the fine linen is the righteous deeds of the saints (Revelation 19:6–8).

And as if to underline the importance of conveying this scene to the saints, the angel tells John to write this down:

"Blessed are those who are invited to the marriage supper of the Lamb. These are the true words of God" (Revelation 19:9).

However, this last proves too much for John. After all that has gone before, he is now overcome with the awesomeness of these words and this scene. He falls on his face to worship the angel. So much has happened in this series of visions that it is easy for us readers to lose our sense of wonder and belief. For John, dealing with an angel face to face, even with the touch of Jesus upon him, was a very testing process. Hurriedly, the angel picks him up saying:

"You must not do that! I am a fellow servant of God, just like you and your brothers who hold the testimony of Jesus. Worship God. For the testimony of Jesus is the spirit of prophecy" (Revelation 19:10).

The angel here underscores once more the deep lesson of *Revelation*. God's people are those whose lives are a living witness to Jesus and who worship God in Spirit, even as the whole company of heaven does.

From the beginning of the *Revelation,* the testimony of Jesus, both his own and that of his people, has been a central theme. Here, the whole issue of what constitutes true prophecy is dealt with in the phrase used by the angel: *"The testimony of Jesus is the spirit of prophecy."* Where any individual witnesses to Jesus out of a believing heart, such witness is invested with the power of God.

Such testimony does not have to be particularly coherent or polished, but it does have to be the expression of the truth of our relationship with Jesus. True witness is neither mechanistic evangelistic technique nor quoting Bible verses; it is first of all the personal experience of Jesus' power to change me, so that I know he can change you too. This is the needed work of God's frontline troops, the work that qualifies us for the marriage feast of the Lamb.

The marriage feast pictured here will be held in accordance with the conventions of Jewish betrothals and weddings. The feast was always a great social occasion within the community, as it is in most communities, and Jesus often used the picture of a wedding to illustrate the coming kingdom of God.

In Matthew 22, we find the parable of the guest who came into the feast but was found to be without a proper wedding garment (i.e., one who had no righteous deeds as the outworking of his faith; Revelation 19:8).

In the parable in Matthew 25:1–13, we find a number of young women who were not ready when the bridegroom came (i.e., their supply of oil had lapsed, as with a lampstand that is no longer giving light).

In Luke 13:27–30, there is an account of those whom Jesus does not recognise despite all their protestations about having worked with him and known him (i.e., knowing him personally is essential; see Matthew 7:21).

Finally, in Luke 14:15–24 on, we read the terrible story of those who were invited to a great dinner but found it all too much trouble; they just wanted to get on with their own lives and social arrangements.

These passages in the gospels all portray those who fail to be conquerors. They may, in fact, want to come to the wedding feast, but unless they are properly dressed, they cannot come. Jesus said sadly:

> *"Many are called but few are chosen"* (Matthew 22:14).

These celebration scenes in heaven are covered in a few short sentences by John. They take little time to read, but we must give them their full value. The description is intended to convey information that our hearts and minds and imaginations can take hold of and convert into comprehension of the spiritual reality of heaven of which we are now a part. This is part of our hope—the glorious Christ in me, now! What glory we witness here! What multitudes are involved. They are waiting for us to join them. What marvellous worship we can discern! What joy! What holiness! We are to receive it by faith and enter in, in obedience.

Further *revelation* of the bride will come later.

HE COMES!
REVELATION 19:11-21

Act V, Scene 2—HE COMES!

Time: The End

Place: On Earth

People: Those Remaining

> *"Then, I saw heaven opened, and behold, a white horse! He who sat upon it is called Faithful and True, and in righteousness he judges and makes war"* (Revelation 19:11).

Here John sees the heavenly counterpart to the scene he described at the end of chapter 16. The armies of the Antichrist have gathered together at Armageddon to destroy Jerusalem-Babylon. But now the Christ himself will ride forth to deliver the desolate city. He is not seen now as the Lamb of God but as the mighty Word of God, fully vindicated. The world has been ruled by reason and science, in contradiction of God's Word, ever since Adam—but no more. Never again will man be able to set aside God's Word, for he is also the awesome King of Kings and Lord of Lords.

> *"His eyes are like a flame of fire, and on his head are many diadems; and he has a name inscribed which no one knows but himself. He is clad in a robe dipped in blood, and a name which is called the Word of God"* (Revelation 19:12–13).

This is the King who, with his armies, now prepares to return to earth to fulfil his destiny. In establishing Jesus' identity, John emphasises the coherence and consistency of the *Revelation* in 19:15 by making reference to his roles revealed in earlier passages.

1 **High Priest and Judge of his churches**: *"From his mouth issues a sharp sword with which to smite the nations"* (cf. Revelation 2:16).

2 **King of the Nations**: *"He (with his disciples) will rule them with a rod of iron"* (cf. Revelation 2:27, 12:5).

3 **God's Avenger**: *"He will tread the winepress of the fury of the wrath of God the almighty"* (cf. Revelation 14:20).

We find it difficult to equate God, who is love, with a God of vengeance. Biblically, it is clearly established that in the end Jesus' righteousness will prevail in everything on earth and in heaven; that is to say, iniquity and sin will have been dealt with forever in a process that began in Eden. God's judgements are righteous. His wrath is righteous also, and vengeance is the righteous payback for deliberate choices of unrighteousness (see Romans 12:19; Hebrews 10:30), not as punishment but as inevitable consequence. Judgement will come later. For now the severity of the vengeance measures the extent of the offence. God's righteous Avenger has come to bring closure to all that has taken place on earth from the beginning of creation.

The coming of Christ with his armies to a devastated, but still rebellious world is a terrible event. It is an occasion that has long been a subject of detailed prophecy and therefore of much speculation. This new *revelation* brings those prophecies together and gives them order and timing.

The prophet Ezekiel was especially chosen to expose the scale of Israel's rebellion against God. More than any other, he revealed the source of all sin as *iniquity*, a word that is almost eliminated from the New Testament by mistranslation and lack of insight. The iniquity that caused Satan to be ejected from heaven (see Ezekiel 28:15) not only captured one-third of all the angels but also replaced the Holy Spirit in the hearts of Adam and Eve. That iniquity, God had said, would be passed on from father to child through all generations (see Exodus 34:7). Its pernicious working is clearly seen in Genesis 6:5, and God's only remedy was to *blot out man and beasts and creeping things and birds of the air from the earth* (v. 7). In Genesis 15:16, the Lord cites iniquity as the reason for the four-hundred-year sojourn of Israel in Egypt. There would come a time when the "*iniquity of the Amorites*" (standing for all the nations in the Promised Land) would be complete or filled up, and then God would bring judgement upon them through his people Israel.

The giving of the law, Paul tells us, was to reveal sin. But such is the power of iniquity that none can live righteously, however hard we try (see Psalm 14:1–3; Romans 7). Under the law, the justification of an individual before the holy God and his reconciliation with the God who is love, was made possible by his continuing in faith-obedience in God's covenant. Ezekiel's task was to make this abundantly clear to a fallen and failing Israel. In Ezekiel 14, he reveals the hypocrisy of the elders of Israel who are going through the motions of religious observances but whose hearts are given over to idolatry. Then in Ezekiel 33, he defines the "watchman's" God-given responsibility to warn the people to repent of their iniquity before the sword of the Lord comes bringing judgement.

What then follows is detailed prophecy concerning the restoration of both Israel and Judah to their land.

> *"The word of the Lord came to me: 'Son of man, when the house of Israel dwelt in their own land, they defiled it by their ways and their doings; their conduct before me was like the uncleanness of a woman in her impurity. So I poured out my wrath upon them for the blood which they had shed in the land, for the idols with which they had defiled it. I scattered them among the nations, and they were dispersed through the countries; in accordance with their conduct and their deeds I judged them. But when they came to the nations, wherever they came, they profaned my holy name, in that men said of them, 'These are the people of the Lord, and yet they had to go out of his land.' But I had concern for my holy name, which the house of Israel caused to be profaned among the nations to which they came. Therefore say to the house of Israel, 'Thus says the Lord God: It is not for your sake, O house of Israel, that I am about to act, but for the sake of my holy name, which you have profaned among the nations to which you came. And I will vindicate the holiness of my great name, which has been profaned among the nations, and which you have profaned among them; and the nations will know that I am the Lord, says the Lord God, when through you I vindicate my holiness before their eyes.*

> *"For I will take you from the nations, and gather you from all the countries, and bring you into your own land. And I will sprinkle clean water upon you, and you shall be clean from all your uncleannesses, and from all your idols I will cleanse you. A new heart I will give you, and a new spirit I will put within you; and I will take out of your flesh the heart of stone and give you a heart of flesh. And I will put my spirit within you, and cause you to walk in my statutes and be careful to observe my ordinances. You shall dwell in the land I gave your fathers; and **you shall be my people, and I will be your God**"* (Ezekiel 36:16–28).

The heart of natural man (the seat of his spirit) has never changed. When speaking of the emptiness of outward religious observances, Jesus said to his disciples:

> *"Then are you also without understanding? Do you not see that whatever goes into a man from outside cannot defile him, since it enters, not his heart but his stomach, and so passes on?" (Thus he declared all foods clean.) And he said, "What comes out of a man is what defiles a man. For from within, out of the heart of man come evil thoughts, fornication, theft, murder, adultery, coveting, wickedness, deceit, licentiousness, envy, slander, pride, foolishness, All these evil things come from within, and they defile a man"* (Mark 7:18–23).

Two Greek words are used in the New Testament to speak of "iniquity," as opposed to just one word in the Hebrew. These are: *adikia*, meaning literally "to be without righteousness" (or unrighteousness), and *anomiia*, meaning literally "to be without law" (or lawlessness). These meanings convey something of the writer's intention, but neither catches the full meaning of the original Hebrew word that effectively combines both of them in the one word.

In Matthew 24:12, when warning his disciples about the end times, Jesus says, "*Because wickedness is multiplied, the love of most will grow cold.*" He is not pointing to the wickedness of the world but to what is going on in the hearts of many in the churches. The word translated "wickedness" here, is the Greek word *anomia (iniquity)*.

When Paul wrote to the Thessalonians about the end times, he used both New Testament words for iniquity several times in describing the activities that would take place (see 2 Thessalonians 2:1–12). When he writes, "*The mystery of lawlessness is already at work*" (v. 7), he is not pointing to lawlessness in the world, for it has never been any different, but to the iniquity that is going unchallenged within the churches of the last days.

The point is this. God was so angry at the unrestrained iniquity in man that he brought the Flood, saving only Noah and his family. And God was so angry with Israel because they chose idolatry and the shedding of blood, thus profaning his name in the world, that he scattered them among the nations for two thousand years, despite their access to his grace through his covenant. How much more, then, will God be angry with a Christian Church, for whom Jesus shed his blood and died, when instead of challenging the iniquity in the hearts of men, it tolerates the idolatry and bloodshed associated with Babylon. All these phases of God's plan are intended to progressively teach us about the Creator and to demonstrate the unacceptability of sin and iniquity in any circumstances. If we deliberately ignore the *revelation* of our God in history, then we must take the responsibility for doing so upon ourselves (see Hebrews 2:1–4). Thus, the wrath of God is justified, because he holds us accountable for the choices we make in life whatever phase of God's plan we live in.

In the *Revelation*, we have now reached a new phase altogether; both the old and new covenants are past and are no longer effective. All those armies gathered against Christ are there as a result of the iniquity that has enabled Satan to mobilise them. Jesus has come to earth to possess that which is rightfully his and to institute a different

141

rule. Now, with the severity symbolised by his iron sceptre, the *"rod of iron,"* he will impose his rule over all the earth's people. He will ensure peace, justice, and prosperity, but the hearts of men will not be changed. Our salvation is by faith in that which is unseen, when sight comes there is no more salvation as we know it.

The Antichrist and his prophet are captured and sent straight to the lake of fire and sulphur in fulfillment of Daniel's prophecy (see Daniel 7:11).

Thank God, it is over—except for a final and necessary lesson that will take one thousand years to complete.

THE REIGN OF CHRIST
REVELATION 20:1-10

Act V, Scene 3—THE REIGN OF CHRIST　　　　　**Time: After Christ's Return**

Place: Heaven　　　　　**People: All**

In chapter 20, John simply but graphically describes the capture and imprisonment of Satan. It appears that this is easily accomplished, but the question it presents to us is this: Why would Jesus want to put Satan in the pit for a thousand years and then release him? Why not finish him along with the Beast and the False Prophet at this time?

The answer is that as part of our growing spiritual maturity, we have a profound lesson to learn concerning our Father's righteousness, his judgements, and his mercy. For this reason, Satan is to be kept out of the way where he cannot influence men and women and then, after a thousand years, released for a short time.

We should understand by now that Satan's activities are totally constrained by Jesus. He is not almighty as many seem to think; he is a renegade angel and is not free to do whatever he wants. It is only by the permission of God that he has been able to act in history as he has. God could have chained Satan up at any time, but without Satan there would have been no spiritual battle to be fought and won by Jesus' followers. Without Satan, there would have been no sanctification of God's people and no conquerors. Without being changed in the process of learning to conquer Satan, no one is fitted to reign with Jesus Christ. All through time he has been the means of our testing and training in righteousness, and God still has one more deep lesson to teach us through this wicked adversary.

King Jesus has arrived on earth with a considerable entourage. The raptured conquerors are with him, completely at one with him as a bride is with her husband. Those who were saved out of the Great Tribulation are reigning with him (see Revelation 20:4), apparently administering order and justice in the world. The leadership in Israel will be reestablished (see Ezekiel 34:11–31), and Ezekiel's prophecy of the miracle of the "dry bones" (37:1–14) will have taken place. The Promised Land of Israel will be inhabited by a divinely raised-up and rejoined Israel and Judah (37:15–28).

Eventually, the great new temple will be built, the Levitical priesthood will be established once more, and the Lord of glory will dwell among his people (see Ezekiel 40–48).

But before this, Christ has to establish his order on the earth and restore its shattered condition. All who live on the ravaged earth once the fighting is over must face a tribunal. John is given no details of this judgement, although it is made clear that the judges (Revelation 20:4) are to be those who *"washed their robes and made them white in the blood of the Lamb"* (7:14). They will be the judges of their persecutors. The rest of the dead will not come to life until the thousand years are over (20:5).

Jesus had said that when he came in his glory with all his angels, all the nations would be gathered together before him for judgement (Matthew 25:31–46). This is not the judgement of the dead from the great white throne, which comes much later, but a judgement of those who are alive at his coming. We can call it *"the sheep-and-goats judgement."* The judgement here is based upon the way the people have behaved during the last seven years of the Antichrist's rule. Did they follow him blindly, or did they resist where possible? We find the basis of their judgement stated twice by Jesus:

> *"Truly, I say to you, as you did it to one of the least of these my brethren, you did it to me"* (Matthew 25:40).

> *"Truly, I say to you, as you did it not to one of the least of these, you did it not to me"* (Matthew 25:45).

This is what we might call today a truth-and-reconciliation tribunal. Did those on trial have compassion on Jesus' brethren, both Jewish and Gentile believers, during the time of the Great Tribulation and even after? The test is whether they fed starving people, clothed those who had no way of clothing themselves, gave refuge to the homeless, and took the risk of visiting those who had been unjustly imprisoned by the regime—all these being the result of a refusal to take the mark of the Beast—or went with the flow of popular consent to the atrocities. Jesus' account makes it clear that the plaintiffs' only acceptable justification will be the good works they did in these testing times; and who better to be their judges than those who were made to suffer and die?

The wicked will go into eternal punishment, as they had been warned so many times.

> *"Just as the weeds are gathered and burned with fire, so it will be at the close of the age. The Son of man will send his angels, and they will gather out of his kingdom all causes of sin and all evildoers, and throw them into the furnace of fire; there men will weep and gnash their teeth. Then the righteous will shine like the sun in the kingdom of their Father"* (Matthew 13:40–43).

> *"So it will be at the close of the age. The angels will come out and separate the evil from the righteous, and throw them into the furnace of fire; there men will weep and gnash their teeth"* (Matthew 13:49–50).

By this means, at the commencement of Christ's reign, all obvious sources of wickedness and rebellion are removed from the world. Jesus is making a fresh start on earth—but how long will it last?

The world gradually will settle down to a millennium of plenty, peace, and justice. It will seem like heaven on earth at last.

There will be total harmony between peoples on the whole face of the earth. Under the authority of Jesus and his appointed rulers, there will be no wars and no need for fighting. Order will be restored to the environment, and the earth will yield its abundant fruits once more. No one will be hungry or destitute. Israel will be established as God's people, and be admired for their example and behaviour. King Jesus will reign in glory and righteousness from Jerusalem. Truly there will be peace on earth and goodwill toward men.

In the light of this, it is quite devastating to consider what John then tells us.

> *"And when the thousand years are ended, Satan will be loosed from his prison, and will come out to deceive the nations which are at the four corners of the earth, that is Gog and Magog, to gather them for battle; their number is like the sand of the sea. And they marched up over the broad earth and surrounded the camp of the saints and the beloved city; but fire came down from heaven and consumed them, and the devil who had deceived them was thrown into the lake of fire and sulphur where the beast and the false prophet were, and they will be tormented day and night for ever and ever"* (Revelation 20:7–10).

After a thousand years, the memories of the past—our times—will have faded away and become as a bad dream, if remembered at all. Mankind will have forgotten what the Adam nature is really like. People will look back over history and believe themselves to be superior to those primitives who were their ancestors, rather as we do today.

At this point Satan is deliberately released once more so that he can be active in society. It is astonishing but true that he will soon muster a massive rebellion against King Jesus, a rebellion against the living and visible Word of God.

What does this tell us? All the lessons and insights learned in our time will be forgotten by new generations. Where there is sight, faith is not required. Without faith one cannot be born again. In this thousand years, Jesus will be present with the people as High Priest and King, but none will be born again by faith. Except a man be born again, he cannot live in the righteousness of the obedience of faith; his heart will always incline to evil, just as it did from the beginning.

We can never change the flesh-nature we inherit from our forefathers no matter how hard we try or what sincerity we have. Because we find it so difficult to believe this deep down, God goes to great lengths to show us ourselves. In this time, the Father answers the question so frequently put concerning the awful events in this world: *Why does God allow this to happen?* His answer is, *"Because there is no way in which a person can be made fit to live eternally with the holy God, other than by working out his salvation amidst the pain, suffering, and temptations of this world."* That is what it means to be a conqueror!

If asked, I would have been inclined to think that if God provided us with all we needed; if he abolished crime; if war and sickness were done away with; if there were no exploitation of the weak; if the earth were restored to its first beautiful, created condition and kept that way; if there was peace and plenty for all; and if justice and fairness were found in all government, then men and women would be content to live, and love, and bring up their families in thankfulness and peace, worshipping a good and loving God who lived among them.

Christ's thousand-year reign shows us that this is not so. Such is the heart of man that, when the first opportunity presents itself, like his forefather Adam before him, he will attempt to grab power and government for himself. God wants us to see how totally depraved unsaved man is and how incorrigible his problem is. If Jesus had not come to die for us, there is no other remedy for our condition.

Ezekiel prophetically anticipated a rebuilt temple in Israel and Jesus' millennial reign. In his wonderful "valley of dry bones" prophecy (Ezekiel 37), he foresees the past nation of Israel being supernaturally resurrected to life and the twelve tribes dwelling peacefully in their promised inheritance in Israel. Then he foretells the last ghastly rebellion led by Gog.

In the end, Satan's reappearance brings a last great testing of human hearts. Amazingly, huge numbers will be persuaded once again to rebel against their God. A thousand years of sublime existence will do nothing to assuage the iniquity that has been passed down from father to son throughout the generations. When the opportunity is provided by a newly released Satan, that iniquity, chafing against the iron rule of Jesus, rises up, and the armies of the world gather against him in a mad endeavour to wrest control from him.

For a full account of this great battle, we can read Ezekiel's amazing prophecy in chapters 38 and 39. We see the leader of the armies coming up against Israel identified as Gog, *"the chief prince of Meshech and Tubal"* (38:3), a chief prince from the uttermost parts of the north. Gog is a descendant of Japheth, the eldest of Noah's three sons from whom all the peoples of the earth are descended. Magog, Meshech, and Tubal are noted as his sons (Genesis 10:2–5). As a people they are prophesied to be *"enlarged"* (Genesis 9:27), which indicates the important part they will play in the world's history.

This Gog features again in Revelation 20. He is not the Antichrist who led the world's armies to battle at Armageddon (Revelation 16:16) but the latter-day tool of Satan. The word *Gog* can carry a meaning in Hebrew of "high" or "mountain." The extensive range of the Caucasian Mountains, which stretch between the Black Sea and the Caspian Sea, includes Mount Elbrus (18,510 ft), which is higher than any mountain peak in Europe.

When General Gog and his armies ride down to tackle Israel, Ezekiel says that he is accompanied by Persia, Cush, and Put (38:5), which in our day are known as Iran, Ethopia, and Libya (see also Daniel 11:43). With him also are Gomer (Turkey) and Bethtogarmah (son of Gomer; Gen 10:3), identified for us as being from the uttermost parts of the north. The descendants of Gomer are reputed to have settled to the north of the Black Sea and then spread southward and westward to the extremities of Europe; so these names from Genesis are the progenitors of our European races today. It is probable that the nations of modern Europe are being identified here.

This great revolt is allowed to flourish, and the armies come up against Israel and Jerusalem like a great tide. However, the outcome is determined by one line in the Revelation:

> *"But fire came down from heaven and consumed them"* (Revelation 20:9).

And at last, it is finally over. Satan is finished. He is captured and thrown into the lake of fire and sulphur.

Paul said:

> *"Flesh and blood cannot inherit the kingdom of God"* (1 Corinthians 15:50).

The one-thousand-year experiment is for us, not for God. He understands the profound corruption of iniquity that infests the hearts of human beings, but we do not. Only faith-obedience to Jesus Christ can cure us. Let us be thankful for his wonderful mercy. Had Jesus not been willing to pay such a terrible price, we would have, and could have, no hope. As these things are revealed to us by our God, are we yet convinced of our need and his mercy?

Only that which is spirit can put on immortality; all that is flesh in us—body, mind, and spirit—must yield to the Holy Spirit in us. To be transformed by the renewal of the mind is to have our fleshly minds replaced by the mind of Christ. This is the outcome of a faith walk with him. Are we yet convinced of our need and his mercy? Herein is the spiritual battle set before our eyes once more and well understood by Satan.

The process of change does not stop until we are dead. In life, we gradually learn how to enter into the abiding rest of God's presence. Each stage of life brings new dimensions and new depths of this relationship with our Father and Jesus. But we must realise that our enemy is seeking always to lull us into a resigned complacency; a sleep of the flesh that is the opposite of God's rest.

It is Christ within me through faith that I need. This miracle is not available to the people born into the thousand-year reign of Christ. Without being reborn through faith, their humanity will fail when Satan once more presents his temptations to them. Once this lesson is learned, Christ is ready to bring creation to its conclusion.

JUDGEMENT AND THE SECOND DEATH
REVELATION 20:11-15

Act VI, Scene 1—JUDGEMENT AND THE SECOND DEATH

Time: After the Millennium

Place: Heaven

People: All

In Revelation 20:11, we come at last to the grand finale of the great story of creation, as we are shown God seated on a great white throne. This scene, which takes place after the end of the thousand-year reign of Christ, seems quite ordinary. It is a court of law, a straightforward place where people are to be judged on the basis of evidence presented formally from the record books.

Countless human beings have walked the earth over the ages. All the unsaved dead are now raised to life. None is forgotten. However remote, unknown, or seemingly lost, God has the record of their lives. This is their time of opportunity to justify themselves before their Creator, for the way they chose to live in the world. The court also has a "*book of life*" to refer to. This book is a mystery to us. It may be the same book as the Lamb's Book of Life referred to earlier (Revelation 13:8), but that is not an important issue. What is important is to realise that God has known each one of us intimately from the beginning. The trial is presented as an opportunity for each plaintiff to make a case against God's righteous judgement. This is a terrible moment of finality, for if one's name is not found in the Book of Life, he is summarily cast into the lake of fire.

Jesus warned:

> "*You will know them by their fruits. Are grapes gathered from thorns, or figs from thistles? So, every sound tree bears good fruit, but the bad tree bears evil fruit. A sound tree cannot bear evil fruit, not can a bad tree bear good fruit. Every tree that does not bear good fruit is cut down and thrown into the fire. Thus you will know them by their fruits*" (Matthew 7:16–20).

We know that everyone who has not been saved by grace through faith in Jesus will be standing here and giving account of himself or herself. All those who think they have a good case to argue will now be able to do that, face to face with Jesus. The books will have the record. Nothing will be hidden. The secrets of every heart will be exposed to public view. All will have the opportunity to justify before God the life they have lived in the world.

Any who think to accuse God of unfairness will be able to state a case, if they can find the words. The cynics, the mockers, and the sinners will all be here. Will any be saved? Atheists, agnostics, scientists, philosophers, religious of all kinds; if anyone's name is found written in the Book of Life, he or she will be saved, but not otherwise. There are many questions about this final judgement we cannot answer now, but we can say with absolute assurance that the Lamb's Book of Life can include anyone who will turn to him. It has been suggested that the Book of Life referred to here is a different book from the Lamb's Book of Life and has to do with those who never heard the gospel. It has always been man's duty to seek God, and God has always been willing to be found by those who will seek him.

If we have used our human capabilities for anything less than this, then we have foolishly misdirected our own life, and we are accountable for it. God respects the integrity of every individual. We can choose to find him, or not. We can live for ourselves or live for God. Paul wrote:

> *"For the wrath of God is revealed from heaven against all ungodliness and wickedness of men who by their wickedness suppress the truth.* **For what can be known about God is plain to them, because God has shown it to them.** *Ever since the creation of the world his invisible nature, namely his eternal power and deity, has been clearly perceived in the things that have been made. So they are without excuse"* (Romans 1:18–20).

The undeniable evidence presented by the wonderful creation of which we are an integral part is that God *is* and he wants us to know him.

Day by day, we all live surrounded by the evidence of God for God. To deny him we must deliberately refuse to accept what is evident to our senses. But whatever our choice may be, we will be judged by his laws. The reply to all questions, doubts, and misgivings about this process is that God's justice is greater than ours, even as his matchless grace and loving kindness exceeds ours.

> *"The God who made the world and everything in it, being the Lord of heaven and earth, does not live in shrines made by man, nor is he served by human hands, as though he needed anything, since he gives to all men life and breath and everything. And he made from one every nation of men to live on the face of the earth, having determined allotted periods and the boundaries of their habitation, that* **they should seek God, in the hope that they might feel after him and find him.** *Yet he is not far from each one of us, for in him we live and move and have our being"* (Acts 17:24–28).

Since we bear something of God's image, we all carry within us some consciousness of his divine nature and righteousness. When lost, helpless, and fearful, there are few who do not secretly pray for help from beyond themselves. In our behaviour we may be a law unto ourselves, but when we break our own laws, we condemn ourselves. We must sear our consciences in order to indulge our lusts. We know ourselves to be guilty. No one will be surprised to stand before God on that day of judgement.

Paul wrote to the Roman Christians explaining this point:

> *"When Gentiles who have not the law do by nature what the law requires, they are a law to themselves, even though they do not have the law. They show that what the law requires is written on their hearts, while their conscience also bears witness and their conflicting thoughts accuse or perhaps excuse them on that day when, according to my gospel, God judges the secrets of men by Christ Jesus"* (Romans 2:14–16).

Thus, all the dead are raised. The sea, death, and the grave yield every soul from Adam onward. This is a mighty task. It must be supposed that those being judged stand in their resurrection bodies. Consider for a moment what this experience will be like. Each individual is restored to eternal life just as Jesus promised.

> *"For as in Adam all die, so in Christ shall all be made alive"* (1 Corinthians 15:22).

Each person will be completely whole, made new, free from everything of the past, and will now see almighty God, their Creator, before them, the one whom they despised and rejected in life. They will then realise what they have lost for the sake of the whore's false promises and their own egotistical disobedience. They will have a glimpse of eternity, but it will be forever lost to them. They are judged by the motivation that directed their lives. Thank God that there are some who, having done well, find that their names are written in the Book of Life, and they will receive their reward.

There is only one Lamb's Book of Life; it contains the names of God's family—those who conquered—and those who wash their robes. It was written before the foundation of the world (Revelation 13:8). We should not think, thereby, that we have a predetermined destiny and therefore are not responsible for our life choices. Jesus made an important promise to those who conquer.

> *"He who conquers shall be clad thus in white garments, and I will not blot his name out of the book of life"* (Revelation 3:5).

It is possible for our name to be blotted out of that book if circumstances warrant it. We who live today are a most privileged generation, but like Paul before us (see Philippians 3:12–16), none of us should take our salvation for granted. We have seen that the battle continues unabated until at last Satan is removed. How do we know how we will fare in the future? Will we stand in the evil day? Without the Word, many are deceived into halfheartedness and compromise, soiling their robes. We are to have assurance, yes, but complacency, no! This is also the *Revelation* lesson to the churches.

Eternity is at hand. Death, which has plagued and terrified our world, now ends forever. It is consigned with the grave and the guilty to the lake of fire and sulphur. This is the end of all vain religion, false hopes, and foolish deception. It is truly the end. Iniquity, sinning, death, pain, sickness, the grave, hate, want, war, greed, selfishness, unkindness, disobedience, and disloyalty are all over now. What a promise we have from Jesus:

> *"Let the time that is past suffice for doing what the Gentiles like to do, living in licentiousness, passions, drunkenness, revels, carousing, and lawless idolatry. They are surprised that you do not now join them in the same wild profligacy, and they abuse you;* **but they will account to him who is ready to judge the living and the dead.** *For this is why the gospel was preached even to the dead, that though judged in the flesh like men, they might live in the spirit like God"* (1 Peter 4:3–6).

The lake of fire and sulphur is the second death—a truly terrible place of eternal separation from God. The devil is there, and the Beast and the False Prophet are there too (Revelation 20:10); and now all those whose names are not written in the Book of Life are consigned to it. It is not oblivion. When Adam ate the forbidden fruit, he died to God, and God had called the life of mankind on earth, "death." It was not oblivion but an inferior state lived in spiritual darkness. It included the pain, poverty, sickness, and frustration of life in this world without God. The second death comes by the deliberate choice of each one, and it will be an even more unpleasant life of constant pain and frustration, as Jesus warned:

> *"The Son of Man will send his angels, and they will gather out of his kingdom all causes of sin and evildoers, and throw them into the furnace of fire; there men will weep and gnash their teeth"* (Matthew 13:41–42).

The weeping is pain, and the grinding of teeth is frustration. There is an eternity of it. We might as "the rich man" did (Luke 16:19), think that someone could be sent to warn others so that they will turn to God and be saved from such a terrible fate. But such a one has been sent. Jesus came, and many witnesses and martyrs followed after. They are the conquerors—countless ordinary, unsung but faithful men and women who witnessed to the truth of salvation in Jesus. But, as with their Lord, they were despised and rejected of men.

Today, much, perhaps most of the church does not believe in hell. On the basis of our own humanistic rationalisation, we want to say, "A loving God would never do such a thing!" Our own sentimental attachment to the things of the flesh shriek out that we are not that bad. We are ready to excuse ourselves, but heaven without holiness would cease to be heaven. The thousand-year lesson of the millennial reign of Christ is clear:

> *"Truly, truly, I say to you, unless one is born anew, he cannot* **see the kingdom of God***"* (John 3:3).

> *"Truly, truly I say to you except a man be born of water and the spirit he cannot* **enter the kingdom of God***"* (John 3:5).

Even among Christians there is such a low comprehension of the holiness of God that we want to rationalise away the *revelation* of God's Word. We even suggest that for unredeemed man to be consigned to the lake of fire and sulphur would be itself an unholy and unloving act; therefore, God cannot do it—the Bible must be mistaken! Because we cannot comprehend it, we deny it and attribute to God a substituted sentimentality that wants to say that everything will all be all right in the end. A little earlier in *Revelation* we read:

> *"If anyone worships the beast and its image, and receives a mark on his forehead or on his hand, he also shall drink the wine of God's wrath poured unmixed into the cup of his anger, and he shall be tormented with fire and sulphur in the presence of the holy angels and in the presence of the Lamb. And the smoke of their torment goes up for ever and ever; and they have no rest, day or night, these worshippers of the beast and its image, and whoever receives the mark of its name"* (Revelation 14:9–11).

These words cannot be made into allegory. They are crystal clear, spelled out extremely carefully so that there is no room for misunderstanding. The second death is the only alternative to heaven. It is terrible, it is unimaginable, and yet people freely choose this alternative for themselves rather than live under the benign authority of their Creator.

THE NEW HEAVEN AND EARTH
REVELATION 21:1-22:5

Act VI, Scene 2—THE NEW HEAVEN AND EARTH   **Time: Eternity**

Place: The New Heaven and New Earth   **People: The Redeemed**

I think one of the reasons we are so disinclined to accept the scriptural account of hell is that we have learned to live without the concept of heaven afforded us in the *Revelation*. At the beginning of Revelation 21, John simply says, "*I saw a new heaven and a new earth; for the first heaven and the first earth had passed away.*" The one detail he gives us is that the sea is gone, thus making a vast area of the earth's surface available for habitation. He does not try to excite us with what he sees. He makes a matter-of-fact statement, almost as if this were an altogether unremarkable event he is witnessing.

Perhaps, in the context of all the shocking and disturbing scenes that have gone before, he is relieved to reach the relative calm and peace of this one. The world of the thousand-year reign of Jesus has been described to some extent in Old Testament prophecy, but the new heaven and the new earth is nowhere described. Paul said that it was not subject to decay like our present world (Romans 8:21), but otherwise it is quite beyond our imagination (see 1 Corinthians 2:9). Because of this lack of information, our concept of heaven is restricted to an apprehension that it might turn out to be rather dull. After all, perhaps it will be a puritanical existence with a lot of religious activity and even frequent church services, which we ought to enjoy but secretly find boring and repetitive.

Naturally, we hold the idea that we live in a material universe made of numerous physical substances and that the unseen spiritual world is insubstantial. But John's revelation enables us to see heaven. It visibly demonstrates that while our world is temporary and already passing away, heaven is eternal. Heaven is not material in the earthly sense, but it is substantial. It is formed of quite different substances that are not subject to decay; and not being governed by the forces that control our universe, it behaves differently from anything we know. To be there, we will inherit an eternal body just like Jesus' body. We will live in a real and exquisite environment, interacting with angels and others in a complex and comprehensive social fellowship. And we shall be one with Jesus and our glorious, substantial Father.

We see that the main feature of the new creation is God's presence. This is the wonderful message announced from the throne itself (Revelation 21:3). It is calculated to be a sufficiently wonderful thing that all the other details pale by comparison. God is living with his people in close and personal relationship. Is it likely that we will view this news with much enthusiasm if the development and enjoyment of our relationship with him in this life has not been our first priority?

Who are these among whom God is pleased to dwell? They are the ones whose names were written in the Book of Life from before the foundation of the world. It seems clear that the new earth is to be populated with those people who have been featured in the scenes in heaven and that we have seen in the *Revelation*, although they have different roles and responsibilities, as do the angelic hosts.

Included are those believing people who did not side with Satan at the last temptation after the thousand-year rule of Christ. Their commitment to Jesus was proved and is the basis of their salvation. It seems that there will have been a real cost involved in standing for Christ at the end of his millennial reign, because John hears the promise given to them that God will wipe away every tear from their eyes, and death, mourning, crying, and pain will have passed away forever for them (v. 4).

These are the thirsty, to whom God gives the water of life without payment (v. 6). These are the multitudes to whom John refers when he speaks of the *"nations . . . and the kings of the earth"* (v. 24). And it is these nations who are to enjoy the fruit of the Tree of Life, the leaves of which are for the healing of the nations (22:2). These are a recreated people who will enjoy the Edenic blessings that Adam forfeited. These people will never die, but they will marry and increase, and in holiness and happiness they will fill the new earth (Genesis 1:28). Without the oceans and seas, in a wonderfully productive environment, there will be room for untold numbers to live. And *"God himself will be with them"* (21:3). What a marvellous prospect!

Then he who sat upon the throne (the Almighty himself), as if to underline his purposes, speaks directly to John *for us*.

> *"Behold, I make all things new."* [Every corrupted thing has passed away] . . .

> *"Write this, for* **these words are trustworthy and true***"* (Revelation 21:5).

This is one of those statements that seems to say: "You need to pay careful attention to this."

> *"And he said to me, "It is done! I am the Alpha and the Omega, the beginning and the end:*

> *"To the thirsty I will give from the fountain of the water of life without payment.*

> **"He who conquers shall have this heritage, and I will be his God, and he shall be my son.**

> *"But as for the cowardly, the faithless, the polluted, as for murderers, fornicators, sorcerers, idolaters, and all liars, their lot shall be in the lake that burns with fire and sulphur, which is the second death"* (Revelation 21:6–8).

God shows us three categories of people in this summary statement:

1. Those who are citizens of the new earth: the thirsty
2. Those, his sons, who populate the New Jerusalem
3. Those who have refused God's grace: the lost

Group 2, as we have seen, divides into four subgroups:

1. Those who share God's throne: the conquerors (3:21)
2. Those who serve him in his temple and have washed their robes (7:14–15, 22:3)
3. The 144,000 from the twelve tribes of Israel, who stand before his throne (14:3) and follow the lamb wherever he goes (14:4)
4. Those standing beside the sea of glass with harps of gold, singing the song of Moses (15:2–3).

Remember that John has seen the devastation of Jerusalem-Babylon—the whore. Now he is carried away into a high mountain to see the gleaming New Jerusalem actually coming down out of heaven, prepared as a bride adorned for her husband. A simply glorious sight! What a contrast! This is a picture of what Jerusalem could have been for God. As we consider this sublime sight, we must suspend our understanding of the physical limitations imposed by our present creation. This city is *"the Bride, the wife of the Lamb"* (Revelation 21:9).

As the first creation was a kind of wife for God, so the New Jerusalem is wife for the Son. Once more we are to open our hearts to the Holy Spirit's revelation. The lampstand-churches that reign with Christ in eternity are so identified with New Jerusalem that they are an integral part of the city. The promise of Jesus to his faithful conquerors is now to be consummated.

> *"I am coming soon; hold fast what you have, so that no one may seize your crown. He who conquers, I will make him a pillar in the temple of my God; never shall he go out of it, and I will write on him the name of my God, and the name of the city of my God, the new Jerusalem which comes down from my God out of heaven, and my own new name. He who has an ear,* **let him hear what the Sprit says to the churches"** (Revelation 3:11–13).

The bride is unworldly. She shines with the radiance of a most rare jewel because the glory of God's presence is within; and because the whole gigantic structure is of crystal, this glory penetrates from inside to out. Consider the wonder of the gates, with their inscriptions bearing the names of the twelve tribes of Israel, and the wonder of the foundations with the names of the twelve apostles of the Lamb in equal honour. We are told that each gate is made of a single pearl. John has to convey to us what he is seeing by the use of the best imagery he can find. In the same way, he sees the foundations different from one another, each one coloured and magnificent, like a unique jewel.

Then on these foundations there are built walls of glittering jasper surrounding an interior city made from such pure gold that he compares it to glass (v. 18). But what walls they are! They are about 100 meters high. The city they enclose is unimaginable; it is 2,400 kilometers in length, breadth, and height. It could be shaped like a cube or pyramid—and it permanently shines with the glory of God—a beacon of light in the universe.

We are given the measurements of this glorious, shining, gold-crystal city. Its footprint, of a size that would cover most of Europe today, is 2,400 kilometers square, and its top is 2,400 kilometers above its base. The space enclosed within it could easily accommodate every person who has ever lived. Jesus told us that his Father has many mansions in his house. Here we get some idea of what he meant. This city is not limited to the low-level constructions of our society, which have to take account of the natural stresses encountered under gravity and the difficulties of access.

The streets in the city are three-dimensional and lead to all parts of the city. The River of Life seems to have a course that is coincident with the main street and flows directly from the throne of God and the Lamb. The beautiful Tree of Life is also freely available in the city. The very tree of which Adam was not permitted to eat can now be freely eaten by all who are entitled to be there.

The kings of the earth will come to pay homage (21:24). They will be glad to leave their part of the earthly paradise and make their journey through the wonders of a worldwide, reconstituted Eden, which is being enjoyed by all, in order to worship their Creator in his temple.

We are to imagine a universe with the earth as its focal point. On this earth is situated a crystal structure from which streams light that enlightens all creation. God the Creator has made his dwelling place in the midst of his chosen people. The four living creatures are there. The elders are there. The angels are there. The Lamb and the conquerors are there. Wondrous things happen, things the Father has stored up in his heart for his beloved.

> "There shall no more be anything accursed, but the throne of God and of the Lamb shall be in it, and his servants shall worship him; they shall see his face, and his name shall be on their foreheads. And night shall be no more; they need no light of lamp or sun, for the Lord God will be their light, and they shall reign for ever and ever" (Revelation 22:3–5).

With this concluding statement showing us a worldwide pastoral people, totally at peace within itself and with its Maker, the *Revelation* is concluded. The great, panoramic drama of God's purposes draws to a fitting climax.

EPILOGUE
REVELATION 22:6-21

Act VI, Scene 3—EPILOGUE   **Time: Eternity**

Place: The New Heaven and New Earth   **People: The Redeemed**

John has been taken on a conducted tour of heaven; the home where he will spend eternity as part of God's family. This important last chapter of the *Revelation* begins with a series of statements that at first sight may seem to be somewhat disjointed, but they are invested with great authority by the words the angel uses.

> *"These words are trustworthy and true. And the Lord, the God of the spirits of the prophets, has sent his angel to show his servants what must soon take place. And behold I am coming soon. Blessed is he who keeps the words of the prophecy of this book"* (Revelation 22:6–7).

As the angel makes this statement to him, John is struggling to handle what he is seeing and hearing, and he has to make a response. We see a scene almost exactly like that which we saw earlier (cf. 19:10). Understandably overwhelmed, John falls down at the feet of the angel to worship him. This is a reminder to us of the immensity of the task that he was undertaking and how the frailty of his flesh affected him even at this late stage of the *Revelation*. This time, the angel gently chides him.

> *"You must not do that!* **I am a fellow servant with you and your brethren the prophets and with those who keep the words of this book.** *Worship God.*

> *"And he said to me, 'Do not seal up the words of the prophecy of this book, for the time is near. Let the evil doer still do evil, and the filthy still be filthy, and the righteous still do right, and the holy still be holy.'*

> *"Behold, I am coming soon, bringing my recompense,* **to repay everyone for what he has done.** *I am the Alpha and Omega the first and the last, the beginning and the end.*

> **"Blessed are those who wash their robes,** *that they may have the right to the tree of life and that they may enter the city by the gates. Outside are the dogs and*

sorcerers and fornicators and murderers and idolaters, and everyone who loves and practices falsehood.

"I Jesus have sent my angel to you with **this testimony for the churches.** *I am the root and the offspring of David, the bright morning star"* (Revelation 22:9–16).

The angel's description of himself here is significantly different from the one we read in 19:10. Now John is formally identified as one of the prophets not only because of his long testimony to Jesus, but also because of this prophetic *Revelation* to the churches. Thus, *"keeping of the words of this book"* is to become a key factor in the life of the conqueror (see Revelation 1:3).

The second phrase of the angel's statement speaks of a time when the world will be experiencing the impact of these prophesied events. For those believers who recognize what is going on, it is a time for perseverance and faith. Those who do not, will continue in their ways and so will reap what they have sown.

This is the promise of God, the Beginning (Alpha) and the Ending (Omega) of all things (cf. Revelation 1:8), **who is "*coming soon!*"**

These passages are like a quick rehearsal of God's undoubted purpose in what is to take place, given so that the reader is in no doubt of the significance to him personally of what has been revealed. In discerning the mysteries of the future, we must not lose sight of their practical application to our lives today. That which is true prophecy will have immediate significance for our current walk with God. For many who read this book, it is time to "wash your robes" free from the compromise and halfheartedness with which you have grown comfortable and familiar. Only this will give you the right to enter the Holy City and partake of the Tree of Life.

Let us agree together, there is no place for iniquity, sins, or transgressions in our Father's house. The only effective cleansing agent is not regret, apology, sadness, or excuse; it is the blood of the Lamb. If we don't use it, he cannot.

We have learned from the *Revelation* that at the conclusion of Jesus' thousand-year reign, there will come another time of testing for men and women, for in all that time sin and iniquity will still reside in the hearts of men. Once more, men and women will *"wash their robes"* by faith, and so be saved. This time the outcome of their victory is that they too can literally enter the New Jerusalem, and the angel encourages the reader with this guidance (v. 14).

When the time is right, the understanding of the *Revelation* will no longer be hidden from those who seek to know it. I believe it is available to us now and is of ever-increasing importance as the day of the Lord draws nearer. Many make little attempt to understand it, excusing themselves by fearing they might get it wrong, as countless others have done down through the ages. We must understand that the Revelation is "***for the churches,***" that is for you and me, would-be conquerors.

While it is not easy, we must all enter the struggle on our own behalf. We are instructed to read it first, so that we know what is written there. Its study can follow. It is more harmful to live without an anticipation of the soon return of the Lord and to ignore the prophecies of these Scriptures, than it is to make the effort and get some of the details wrong.

The *Revelation* is for lampstand-churches today; it is not for the world. If, because of unbelief in *all of* God's Word, a church cannot say what the future holds, what chance does the world have? Such a church is not part of Jesus' church, for it cannot be a lampstand.

The bride of Christ can be recognised by the ministry she brings, and now we have this wonderful and succinct summary:

> *"The Spirit and the Bride say, 'Come.' And let him who hears say, 'Come.' And let him who is thirsty come, let him who desires take the water of life without price"* (Revelation 22:17).

The bride and the Holy Spirit always agree. *If a church is not found by Jesus as a "lampstand," it is not part of the bride.* Unless we know where to find the living water for ourselves, we cannot show others where to find it. *"Come"* is an invitation that means that I know personally where the source of the living water is to be found. The river flows from the throne of God and the Lamb, and that is where I too must find my ministry.

"Come!"* This is the heart of the gospel today because it is the heart of Father-God.** For two thousand years it has been proclaimed from heaven as Jesus opens the four seals. The water of life, which flows from the throne of God in the New Jerusalem, is still available today to those who come through faith in Jesus Christ. It is the gift of the Holy Spirit, which God longs to give to all people (John 7:38–39). A day is coming when the water of life may no longer be available. Until that day, the command goes out from the throne of God through his lampstand-churches to all people, ***"Come!" The cry goes out from the Holy Spirit, ***"Come!"*** Let all who are hearing the Holy Spirit make the offer known and cry, ***"Come!"***

And if it seems that our ministry is a failure, if our witness to Jesus is rejected, what then?

> *"I warn every one who hears the words of the prophecy of this book: if any one adds to them, God will add to him the plagues described in this book, and if any one takes away from the words of the book of this prophecy, God will take away his share in the tree of life and in the holy city, which are described in this book. He who testifies to these things says, 'Surely, I am coming soon.' Amen. Come, Lord Jesus!"* (Revelation 22:18–20).

All who drink will surely say with John, *Maranatha*—"Come, Lord." And until then, the grace of the Lord Jesus is with you and all the saints.

HOW SOON?

All through Scripture periods of forty (days or years) have had prophetic significance. They served as times of preparation, probation, or testing of God's people. Thus, Israel wandered in the wilderness for forty years after they left Egypt, and the Lord said of them:

> *"And you shall remember all the way which the Lord your God has led you these forty years in the wilderness, that he might humble you, testing you to know what was in your heart, whether you would keep his commandments, or not"* (Deuteronomy 8:2).

Although God entered into a comprehensive covenant with his people Israel, he was in no doubt as to the likelihood of their keeping it. He laid out detailed laws by which their lives and their relationship with him were to be governed, and then he began to train them in obedience. The book of Hebrews gives us a detailed analysis of Israel's failure in that special time of training and testing. God kept his part of the agreement, but his people constantly failed in keeping theirs.

> *"Your fathers put me to the test and saw my works for forty years. Therefore I was provoked with that generation"* (Hebrews 3:9–10).

The lessons that Israel had to learn under the old covenant exactly parallel those we must learn under the new covenant if we are to conquer our enemy. Their struggle as a nation to enter, conquer, and subdue the land of Canaan mirrors the individual spiritual battle by which we are to reach spiritual maturity. It is God himself who brings or allows the testing circumstances that challenge our obedience and perseverance.

Even Jesus was led by the Spirit into the wilderness to be tested by the devil for forty days. God permits us to be tempted, but as we have seen in *Revelation*, he is not the tempter: that is the work Satan and his forces do in the world (see James 1:13).

> *"Then Jesus was led by the Spirit into the wilderness to be tempted by the Devil. And he fasted forty days and forty nights"* (Matthew 4:1–2).

Precisely forty years after Jesus died in Jerusalem in AD 30, Jerusalem and its great temple were destroyed by the Romans; and the promised dispersion of the Jews began in earnest. Their time of probation was over. The gospel of the kingdom of God had been preached to them, and once more Israel had failed the test by rejecting it.

Jesus was questioned about the signs of his coming and the signs of the close of the age on at least two occasions. Matthew 24 records one of those occasions, when he was speaking to his disciples on the Mount of Olives, and Mark 13 also covers this account. Luke 21 records another occasion when Jesus spoke in the temple. As happens to any speaker who is dealing with a particular subject on different occasions, the two accounts cover much the same ground, but they emphasise different aspects of a series of very complex events (the details of which we have understood from our study in the *Revelation*).

In these three relatively short gospel passages, we find Jesus referring to a series of end-time events that would take place before his return. He used very concise terms that need careful study, for he was prophesying not only about events that would take place in Israel after his death but also about events that would precede his return. He was, in effect, speaking to two generations separated from one another in time (as we now know) by two thousand years. Those living in that first generation, who were hearing him even as he spoke, could not understand this; they understood that the events he was describing would occur within their lifetime (i.e., within about the next forty years). But we, living in a generation nearly two thousand years after, have hindsight and insight. We are able to see and evaluate Jesus' words in the light of history.

At the time he was speaking, of course, Jesus had not yet been formally rejected by Israel. When we look back, we should remember that hypothetically speaking, Israel could have accepted Jesus as their Messiah, either at his appearing and during his ministry or at the preaching of the apostles after his death. This being so, Jesus' prophetic words had to encompass both the fate of the nation of Israel, to whom he had come and who would reject him, and the fate of the church that would be raised up in the event that Israel rejected him a second time. His prophetic words, carefully taking account of these issues, intermingled these topics in such a way that the sequence of events is difficult to understand. When we realise that his words address two distinct generations—one listening to him and one that would be living at the time of the end—then we begin to find the truth. In *Revelation* we have been given the essential key that brings together all biblical prophecy and opens the door to a comprehensive understanding of it.

After Jesus' death, the political scene in Israel became increasingly chaotic, and eventually the Romans were forced to send an army to put down a full-scale insurrection. Jesus foretold these events, which led ultimately to the destruction of the temple and of Jerusalem itself in AD 70, followed by the dispersion of the Jews among the nations.

Jesus' words in Luke 21:5–36 appear to suggest that the destruction of the temple and the scattering of the Jews would be followed shortly afterward by signs of his return. His statements appear to take no account of the yet-future "church-age." Because the questions put to him (v. 7) are tied to the destiny of Israel, his answers relate specifically to their destiny. The Gentiles do not feature openly in end-times prophecy until after Jesus' death and the second rejection of the gospel by Israel.

However, Jesus makes one reference to the "times of the Gentiles" (Luke 21:24) without expanding on what he means. It was left to Paul to spell out all the implications for the Gentile nations of Israel's unbelief. And it was not until the *Revelation* was given to John much later that Jesus spelled out the long-term consequences of the unbelief of the Gentile nations.

History tells us that the generation in Israel who heard Jesus' words suffered terribly over the next forty years. Although the gospel was proclaimed in all Israel by the apostles for forty years after his death and resurrection, with accompanying signs and wonders, relatively few believed. Paul, a highly trained theologian, was chosen specifically to bring the gospel to the Gentiles. His training qualified him to explain the connection between God's old covenant, made exclusively with Israel, and his new covenant, made with any individual who would receive it. So for a period after Jesus' death, the gospel was preached both in Israel and to the Gentiles. But in

Acts 28:28 we read Paul's exasperated words, announcing a judicial cutting off of Israel and a turning fully to the Gentile nations.

The phenomenal rejection of the gospel during this time was not peculiar to Israel, however. The response of the Gentiles to whom the gospel was preached by Paul, although warmly received by a few, was generally lukewarm. Paul even records in his letters how many of those who were saved subsequently fell away. The testing was always there—it has never been easy to conquer for Jesus.

> "You are aware that all who are in Asia **turned away from me**, and among them Phygelus and Hermogenes" (2 Timothy 1:15).

Thus, it was that before the end of the first century, Jerusalem, which had been the early headquarters of a thriving church, had been wiped out. Christianity and individual Christians were having a tough time throughout the Roman Empire. Some churches were being persecuted, false prophets abounded, leaders were divided, and the believers were puzzled; and Jesus had not returned as expected. The "new life" that was being preached was certainly going to cost converts their old lifestyle, social standing, and business potential, and they were only getting trouble in exchange.

For many of them, it was only the expectation of an imminent return of Jesus in glory and triumph that enabled them to persevere through their troubles. The letters of Paul and John, and even the words of Jesus himself, seemed to encourage them to expect his return at any time. And yet Jesus had not come. Many came pretending to be him, and many were led astray by false prophets doing signs and wonders, just as Jesus had warned. These experiences led to much disillusion and disappointment.

It was even suggested by some that Jesus had already returned and there was nothing more to expect of him. As the first sense of immediacy and urgency disappeared, it is easy to imagine those early Christians beginning to feel doubt and even despair creeping in. Was the promise true? Or was something wrong?

Jesus wants all of his people to live with the expectancy of his return, because it is only this attitude of mind that will protect us from the subtle pressure of the world to conform to its standards. It is the expectation of Jesus' return that sets us irrevocably apart from all others because we press on in obedience during our *testing times*, knowing that whether we die first or are raised up at his coming, we are to be found "wide awake" by him at any given moment.

Our study of the *Revelation* has shown that there are certain conditions that must be fulfilled before Jesus' return. Ignorance of these conditions is widespread in the church today because the prophetic Scriptures and especially the *Revelation* are not taken seriously. We find that this careless attitude in God's people at the time of the end is itself the subject of prophecy. Thus Peter says:

> "You must understand this, that scoffers will come in the last days, with scoffing, following their own passions and saying, 'Where is the promise of his coming? For ever since the fathers fell asleep, all things have continued as they were from the beginning of creation'" (2 Peter 3:3–4).

This attitude prevails in many churches today, and it lulls their folk into a false sense of security. Specifically, we have learned from the *Revelation* that *the day of the Lord will be preceded by the coming of the Antichrist* (Seal 5). His coming into his supremo role in the world will itself be preceded by, and facilitated by, the terrible disasters with which the time of Seal 4 concludes. The significance of these shocking events will be as unrecognised by the world at large as were the traumatic events, which preceded the fall of Jerusalem and the destruction of the temple in AD 70.

It was in about AD 90–100 that Jesus gave the *Revelation* to John. By then, Israel had rejected him twice, and the Gentile nations too had not received the gospel of the kingdom preached to them. It was time for Jesus to unveil his strategy for the rest of the ages, by which he would complete God's purpose in creation.

The strategy he revealed was that *his* churches were to be his long-term witnesses to an unbelieving world.

> *These churches were to be "**lampstands**," revealing the way and the need for God's children to come into his presence in the Spirit.*

> *The church leaders, like angel-messengers, were to receive their ministry for their churches **directly from God's throne**.*

To inherit the promises of God, all believing disciples were required to be **conquerors**, overcoming Satan as they grew to spiritual maturity and so finally entering God's "rest."

Jesus also revealed that at the end the Gentile nations of the world would totally reject the gospel message, even as the Jews had rejected their Messiah, and choose a counterfeit saviour—the Antichrist—for themselves.

We can also derive from these important prophetic teachings of Jesus that the events in Israel and Jerusalem, during the days in which he lived there, will be replicated in modern Israel in the last days. Jesus said, "This generation will not pass away till all these things take place" (Matthew 24:34; cf. Luke 21:32). It is clear to us now that Jesus' words, although capable of referring to a single generation, in fact refer to two quite distinct generations that are separated by "the times of the Gentiles." Each generation is given specific signs to look for so that it can be ready for what is to happen.

In the *Revelation*, we have seen how Jesus took the scroll and opened the first four seals, sending out the four horsemen of the Apocalypse, and thus initiating his strategy for "the times of the Gentiles." We saw that the great sign of Revelation 12—a picture designed to reveal Satan's strategy in the world—is also a picture that gives insight into the four beasts out of the sea that Daniel saw in his dream so many years before (Daniel 7). We who live now see how all this has worked out in the subsequent history of the world, during which, beginning at Pentecost, Jesus has slowly built his church. We understand the truth of who we are—chosen by God, not for fame and fortune in this world, but to be those who are conquerors whatever our circumstances or situations.

In Romans 11, Paul refers to Israel as branches being "broken off because of their unbelief" (v. 20), but he points out that, even in this, God's purposes were being served. He tells us that this happened for the sake of the Gentiles. The passage is important for us because in it Paul seeks to explain the mystery of God's dealing with the Jews and Gentiles.

> *"I want you to understand this mystery, brethren: a hardening has come upon part of Israel, until the full number of the Gentiles come in, and so all Israel will be saved"*
> (Romans 11:25–26).

The mystery has to do with the unresolved tension between man's freedom to operate under his own will and God's foreknown purposes. Israel could have repented at the preaching of the apostles, but they did not do so; and Paul shows us that this was because God also wanted to save the Gentiles.

However, Paul shows us in this brief passage that there will be a point in time when the last of those Gentiles who are predestined to be converted and saved, will have "*come in*." This does not refer just to those who profess a salvation experience or a church affiliation, but to those who, having been saved, have become conquerors. They have "come out" of Babylon in order to "come in" to New Jerusalem in heaven, in the Spirit. They are snatched up to God and his throne in the rapture as Jesus comes in the clouds.

We have seen that after this, Jesus will open Seal 6 and then Seal 7, as once again he deals directly with his people Israel.

> *"And Jerusalem will be trodden down by the Gentiles until the times of the Gentiles are fulfilled"* (Luke 21:24).

Those who heard Jesus speaking these words might have lived to see his return had Israel repented at the preaching of the apostles. His coming would have been to Jerusalem, just when it seemed that it was to be overwhelmed by the enemy. However, they failed their test, and many of them lived to see the fulfillment of Jesus' words that not one stone of the great temple would be left standing upon another (Matthew 24:2).

The *Revelation* given to John was a vision of events on a worldwide scale that would constitute "the times of the Gentiles" of which Jesus had spoken so briefly. This two-thousand-year age of the church had been hidden even from the apostles, who had all anticipated the imminent return of Jesus.

The generation who will see Jesus' return in the clouds has been given a sign to look for: namely, the time when Jerusalem is no longer trodden down by the Gentiles. Because we have seen the arrival of that time, our generation will live to see "all" take place (Luke 21:25–27, 32). Jerusalem is the link between these two generations. It is the key given to us in interpreting the signs of the end. It is a leaf on the fig tree, which those who heed Scripture will understand (vv. 29–30). Jesus gives added weight to his words when he says:

> *"Heaven and earth will pass away, but my words will not pass away"* (Luke 21:33).

Today we live in a time when the events in Israel and Jerusalem continually fill the front pages of the world's press. We have become used to the idea that Israel exists as a sovereign state, with Jerusalem as its capital city. What we take for granted today was unthinkable until the last hundred years. Until 1917, the land of Israel was known as Palestine, an unproductive desert state, largely populated by Palestinian Arabs and governed by the Ottoman Turks for nearly four hundred years.

Before the end, there will be a second Pentecost in Israel, the fulfillment of Joel's great prophecy (Joel 2:28–3:3). This will be "the latter rain" before the harvest of the 144,000 who are saved out of all the tribes of Israel. For that prophecy to be fulfilled, however, Jerusalem had to be restored to something like its original status. Israel had to be reestablished as a nation, and the surrounding Gentile nations had to be restored to something like their New Testament situation as sovereign states. God had to put in place a political order among the nations that had not existed for over two thousand years. These things all came into being as a direct result of the two world wars in the twentieth century.

It took the First World War (1914–1918) to bring the breakup of the Ottoman Empire and to open the way for the reestablishment of the nations of the Middle East. The empire, which had backed the losing side in the war, quickly disintegrated. As a result, various territories in the former empire, such as Lebanon, Syria, Transjordan, Iraq, and Saudi Arabia, were reinstated as independent nations. The British, who were sympathetic to Zionist aspirations for a Jewish state at the time, were given a mandate by the League of Nations to govern Palestine. In spite of all the political machinations of the governments, God was working out his sovereign purposes in the world's affairs.

Then, after a pause of twenty-one years, came the Second World War (1939–1945). This was instrumental in furthering the establishment of the State of Israel. The terrible pogroms and death camps instituted by Nazi Germany had the effect of squeezing the Jews out of Europe, and their demand for a homeland, after all their suffering, could not be resisted. In 1948, after much trouble and bloodshed, Israel came back into existence as a sovereign nation. Even in all the devastations and political calculations of those war years, the hand of God was at work.

The most specific and vital clue that Jesus gave to us was realized in 1967. In that year, Israel annexed East Jerusalem along with the West Bank of the River Jordan, and for the first time since before the birth of Jesus, Jerusalem was once more under the rule of a sovereign Israeli state. That which had appeared to be impossible even one generation previously had come to pass. It was at that precise moment in 1967 that the time clock Jesus gave us in Luke 21:24 was set in motion. The second forty-year period of probation for Israel began.

There is debate about this sign, as to what the particular significance of it is, if any. In order to resolve the debate, we must look at the details of the fulfillment of Jesus' prophecy during that first forty-year period. From this historic record, we can draw important conclusions concerning the second fulfillment in the last forty years.

Although some of the warnings Jesus gave in his prophecies about "wars and rumours of wars" and "famines and earthquakes" can appear to us rather generalized, they were accurate on a localised scale, because such things did occur in Israel. In the *Revelation* we have seen that similar things will happen again, but on a global scale, before "the end." Jesus also gave to his people a specific sign to observe:

> **"When you see Jerusalem surrounded by armies**, then know that its desolation has come near. Then let those who are in Judea flee to the mountains, and let those who are in the city depart, and let not those who are out in the country enter it; for these are the days of vengeance, to fulfil all that is written" (Luke 21:20–22).

In foretelling a climactic siege of Jerusalem, Jesus pointed out that an opportunity would exist for those hearing his words to make their escape from the city. But if a city is surrounded by armies, how can anyone escape? Or in that case, why should anyone wish to enter into the city from outside?

The historical record shows the precision of Jesus' prophecy. In AD 66 Israel was in a state of anarchy and rebellion. The social and political order imposed under Herod the Great had dissipated rapidly under the rule of his heirs and under the rule of hated Roman procurators. Political instability, high taxation, and a breakdown of law and order had combined to bring the nation to a ferment of resentment and rebellion against Rome. On the orders of Nero, General Vespasian, a seasoned campaigner, was sent to bring the country back to order.

Before tackling Jerusalem, now controlled by two mutually hostile Jewish factions, Vespasian saw the subjugation of the rest of Israel as his first task. Having largely achieved this objective, he began preparations for the attack on the Jewish stronghold. But then in AD 68 came news of Nero's death in Rome. This led to a power vacuum in Rome that different generals tried to fill, vying for the vacant position of emperor. Vespasian did not see himself as one of these claimants, but such was his reputation that his troops insisted that he claim the title, and they declared him emperor in July, AD 69. Six months later this was ratified by the senate in Rome.

So it was that one day the inhabitants of Jerusalem found to their astonishment that quite suddenly and without any obvious explanation the Roman Army, instead of preparing for a siege, had withdrawn. The people's relief was enormous, and they considered themselves to be vindicated. This was surely the hand of God delivering them!

In the following year, while ongoing, bitter factional fighting was taking place within Jerusalem with the loss of many lives, it was easy to put the threat of a potential siege out of mind in order to concentrate on daily survival. Normal life was nearly impossible, and leaving or entering the city was fraught with difficulty. But to the Christians, a sign had been given. Those who remembered Jesus' words had seen Jerusalem surrounded by armies, and for them, this was the sign that its desolation was near. Those who were in the city were to get out of it, and those who were outside were not to enter.

It is likely that many would consider the danger now over. Perhaps Jesus had not meant exactly what he said. Perhaps there was some mistaken interpretation of his words. The majority of people would be resuming their trade and hoping to restore their lifestyle to that of pre-siege days. Others who were outside the city might well feel that they could take a calculated risk and return there in order to conduct business. Even if things did go wrong again, they might argue, there would surely be enough warning to allow them to make an escape.

However, the problem of Jerusalem had not been forgotten in Rome. Under the command of Caesar Vespasian's son, Titus, the siege came again to Jerusalem, and this time there would be no escape. The time of Israel's probation, ordained by God, was ended. The city, which had crucified its Saviour and by now had rejected the gospel message of salvation brought to it by the apostles, was to be abandoned to a heathen overlord (see Daniel 9:26). Following incredible suffering and unmitigated wickedness, Jeremiah's words in Lamentations 2 were justified to the full, and in AD 70, exactly forty years after Jesus' prophetic words, the temple was razed to the ground and Jerusalem was destroyed.

Jesus had prophesied that *not one stone would be left standing on another.* And so it was, and apart from the Dome of the Rock and Al Aqsa mosque, both built later by the Muslims, the Temple Mount has remained that way to this day.

Jesus had told his people to come out of the doomed city. In Revelation 18:4, we saw another call from Jesus: *"Come out of her, my people."* We too are to come out of a doomed city. We who are living in modern Babylon are to see in the fulfillment of Jesus' prophetic words then, their application for our own time.

We are the generation that sees Jerusalem no longer trodden down by the Gentiles. As I write, we are already past the forty years of probation that Jesus foretold. The gospel has once more been fully preached in Israel by Messianic Christians, so today there many Christian Jews, but the nation has not turned to God and received Jesus as its Messiah. Jerusalem has used its time to become like every other city in the world and has even overtaken them to become the mother of harlots, an incarnation of Babylon.

If our understanding of the prophetic timetable is correct, God has signalled that the end is in sight for Israel and for the world. In 2 Thessalonians 2, as a warning, Paul gives the church two signs that must precede Christ's return.

> *"Let no one deceive you in any way; for that day will not come, unless **the rebellion** [lit., apostasy] **comes first**, and **the man of lawlessness is revealed**, the son of perdition, who opposes and exalts himself against every so called god or object of worship, so that he takes his seat in the temple of God, proclaiming himself to be God. Do you not remember that when I was still with you I told you this? And you know what is restraining him now so that he may be revealed in his time. For the mystery of lawlessness is already at work; only he who*

now restrains will do so until he is out of the way. And then the lawless one will be revealed" (2 Thessalonians 2:3–8).

The first sign he gives is that in the last days the churches will have become apostate. This is a terrible charge to make, for it means that many lampstand-churches will have turned away from the whole truth, substituting all kinds of other programmes for that of discipleship. In the same chapter, Paul goes on to explain that many will be condemned because they *"did not believe the truth but had pleasure in unrighteousness (or iniquity)"* (v. 12). Today, in an increasingly secular and hedonistic society, we see churches constantly compromising God's Word as they seek to make it easy for people to go to church. It is a downhill process; step by step their leaders become lukewarm and then grow cold (cf. Matthew 24:12).

The second sign Paul gives us is the revealing of the long-awaited man of lawlessness (or iniquity). This is the one of whom we have discovered so much in *Revelation*. Paul is referring to the Antichrist, who will rule the world (i.e. *"the beast out of the sea"*) as its counterfeit saviour before Jesus comes back.

At the time of writing his letter, Paul knew that the *mystery of lawlessness* (the hidden iniquity that is in the hearts of men and women) that is working in the world was being restrained by the Holy Spirit, even while the "four horsemen of the Apocalypse" do their work. Satan does not have a free hand on the earth. But that restraint would have to be removed one day, so as to allow the Antichrist to be revealed.

In August 2007, a near collapse of the world's banking systems began, and the outcomes have been gaining momentum since. The iniquity at the heart of our capitalist system (Babylon) could no longer be hidden. That could be the point when Jesus removed his restraining hand and the full effects of man's greed and institutional corruption began to be revealed. Time alone will tell us the answer, but only if we know what to be looking for.

In this event, we are nearing the moment of appointing of the Antichrist. Exactly when he will appear we do not know, but we can expect him at any time. When he comes, as we have seen, he will be appointed with acclamation by the world in general; but even now, before he comes, the agony of those early birth pains is being experienced by many unfortunate souls (Matthew 24:8). If we recognize it, we will see that we are surrounded by increasing conflict—famine stalks millions, natural disasters, and earthquakes increase—and the time draws near when the latter birth pains will embrace us all.

For the world there will be fear and foreboding, but because the church no longer understands the root cause of its problem, that "mystery of iniquity" will remain a mystery. Only the lampstand-church can teach fallen humans how to conquer the enemy within and without. Only the lampstand-church will show men, women, and children how to "come out" of Babylon so that they can "come in" to God's presence. Only the salvation process of obedient discipleship that brings holiness can usher us in to the Holy of Holies. Iniquity can be dealt with only by sanctification.

In Revelation 13:5, we saw that the blasphemous Beast is allowed to exercise authority for forty-two months and make war on the saints and conquer them. This passage relates back to Jesus' prophecy, which covers the same period of time.

> *"Then they will deliver you up to tribulation, and put you to death; and you will be hated by all nations for my name's sake. And many will fall away and betray one another, and hate one another. And many false prophets will arise and lead many astray. And because wickedness [iniquity] is multiplied, most men's love will grow cold.* **But he who endures to the end will be saved"** (Matthew 24:9–13).

When the Bible gives specific time periods, they may be taken literally. This counterfeit Christ will persecute the saints for three and a half years when he comes (Seal 5). So Jesus' prophecy in Matthew 24:9–13 will be fulfilled. Are *you* preparing for what is to come? Are you ready to be raptured as a conqueror? Or perhaps you risk being left behind to face the Great Tribulation of Seal 6?

"***Surely I am coming soon!***" (Revelation 22:20) means that the end is imminent. *"Amen. Come, Lord Jesus."*

FINALLY . . .

Finally the fog of ignorance that separates man from God is blown away by the *Revelation of Jesus Christ*. The full wonder and glory of the salvation achieved for us by Jesus is revealed as God opens the doors of heaven so that we see the amazing generosity of the covenant he has made available to us. How parsimonious, dull, lifeless, and useless are the fig-leaf religions invented by men to cover their nakedness before God.

The sacred buildings, liturgies, formulaic worship, prayer meetings, hierarchies, and organisations that seem necessary to our practice of Christianity, however well intentioned they may be, are all swept away in the flood of liberating truth that dawns upon us as we absorb the *Revelation*. God requires none of them. He wants only our love of him and our acceptance of him in response to his love and acceptance of us. When we know that we are each a temple of God all the time, then our meetings together for praise and fellowship become what he wants them to be.

What a gospel we have! Our salvation is not a religion that we join; it is a personal gift from God to us. From the moment of our new birth, he has invested us with everything we need to be his children on earth, conquering the enemy, conquering the flesh of our old life and its lusts, and conquering the society in which we live. God is literally at one with us from that moment forward. As any father who loves his children would do, he gives us the freedom to work out our salvation, guiding us even as he oversees the process.

His promises for our future inheritance are already guaranteed and are waiting for us in heaven. There is nothing sensational or triumphalistic about this. Conquerors are ordinary human beings going about their everyday business in countless environments, experiencing the same pains, frustrations, sicknesses, failures, and even terrors as the rest of the world, but inside they understand God's plan and treasure his promises. Inside, they know that in the course of this life they must be changed from one degree of glory to another in order to be ready for their role in heaven. Inside, they know that even suffering is for their good. And inside they know that no matter what, Jesus will never leave us or forsake us.

Ours is the abundant life of the Spirit—inside. We understand Satan's impotence in the face of our faith; he can do nothing that God does not allow, and what God allows is for the purpose of making us stronger. We know we are living in Babylon on the outside, but inside we live with the Father and Jesus on his throne. We know that God's judgement of our world is inevitable and imminent, but before the worst happens, those who are ready will be snatched to glory. For those who have not pursued their sanctification, there will be a time of testing and cleansing—inside—before they too go to glory.

Once we are saved, two things are common to us all. We each have God's Holy Spirit dwelling in us, and we have his written Word available to us. It is our responsibility by all means to transfer that written Word into our hearts so that it becomes our direction for life. God's anointing abides in us to teach us all things

(1 John 2:20–27). *Secondhand revelation will not do in this battle we are engaged in.* We have seen that the enemy's major weapon against God's people is *deception*. If he was able to use it effectively to destroy the faith of countless believers under the old covenant, how shall we stand if we refuse to hear his Word to us under the new covenant (see Hebrews 3 and 4)?

We must make no mistake about this. As it unfolds from beginning to end, the Bible provides us with a progressive *revelation* of God our Father. No one comes to a mature relationship with God in an instant; it is the Holy Spirit who nurtures us and the Word that instructs us to know our spiritual Father. This does not happen automatically as some suppose: time, much time, and a commitment to learning of him is necessary.

Neither must we make the error of thinking that only certain parts of the Bible will be sufficient for us. We all need the *revelation*, from Genesis to *Revelation*. To consider that the final book of the Bible is impossible to understand and therefore is of little real significance or value to us is a heresy that saps our faith, for it speaks directly against what the *Revelation* says of itself. To be satisfied with partial truth at best will leave us with a limited relationship with our Father and at worst will make our Christian life a painful, stumbling trial. What purpose would be served by God giving the *Revelation* to his churches at the end of the first century and then making it too complicated for them or us to understand?

But there is a reason why the truth of the *Revelation* is hidden. It is not because of the complex pictures and seemingly impossible events that John sees but because discernment from God is required for its understanding, and such discernment is given only to the obedient. Just as the parables Jesus spoke to Israel and its leaders in his day were not understood, the meaning of these visions is hidden.

> *"To you it is given to know the secrets of the kingdom of heaven, but to them it has not been given. For to him who has will more be given, and he will have abundance; but from him who has not, even what he has will be taken away. This is why I spoke to them in parables, because seeing they do not see, and hearing they do not hear, nor do they understand. With them indeed is fulfilled the prophecy of Isaiah which says:*
>
> *'You shall indeed hear but never understand,*
> *And you shall indeed see but never perceive.*
> *For this people's heart has grown dull*
> *And their ears are heavy of hearing,*
> *And their eyes they have closed,*
> *Lest they should perceive with their eyes,*
> *And hear with their ears,*
> *And understand with their heart,*
> *And turn for me to heal them.'*
> *But blessed are your eyes, for they see, and your ears, for they hear. Truly, I say to you, many prophets and righteous men longed to see what you see, and did not see it, and to hear what you hear, and did not hear it"* (Matthew 13:11–17).

The spiritual leaders of Israel had long abandoned the spirit of God's Word in favour of outward appearances, intellectual argument, and political power. It was over four hundred years since they had heard directly from God through a prophet, so why would they now have the insight to prepare the people for the appearing of the Messiah? Is it any different for us today? It is nearly two thousand years since Jesus promised to return; why would we now have the insight to anticipate his soon coming?

The point is this. The *Revelation* intentionally embraces all previous Scripture and places it within the context of God's plan for this world. If we are unwilling for our understanding of God's Word to be brought into line with the new *revelation* of the *Revelation* as we study it, then we will reject its truths in favour of our prejudices, and we will suffer significant loss from doing so.

The question I ask is this: why are the churches today not representing the whole truth of God's Word (including the *Revelation*) to their people? We must face up to the biblical answer. As it was with Israel under the old covenant, so it is with the churches under the new covenant. We are living in that time of apostasy that must precede the return of Jesus (cf. Matthew 24:9–14; 2 Thessalonians 2:3). This apostasy itself is to be a challenge for the conqueror.

In the *Revelation*, we have seen the call of Jesus to every church member and to every church:

> *"He who has an ear, let him hear what the Spirit says to the churches"* (Revelation 2:7, 11, 17, 29, 36, 3:6, 13, 22).

It is the *"one who conquers"* who will share the throne of God and thus fulfil his desire for union with us.

When the *Revelation* was given a mere seventy years after Pentecost, the churches were already failing in their new covenant calling because they were not "lampstand-churches," just as Israel had failed in its calling to be God's witness to the Gentile world. Although God has restored the church through revivals and reformations from time to time, now, 1900 years later, so widespread is apostasy in every denomination that it passes for orthodox biblical faith. Instead of making *"conquerors"* who have learned to live in God's throne room, we are making *"church members"* who live in Babylon with no idea of their citizenship in heaven. We practise corporate religion instead of personal faith. So many churches are in the world, and the world is in the churches.

None of this is intended as criticism, for without *revelation* we must remain blind and deaf to life-changing truth. The *Revelation* was specifically given to John to open the eyes and ears of believers so that they might become *"conquerors"* and inherit all the promises of God.

It is my conviction that this wonderful, prophetic book is profoundly relevant, urgent, and necessary truth for God's people, and all the more so as the end of time approaches. Any study, however scholarly it may be, that fails to recognise the *revelation* of the book of *Revelation* is not truth, and it can have no power to help its reader to be a conqueror.

In *The Revealing of God*, I have sought to give equal weight and value to every passage of the *Revelation* that John wrote down, however extraordinary it may appear to be at first sight. At its beginning, I made a case for considering that *"every word that proceeds from the mouth of God"* is necessary for our growth to spiritual maturity, and as I conclude and rest my case, it is my prayer that this book might have helped you and many others who hunger and thirst after righteousness to be filled with all the fullness of God.

Lightning Source UK Ltd.
Milton Keynes UK
174882UK00002B/5/P